CW00858589

AFTERLIFE

THE PROOF

2

Also by John Burrows

DEAD AGAIN
DEAD AGAIN (The Sequel)
AGELESS

Material used from *Your Eternal Self* (R, Craig Hogan)
(http://youreternalself.com)

John Burrows

AFTERLIFE

THE PROOF

A Look at the Vast Amount of
Scientific Evidence about the Afterlife

JohnBurrowsBooks.com

Burrows, John

© 2012 Lulu Author. All rights reserved.
ISBN = 978-1-326-19640-0

2015

JohnBurrowsBooks.com

To Margaret – until we meet again.

Something strange is going on !!

"This world, after all our science and

sciences, is still a miracle; wonderful,

inscrutable, magical and more ...."

THOMAS CARLYLE ... 1841

Introduction

In recent times it seems that science has become our God. There have been great discoveries such as the structure of the DNA molecule, and in many ways it has brought us a better standard of living and health. This has brought about a general euphoria and a general feeling that science knows it all and that we are on the brink of a full explanation of what life is about. Nothing could be further from the truth. In fact, every day, I see things which tell me that we have only just scratched the surface. Unfortunately, pursuit of the scientific method has drawn us away from our ability to understand the nature of living things.

The mainstream media, too, has a lot to answer for. For many years they have been hostile towards the honest findings of courageous scientists who have worked to prove the Afterlife. They have been misreported and results have been distorted so that they have been seriously discredited. Some churches, too, fall into this same pattern.

Since I was raised with the Scientific Method I learned to question anything which couldn't be proved. It was very easy to be sceptical about such things as the Afterlife.

In fact, for many years in the Middle East I used to argue with the Arabs about how, from this tiny speck in the vastness of space, we could possibly have any idea what was going on. I used to poo poo the idea that there could be a God or an Afterlife and I used to chuckle to myself about their naivety.

However, I began to realize how wrong I was when I read in scientific journals about the strangeness of Quantum

Mechanics and its unbelievable implications. I came to realize that it was me, and not the Arabs, who were crazy.

I still have intense scientific curiosity but try (hopefully) to look at all new things with an open mind.

The beliefs that we are raised with become very powerful and it is always more comfortable to remain with them than venture out into uncertain and unknown territory

I accept that you may be sceptical but I do ask, if you can, to throw away the beliefs you have been raised with or the religious beliefs which became the model for your life. By all means be sceptical, but please try to look at new ideas with an open mind and look at things with a 'scientific curiosity'.

Open-minded curiosity has led to all great scientific discoveries.

The right way is to be open-minded, to state the facts as you see them, and be willing to acknowledge it frankly if you are shown to be wrong. And, above all, to remain good humoured. (1)

In some places this book tends towards the technical. I'm sorry about that but I needed to do that in order to deal with the way that God had to use very complex stuff to produce the simple world we live in. I have tried to keep these technical bits to a minimum, and it is possible to steer around them if you so wish.

The subject matter in this book is so controversial that I have given references for all material. Where no reference appears then the flights of fancy are my own.

There is no need to read this book from beginning to end. It is possible to select those things which appear of particular interest and go straight to them.

I have not written this book for profit, nor with the intention of converting anyone to, or from, any religion. I do not (even if I could) aim to change scientists from their logical and analytical way of thinking. I simply hope that, for those with open minds, I can reveal amazing things about life here on earth and about the afterlife, and that that leads to a more meaningful way of life here on earth

John Burrows
2015

--o--

CONTENTS

CHAPTER ONE

SCIENTISTS & SCEPTICS

The Oxford Dictionary describes a scientist as 'a student or expert in science' and describes science as 'a branch of knowledge involving systematic observation of, and experiment with, phenomena. It goes on to describe a sceptic as 'a person who doubts the truth of (especially religious) doctrine or theory.

It does, however, seem to me that scientists can be very choosy about the kind of phenomena that they will investigate and, often, they deny the existence of something just because it doesn't fit into their framework about life.

Scientific Benefits

There can be no doubt that, in recent times, science has brought us many benefits. The standard of living continues to improve and our age continues to increase.

There have been many great scientific discoveries such as antibiotics and the DNA Helix (the key to life). It has led scientists, however, to believe that we are on the verge of discovering everything. Nothing could be further from the truth. In fact there are many indications that we have hardly scratched the surface of what is really going on.

Quantum Mechanics has been another of science's great discoveries and while it has been tested more than any other theory, many scientists find themselves unable to believe the peculiar implications it brings with it. They deny what it suggests and believe that some other discovery will eliminate the need for quantum mechanics.

Scientists discard Spirituality
Traditional Western scientists discard any notion of spirituality as primitive superstition, magical thinking, or lack of education. (2) However, modern physics includes many concepts that even today are not confirmed by anything more than informed speculation and even suggest that the mind and possibly consciousness are normal properties of nature and the cosmos. (3)

Hogan says: "New discoveries that matter to mankind will never come from the herd of sceptics. They are prisoners of their paradigms.

The Need to be Open Minded
"When you examine the evidence for the afterlife, listen to either ordinary people who speak with genuine excitement and candour, or to the educated intellectuals who acknowledge themselves to be open-minded and willing to let truth be found wherever it lies, even if that is outside of their present understanding. If you are willing to listen to these genuine open-minded people and not the ever-present herd of uninformed sceptics, you will become convinced of the reality of the afterlife. The evidence is incontrovertible. If instead, you shrink back from the newly emerging truth, you will be destined to live huddled in darkness with the sceptics" (4)

Historically, the first explicit formulation of this attitude (that happiness depends on external factors including success) can be traced to Francis Bacon, who defined the basic strategies for the new empirical method in Western science. Referring to nature he used such terms as: "nature has to be hounded in her wanderings, raped, placed on a rack, tortured, and forced to give her secrets to the scientists, put in constraint, made a slave, and controlled" (Bacon 1870).

It has taken over a century to realize that Bacon's suggestion was dangerous and ultimately destructive and self-destructive. With the development of modern technology it proved to be a reliable recipe for planetary suicide.

On a collective and global scale, this frame of mind generates a philosophy and strategy of life that emphasises strength, competition and unilateral control. It glorifies linear progress and unlimited growth. In this context, material profit and increase in the gross national product are considered to be the main criteria of well-being. This ideology and the economic and political strategies resulting from it bring humans into a serious conflict with their natures as living systems and with basic universal laws (5)

The Big Bang

Scientists say that the Big Bang started from an almost infinitely small speck. That speck was the entire universe. Not a speck within some vacuous space. A vacuum in space. The speck was the entire universe. There was no other space. No outside to the inside of creation. Creation was everywhere at once. And then the space and the energy stretched out to form all that exists today in the heavens and on earth. (6)

At the beginning of the twentieth century, most scientists assumed a universe with no beginning and no end. This created certain physical paradoxes, such as how the universe managed to remain stable without collapsing back on itself due to the force of gravity. But other alternatives did not seem so attractive. When Einstein developed the theory of general relativity in 1916, he introduced a "fudge factor" to block gravitational implosion and retain the idea of a steady state universe. He later reportedly called it "the greatest mistake of my life."

Other theoretical formulations proposed the alternative of a universe that began at a particular moment, and then expanded to its present state; but it remained for experimental measurements to confirm this before most physicists were willing to consider that hypothesis seriously. That data was initially provided by Edwin Hubble in 1929, in a famous set of experiments in which he looked at the rate at which neighbouring galaxies are receding from our own.

Using the Doppler Effect (the same principle that allows the police to determine the speed of your car as you pass by their radar equipment, or that causes the whistle of an oncoming train to have a higher pitch than after it has passed you) Hubble found that everywhere he looked galaxies suggested that they were receding from ours. The farther away they were, the faster the galaxies were receding.

If everything in the universe is flying apart, reversing the arrow of time would predict that at some point all of these galaxies were together in one incredibly massive entity. Hubble's observations started a deluge of experimental measurements that over the last seventy years have led to the conclusion by the vast majority of physicists and cosmologists that the universe began at a single moment, commonly now referred to as the Big Bang. Calculations suggest that it happened approximately 14 billion years ago.

A currently unanswered question is whether the Big bang has resulted in a universe that will go on expanding forever, or whether at some point gravitation will take over and the galaxies will begin to fall back together, ultimately resulting in a "Big Crunch." Recent discoveries of little understood quantities known as dark matter and dark energy, which seem to occupy a very substantial amount of the material in the universe, leave the answer to the question hanging, but the best evidence at the moment predicts a slow fade, rather than a dramatic collapse. (7)

The further philosophical problem of there having been a beginning arises with the idea that the beginning of our universe marks the beginning of time, space, and matter. Before our universe came into being, there is every scientific indication that time did not exist. Whatever brought the universe into existence must, of course, predate the universe, which in turn means that whatever brought the universe into existence must predate time. That which predates time is not bound by time. Not inside of time. In other words, it is eternal. If the laws of physics, or at least some aspect of the laws of physics, did the job of creation, those laws by necessity are eternal. (8)

Creation

The existence of the Big Bang begs the question of what came before that and who or what was responsible. It certainly demonstrates the limits of science as no other phenomenon has done. The consequences of Big Bang theory for theology are profound. For faith traditions that describe the universe as having been created by God from nothingness, this is an electrifying outcome. Does such an astonishing event as the Big Bang fit the definition of a miracle?

The sense of awe created by these realizations has caused more than a few agnostic scientists to sound downright theological. In God and the Astronomers, the astrophysicist Robert Jastrow wrote this final paragraph: "At this moment it seems as though science will never be able to raise the curtain on the mystery of creation. For the scientist who has lived by his faith in the power of reason, the story ends like a bad dream. He has scaled the mountains of ignorance; he is about to conquer the highest peak; as he pulls himself over the final rock, he is greeted by a band of theologians who have been sitting there for centuries.

For those looking to bring the theologians and the scientists closer together, there is much in these recent discoveries of the origin of the universe to inspire mutual appreciation.

The Biblical View of the World

In his provocative book, Jastrow writes: "Now we see how the astronomical evidence leads to a biblical view of the world. The details differ, but the essential elements and the astronomical and biblical accounts of Genesis are the same; the chain of events leading to man commenced suddenly and sharply at a definite moment in time, in a flash of light and energy.(9)

Amo Penzias, the Nobel Prize-winning scientist who co-discovered the cosmic microwave background radiation that provided strong support for the Big Bang in the first place, states, "The best data we have is exactly what I would have predicted, had I nothing to go on but the books of Moses, the Psalms, and the Bible as a whole. (10) Perhaps Penzias was thinking of the words of David in Psalm 8. "When I consider your heavens, the work of your fingers and the stars, which you have set in place, what is man that you are mindful of him?"

--o--

CHAPTER TWO

QUANTUM

> The implications of Quantum Mechanics are quite unbelievable. They turn the world, as we know it, upside down. Things can be in many places at the same time; things can travel at infinite speeds; and time, as we know it, seems not to exist. No wonder many scientists still fail to believe in its many weird implications.

The Greek Philosophers sliced matter up into thinner and thinner sections until Democritus put a stop to the discrimination by declaring that there was a limit beyond which particles became indivisible or a-tomic. More than two thousand years later John Dalton showed that all matter in the universe was composed of basic building blocks, or atoms.

The Atom
Both of them were right but we now know that one further division is possible and that atoms can be split into even more fundamental particles. At first it seemed as though these operated on a planetary principle, with electrons travelling in orbit around a central nucleus. More recently it has become apparent that electrons are more like clouds of electricity vibrating with wave patterns. None of this can be seen, but there is clear evidence that at the centre of the fog is a collection of nuclear bits and pieces that contain nearly all the mass of the atom and nearly all of its energy. If the atom were to be inflated until it filled an Olympic stadium, this nucleus would be the size of a pea

lying alone in the centre of the track. There is proportionally as much empty space inside the atom as there is in the universe.

Solid Matter is mostly Space

All matter is like this. Take a man and squeeze the empty spaces out of him like the holes in a sponge, and you are left with a little pile of solid substance no larger than a fly speck. We are the hollow men and our insubstantial bodies are strung together with electromagnetic and nuclear forces that do no more than create the illusion of matter. In this respect there is little to separate the living from the non-living; both are composed of the same sparse fundamental particles interacting with each other in the same elementary ways.

The only real difference is that the atoms of life are organized. They have become arranged into self-replicating patterns that defy cosmic chaos by constantly repairing and replacing themselves. Feeding on order, they learn to recognize and respond to it; the more organized they are, the more responsive they become. Life must be in close touch with matter, and at the highest levels this means that it not only takes energy and information from its surroundings but returns them as well. (11)

The solidity of iron is actually 99.9999999999999 percent startlingly vacuous space made to feel solid by ethereal fields of force having no material reality at all. Hollywood would have rejected such a script out of hand and yet it is the proven reality. But don't knock your head against that space. Force fields can feel very solid.

Quantum Physics

But that was the atom, and then quantum physics came on to the scene with its micro, micro world, only to prove to us that there is no reality. Not even the one part in a million billion that seemed to be solid. Ask a scientist or a physicist, what an electron or the quarks of a proton are made of. She or he will have no answer. Ask the composition of photons, the wave / particle packers of energy that underlie all those micro-particles of matter. The reply will be along the lines of "Huh?" (12)

A Strange New World
Despite its incredible implications (such as travel faster than the speed of light, and instantaneous connection between events here and the other side of the universe) it remains one of the most tested theories, ever. Even Einstein found it difficult to come to terms with.

It is easy to understand. The strange new land that physicists had found lurking in the heart of the atom contained things that were more wondrous than Cortes or Marco Polo ever encountered. What made this new world so intriguing was that everything about it appeared to be contrary to common sense. It seemed more like a land ruled by sorcery than an extension of the natural world, an Alice in Wonderland realm in which mystifying forces were the norm and everything logical had been turned on its head

An even more surprising feature of the quantum was its implications for the nature of location. At the level of our everyday lives things have very specific locations, but Bohm's interpretation of quantum physics indicated that at the sub-quantum level, the level at which the quantum potential operated, location ceased to exist. All points in space become equal to all other points in space, and it was seemingly useless to speak of anything being separate from anything else. Physicists call this property 'non locality'

Or as Grof puts it:

The world appears to be made of separate material objects and has distinctly Newtonian characteristics; time is linear, space is three dimensional, and all events seem to be caused by chains of cause and effect. Experiences in this support, systematically, a number of basic assumptions about this world such as matter is solid; two objects cannot occupy the same space; past events are irretrievably lost; future events are not available; one cannot be in more than one place at a time; one can exist in only one time frame at a time; a whole is larger than a part; or something cannot be true and untrue at the same time

Also, we are so deeply convinced that our bodies are solid and objectively real that it is difficult for us to even entertain the idea that we, too, may be no more than will-o'- the-wisps.

One startling discovery made by quantum physicists was that if you break matter into smaller and smaller pieces you eventually reach a point where those pieces --- electrons, protons, and so on, no longer possess the traits of objects. For example, most of us tend to think of an electron as a tiny sphere or a bee whizzing around, but nothing could be further from the truth. Although an electron can sometimes behave as if it were a compact little particle, physicists have found that it literally possesses no dimension. This is difficult for most of us to imagine because everything at our own level of existence possesses dimension. And yet if you try to measure the width of an electron, you will discover it's an impossible task. An electron is simply not an object as we know it.

Another discovery physicists made is that an electron can manifest as either a particle or a wave. If you shoot an electron at the screen of a television that's been turned off, a tiny point of light will appear when it strikes the phosphorescent chemicals that coat the glass. The single point of impact the electron leaves on the screen clearly reveals the particle like side of its nature.

But this is not the only form the electron can assume. It can also dissolve into a blurry cloud of energy and behave as if it were a wave spread out over space. When an electron manifests as a wave it can do things no particle can. If it is fired at a barrier in which two slits have been cut, it can go through both slits simultaneously. When wave-like electrons collide with each other they even create interference patterns. The electron, like some shape shifter out of folklore, can manifest itself as either a particle or a wave.

This chameleon like ability is common to all sub atomic particles. It is also common to all things once thought to manifest exclusively as waves. Light, gamma rays, radio waves, X rays-all can change from waves to particles and back again. Today physicists believe that sub-atomic phenomena should not be classified solely as either waves or particles, but as a single category of somethings that are always somehow both. These somethings are called quanta, and physicists believe they are the basic stuff from which the entire universe is made.

Particles only Appear When we look at Them

Perhaps most astonishing of all is that there is compelling evidence that the only time quanta ever manifest as particles is when we are looking at them. For instance, when an electron isn't being looked at, experimental findings suggest that it is always a wave. Physicists are able to draw this conclusion because they have devised clever strategies for deducing how an electron behaves when it is not being observed (it should be noted that this is only one interpretation of the evidence and is not the conclusion of all physicists; Bohm himself has a different interpretation). Once again this seems more like magic than the kind of behaviour we are accustomed to expect from the natural world. Imagine owning a bowling ball that was only a bowling ball when you looked at it. If you sprinkled talcum powder all over a bowling lane and rolled such a "quantum" bowling ball toward the pins, it would trace a single line through the talcum powder while you were watching it. But if you blinked while it was in transit, you would find that for the second or two you were not looking at it the bowling ball stopped tracing a line and instead left a broad wavy strip, like the undulating swath of a desert snake as it moves sideways over the sand.

Such a situation is comparable to the one quantum physicists encountered when they first uncovered evidence that quanta coalesce into particles only when they are being observed. Physicist Nick Herbert, a supporter of this interpretation, says this has sometimes caused him to imagine that behind his back the world is always radically ambiguous and like a ceaselessly flowing quantum soup. But whenever he turns around and tries to see the soup, his glance instantly freezes it and turns it back into ordinary reality. He believes this makes us all a little like Midas, the legendary king who never knew the feel of silk or the caress of a human hand because everything he touched turned to gold. "Likewise humans can never experience the true texture of quantum reality," says Herbert, "because-everything we touch turns to matter."(13)

Or as Meek states: "First of all it is now concluded that the mind of the experimenter can in some way influence matter. The second finding is that matter-energy can neither be created nor destroyed. All matter is energy and as the energy is changed or modified the "matter" is merely matter at a different level of "existence." (14)

Indeed, because the quantum potential permeates all of space, all particles are non-locally interconnected. More and more the picture that Bohm was developing was not one in which sub-atomic particles were separate from one another and moving through the void of space, but one in which all particles were part of an unbroken web and embedded in space that was as real and rich with process as the matter that moved through it. (15)

Max Planck put forward the bold proposition that, energy was given out (or absorbed) in 'packets' of energy when an electron moved between orbits. Also, that the electrons could only possibly exist in very discrete orbits and that the space between orbits was banned. The implications of this were immense. If electrons orbiting a nucleus can reside only at specific levels of energy, with no immediate stages allowed, then how does the electron change from one energy level to another? Not by gradually or even rapidly moving across the divide between orbits. Such a transition would imply that for a finite time, no matter how brief, the electron had an energy intermediate between the higher and lower orbits. But observations showed that such gradualism is forbidden. The electron simply leaps from one orbit to another in zero time.

The Universe clashes with Human Reason
The universe we have discovered behaves in a manner most illogical. It does not comply with human reason. (16)

One hundred years ago, a physics professor would have lost tenure on the spot if caught teaching the concept that matter in all its forms of solids, liquids, and gases was actually condensed energy. What hokum it would have seemed. There is conservation of energy and conservation of matter, or so it was believed. Energy may change form, perhaps from radiant to thermal, or from kinetic to potential, and so might matter change, from solid to liquid or gas, but in a closed system the sum total of energy and the sum total of matter remained fixed. That each was distinct from the other seemed too obvious to be questioned.

Einstein
Then came Einstein, relativity, and $E = mc^2$ Einstein hypothesized, and it has since been confirmed, that matter, (m), intrinsically represents a specific amount of energy, (E). And the type of matter was immaterial. As bizarre as it seems, a gram of rose petals and a gram of uranium contain identical amounts of energy. The constant, c^2, in the equation, is the speed of fight squared or multiplied by itself. That "c" is a massive value and that

tells us that even a tiny amount of matter contains a huge quantity of energy. (17)

Physics deals with shadows. It always did, but the new physics has become aware of the fact, while the old physics operated under the illusion that it dealt with the world itself. (18)

To most of us still, the shadows seem real enough. They appear to be the whole world, unless something happens to make you doubt your perceptions. Sir James Jeans and other sensitive physicists party to the complex mathematics became aware of the shadowy nature of the whole enterprise, and turned round to look at the light. They found, to their surprise, that even their new physics could tell them nothing whatsoever about the world outside the cave. To go beyond the shadows, they discovered, was to go beyond physics altogether and into metaphysics. With the result that every one of them - Einstein, Schrodinger, Heisenberg, De Broglie, Planck and Pauli included - became a mystic. (19)

The leading edge of physics is now more like mysticism and magic.

Talbot put it this way, electrons and all other particles are no more substantive or permanent than the form of a geyser of water takes as it gushes out of a fountain. They are sustained by the implicate order, and when a particle appears to be destroyed, it is not lost. It has merely enfolded back into the deeper order from which it sprang.

The constant and flowing exchange between the two orders explains how particles, such as the electron in the positronium atom, can shape-shift from one kind of particle to another. Such shiftings can he viewed as one particle, say an electron, enfolding back into the implicate order while another, a photon, unfolds and takes its place.

32

It also explains how a quantum can manifest as either a particle or a wave. According to Bohm, both aspects are always enfolded in a quantum's ensemble, but the way an observer interacts with the ensemble determines which aspect unfolds and which remains hidden. As such, the role an observer plays in determining the form a quantum takes may be no more mysterious than the fact that the way a jeweler manipulates a gem determines which of its facets become visible and which do not. Because the term hologram usually refers to an image that is static. It does not convey the dynamic and ever active nature of the incalculable enfoldings and unfoldings that moment by moment create our universe, Bohm prefers to describe the universe not as a hologram, but as a "holomovement." (20)

Talbot goes on to say: "as for me, as a result of my own experiences I agree with Don Juan when he states, "We are perceivers. We are an awareness; we are not objects; we have no solidity. We are boundless. The world of objects is a way of making our passage on earth convenient. It is only a description that was created to help us. We, or rather our reason, forget that that the description is only a description and thus we entrap the totality of ourselves in a vicious circle from which we rarely emerge in our lifetime. (21)

The Quantum is extraordinary. It is dimensionless, can exist in more than one place at a time, can travel faster than light and communicate instantaneously with the other side of the universe. As if that wasn't enough, it has no respect for linear time as we know it.

No wonder Einstein found difficulty in coming to terms with these and many other strange properties of the Quantum.

--o--

CHAPTER THREE

TIME

> *It is often referred to as "the arrow of time". It is given that name with good reason. Everything moves forward. What is gone is gone, and what is to come remains unknown until we get there. However, this is not so. It has been demonstrated to be completely false. We **can** go back in time, and we **can** also visit the future.*

Einstein showed that time wasn't constant and that it could change with acceleration and gravity, but it didn't end there. Precognition (see later notes) tells us that the future is not forbidden to us, nor is going backwards in time.

Precognition

In another equally astonishing personal flash forward a female NDE'r (Near Death Experiencer) was shown a photograph of Raymond Moody, told his full name, and told that, when the time was right, she would tell him about her experience. The year was 1971 and Moody had not yet published *Life after Life* so his name and picture meant nothing to the woman. However the time became "right" four years later when Moody and his family unwittingly moved to the very street on which the woman lived. That Halloween, Moody's son was out trick-or-treating and knocked at the woman's door. After hearing the boy's name the woman told him to tell his father that she had to talk to him and when Moody obliged she related her remarkable story (22)

Predestination
Dare we accept predestination? Must we, if we do, deny the freedom of the will? That freedom, in any case, is strictly limited, but such as it is we cling to it with tenacity. Perhaps this rather depends on what we mean by the term free will. As I have pointed out elsewhere, our choice of action (subject to the circumstances in which we find ourselves placed) depends upon our own characters. We act as we do under gives circumstances because our characters are what they are, and for no other conceivable reason. Had we different characters, or were the circumstances altered we should act differently. From our own point of view, therefore, we have free will, as we make our own choice. Character is the mainspring of action. John Jones in given circumstances does not act like Tom Smith, because he is John Jones. Character and circumstance between them determine the history of the world and the fate of nations. If John Jones were to act differently from what he does, it would be because he had a different character to what he has, because in short he was not John Jones. Must we not admit that the Omniscient Wisdom could foresee everything?

If it were otherwise we should be compelled to maintain that there was some element of causation which had been overlooked, and which led to a variation of the anticipated consequences.

Fate & Free Will
Why should such a belief lead to an apathy engendered by fatalism? The truth is, we find the main-spring of our actions in character, and not in whimsy. Would it stimulate my efforts to reflect that, being John Jones, I acted as if I were Tom Smith? Hardly is such a thing conceivable. Fate and free will, I would suggest, are only the same truth looked at from different angles, and the knowledge that we act as we do is because we are what we are, and is no way deterrent to our

effort, but rather an incentive to correct our deficiencies. The determinist hypothesis has never yet been broken down. There may be a way out of it, but if so it still awaits discovery. (23)

Space & Time

Space and time become inseparable, and when we cannot think of one without the other, time ceases to be the old, one-dimensional unit of classical physics, and the combination space-time becomes a four-dimensional continuum.

The idea of a dimension that no one, not even the mathematician, has been able to imagine, let alone see, is difficult to grasp. It is uncomfortable to think of the here-and-now as the past, but it does seem to be true. Space-time is a continuum, and it is impossible to draw distinctions between past and present and perhaps even future. In biological terms the fourth dimension represents continuity. A wheat seed that germinates after four thousand years in the tomb of an Egyptian pharaoh is no different from the other seeds in that husk that sprouted the year after they were first grown on the banks of the Nile. Bacteria normally divide every twenty minutes, but under unfavorable circumstances they can become resistant spores that are sometimes entombed in rock and wait for millions of years to be released and continue multiplying as though nothing had happened. Life conquers time by suspending it in a way that is almost as good as having a time machine. It may deal with space in the same way. (24)

Puthoff and Targ carried out a large number of precognitive remote-viewing experiments. Their findings have been duplicated by numerous laboratories around the world including Jahn's and Dunne's research facility at Princeton. Indeed in 334 formal trials, Jahn and Dunne found that volunteers were able to come up with accurate precognitive information 62 percent of the time.

Precognitive "Chair Tests"

Even more dramatic are the results of the so-called "chair tests," a series of experiments devised by Croiset. First, the experimenter would randomly select a chair from the seating plan for an upcoming public event in a large hall or auditorium. The hall could be located in any city in the world and only events that did not have reserved seating qualified. Then without telling Croiset the name or location of the hall, or the nature of the event, the experimenter would ask the Dutch psychic to describe who would be sitting in the seat during the evening in question.

Over the course of a twenty-five year period, numerous investigations in both Europe and America put Croiset through the rigours of the chair test and found that he was almost always capable of giving an accurate and detailed description of the person who would be sitting in the chair, including describing their gender, facial features, dress, occupation, and even incidents from their past. (25)

Some NDEs even support LOYe's proposal that several holographic parallel universes, or time tracks, exist. On occasion NDEers are shown Personal flashforwards and told that the future they have witnessed will come to pass only if *they continue on their current path.* In one unique instance a NDEer, was shown a completely different history of the earth, a history that would have developed if "certain events" had not taken place around the time of the Greek Philosopher and mathematician Pythagoras three thousand years ago. The vision revealed that if these events, the precise nature of which the woman did not disclose, had failed to take place, we would now he living in a world of Peace and harmony marked "by the absence of religions, wars and of a Christ figure." Such experiences suggest that the laws of time and space operative in a holographic universe may be very strange indeed. (26)

People Avoid Trains going to be involved in an accident
William Cox, an American mathematician, has recently
completed an interesting survey in an attempt to discover
whether people really do avoid travelling on trains that were
going to be involved in an accident. Cox collected
information on the total number of people on each train at
the time of the accident and compared these with the
number of passengers who travelled on the same train
during each of the preceding seven days and on the
fourteenth, twenty-first and twenty-eighth day before the
accident. His results, which covered several years of
operation with the same equipment at the same station,
show that people did in fact avoid accident-bound trains.
There were always fewer passengers in the damaged and
derailed coaches than would have been expected for that
train at that time. The difference between expected and
actual number of passengers was so great that the odds
against its occurring by chance were over a hundred to one.
(27)

It is important to note that the existence of such
unconscious agendas does not mean that our lives are
rigidly predestined and all fates unavoidable. The fact that
many of Whitton's subjects asked not to remember what
they said under hypnosis implies again that the future is
only roughly outlined and still subject to change.

A Curious Story
This problem of space--time has been raised in a somewhat
curious form in a description given by Sir Auckland Geddes
to a meeting of the Royal Medical Society in Edinburgh
(February 26th, 1937). Sir Auckland Geddes is entitled to
claim the ear of the orthodox as being himself an M.D., and
a former Professor of Anatomy. The experience which he
narrated was not his own but that, as one gathers, of a
medical friend, who for professional reasons asked that his
anonymity should be respected. The "percipient" (as

members of the S.P.R. would describe him), was taken ill on Saturday, November 9th, in the middle of the night with acute gastroenteritis. He gradually grew worse and by 10 o'clock had developed all the symptoms of acute poisoning. He wanted to ring for assistance but found himself quite unable to do so and finally gave up the attempt.

The description as recorded and summarized here was dictated by him to a skilled secretary, who took it down in shorthand after he had regained conscious-ness. (It was reported in The Scotsman of February 27th).

"I realized" (runs this curious narrative), that I was very ill and very quickly reviewed my whole financial position. Thereafter at no time did my consciousness appear to me to be in any way dimmed, but I suddenly realized that my consciousness was separating from another consciousness which was also me. These for purposes of description we might call the A and B consciousness, and throughout what follows the ego attracted itself to the A consciousness."

The A consciousness was what psychical researchers would describe as the externalized personality. The B consciousness was the consciousness still manifesting in the physical body. This B consciousness, says our percipient, gradually "began to disintegrate while the A consciousness, which, was now me, seemed to be altogether outside my body which it could see.

By degrees "Mr. Smith", as we will call him for convenience sake, began to realize that he could see not only his own body lying on the bed, but everything in the house where he was and also the garden, and after a time anything that he desired in London or even in Scotland. He had in short only to concentrate on the place he desired to visualize in order to see it, and here we come to the most curious point, which must be recorded in his own words.

"The explanation I received---from what source I do not know but which I found myself calling to myself my mentor---was that I was free in a time dimension of space wherein 'now' was in some way equivalent to 'here' in the ordinary three dimensional space of everyday life. I next realized that my vision included not only 'things' in the ordinary three dimensional world but also 'things' in those four or more dimensional places that I was in. I understood from my mentor that all our brains are just end-organs projecting, as it were, from the three dimensional universe into the psychic stream and flowing with it into the fourth and fifth dimensions. Around each brain, as I saw it, there seemed to be what I can only describe in ordinary words as a condensation of the psychic stream, which formed in each case as though it was a cloud; only it was not a cloud. (28)

--o--

CHAPTER FOUR

REALITY & CONSCIOUSNESS

Consciousness is precisely that part of ourselves which does not exist as an object within the physical universe and it is composed of those thoughts and emotions and dreams in which we realize ourselves most intimately. (29)

Psychologist William James said: "Our normal waking consciousness, is but one special type of consciousness, whilst all about it, parted from it by the flimsiest of screens, there lie potential forms of consciousness entirely different...... No account of the universe in its totality can be final which leaves these other forms of consciousness quite disregarded. They forbid a premature closing of our accounts with reality." (30)

The Subterranean Labyrinth of the Unconscious
It was almost as if LSD provided the human consciousness with an access to a kind of infinite subway system, a labyrinth of tunnels and byways that exited in the subterranean reaches of the unconscious and one that literally connected everything in the universe with everything else.

After personally guiding over three thousand LSD sessions (each lasting at least five hours) and studying the records of more than two thousand sessions conducted by colleagues, Grof became unalterably convinced that something extraordinary was going on. "After years of conceptual struggle and confusion, I have concluded that the data from LSD research indicate an urgent need for a drastic revision of the existing paradigms for psychology, psychiatry, medicine, and possibly science in general. There is at present little doubt in my mind that our current understanding of the universe, of the nature of reality and particularly of human beings, is superficial, incorrect, and incomplete. (31)

Thus we may never discover the nature of consciousness by studying the physiology of the brain. As the Swedish neuroscientist Ragnar Granit says: 'It is a futile task to hunt for structural parallelism or likeness between the physical processes and conscious awareness when all we can do is to establish correlations.' The time has come to accept consciousness as an independent principle and to cease trying to treat it as something derived, as a mere 'epiphenomenon'. We are organisms and not things by virtue of an unforeseeable miracle - the emergence of consciousness - and this differentiates us decisively and permanently from machines.

> Tiller thinks the universe is also a
> kind of holodeck created by the
> "integration of all living things.

"We've created it as a vehicle of experience, and we've created the laws that govern it," he asserts. "And when we get to the frontiers of our understanding, we can in fact shift the laws so that we're also creating the physics as we go along." (32)

This shaping of reality can be a highly creative process. "Nature," in the view of philosopher Alfred North Whitehead, "is a dull affair, soundless, scentless, colourless, merely the hurrying of material, endless and meaningless. It is we who give the rose its scent and the nightingale its song. "We are the music," said T. S. Eliot, "while the music lasts."

As a sculptor takes responsibility for releasing one of a multitude of potential statues trapped in a block of stone, so we reveal the beauty in nature and in data, running always the risk of losing something in translation. We all have access to what Aldous Huxley called "Mind at Large", but most people, most of the time, know only what comes through the reducing valve of their own sense systems and becomes petrified in language. Reality is rife with "seas like millponds" and "nights as black as pitch".
But all is not lost.

Some people seem to be born with a kind, of bypass that circumvents the reducing valve. In others, temporary bypasses may be acquired through these flows, not indeed the perception of "everything that is happening everywhere in the universe", . . . but something more than, and above all, some-thing different from, the carefully selected, utilitarian material which our narrow individual minds regard as a complete, or at least sufficient, picture of reality. (33)

Unusual Things Do Sometimes Happen
The fact is that unusual things do sometimes happen. I have seen them happening often enough now to be certain of that. And, as a scientist myself, I admit that they present us with a problem. But it is not insoluble and it does not require any desperate mental gymnastics. I see it, in truth, as more of a paradox than a problem. An apparent contradiction produced by poor definition rather than faulty procedure.

The Normal Versus the Paranormal

Science decides what is possible by reference to its definition of reality. Anything which fits the definition is acceptable. Anything which doesn't fit it is impossible and must be rejected. And the problem is that the facts of dowsing or poltergeist phenomena stand in direct contradiction to the current definition. So the issue is reduced to a choice between rival facts. The normal versus the paranormal. And, of course, the normal wins - even if it does have to stand on its head to do so.

Such contortions ought to make us suspicious of the premises that made them necessary. There has to be a flaw somewhere in the argument. And there is. What is being ignored is the point that our definition of reality is a theory, not a fact. We don't know exactly how things work. All we have is a reasonably good hypothesis, and it never was a matter of choosing between rival sets of facts. The debate concerns a set of discordant facts and their relationship to a theory of how things happen. All that is at stake is the validity of a working hypothesis. And all that is necessary to reconcile the new facts with the old theory, is an admission that the theory might be incomplete. There is no need for anyone to stand on their heads. There is no assault on the laws of nature or the principles of science, and no need for protectors of the faith or charges of heresy.

What we need is a slightly broader definition of reality. One which includes the possibility of certain things happening when humans are involved. A definition that is not so exclusive; one less inclined to dismiss certain things as impossible, and better able to deal with what actually happens in terms of probability rather than outright and unreasonable denial. (34)

The Phantom Helmsman

'Sensory deprivation', according to the accepted theory, has the effect of making us attend to internal imagery. But there are numerous accounts of hallucinatory experience which seem to have resulted from sensory isolation plus physical and mental strain rather from just sensory isolation. For example, the lone yachtsman, Joshua Slocum, (whose single handed voyage round the world in 1895 – 1898 was a 'first') was attacked by sea sickness in the Atlantic and unable to steer his boat. He describes how a phantom helmsman appeared and took control. Slocum had a long conversation with him – and he disclosed that he was the pilot on one of Christopher Columbus' ships. (35)

Contrary to what everyone, knows is so, it may not be the brain that produces consciousness, but rather consciousness that creates the appearance of-the brain. (36)

A thought is an action. A dream is as much an action as a breath is an action. Although we speak in terms of separation, all reality is a part of action. When we divide action in order to discuss it, we in no way change the reality of action, nor alter its nature. (37)

Does the Objective World Really Exist?

Pribram realized that if the holographic brain model was taken to its logical conclusions, it opened the door on the possibility that the objective reality world of coffee cups, mountain vistas, elm trees, and table lamps, might not even exist, or at least not exist in the way we believe it exists. Was it possible, he wondered, that what the mystics had been saying for centuries was true, reality was Maya, an illusion, and what was out there was really a vast, resonating symphony of wave forms, a "frequency domain" that was transformed into the world as we know it only after it entered our senses?

Realizing that the solution he was seeking might lie outside the province of his own field, he went to his physicist son for advice. Hisson recommended he look into the work of a physicist named David Bohm. When Pribram did he was electrified. He not only found the answer to his question, but also discovered that according to Bohm, the entire universe was a hologram. (40)

--o--

CHAPTER FIVE

MIND & BRAIN

> *Sir John Eccles, a great Australian neurophysiologist, described the brain as a system of "ten thousand million neurones... momentarily poised to a just-threshold level of excitability. It is the kind of machine that a ghost could operate, if by 'ghost' we mean in the first place an 'agent' whose action escapes detection even by the most delicate instruments."* (41)

The classic view, known as dualism, sees mind as a mysterious unsubstantial something acting on the brain but independent of it and capable of continued existence after the brain has turned to dust. (42)

The Enchanted Loom
The human brain hums along like "an enchanted loom, where millions of flashing shuttles weave a dissolving pattern", but it does so within a narrow range of frequencies. (Man on his nature) (Sherrinton) (1951)

A sleeping brain produces voltages that peak between 1 and 4 times a second (the delta rhythm); while dreaming or in a meditative state, the shuttle accelerates from 4 to 7 cycles per second (the theta rhythm); in a condition of "relaxed awareness", a sort of neutral position, it fluctuates between frequencies of 8 and 13 (the alpha rhythm); and in a normal active or calculating state, the loom usually operates in the range from 13 to 30 cycles a second (the beta rhythm). Under ordinary circumstances, we remain unaware of these rhythms. But if electrodes are placed on the scalp at several points, and sensitive equipment is used to detect, amplify and announce the weak internal signals, we become conscious of them and enter into a new and more intimate relationship with ourselves.

One consequence of this awareness is an ability to control the brain-waves almost at will, concentrating on the production of one rhythm rather than another. And as sustained alpha rhythms in the frontal and central regions of the brain are known to be characteristic of Zen, Yoga and Sufic adepts in a state of deep meditation, numbers of people in the West began to look at biofeedback techniques as short cuts to mystic enlightenment. Electric Zen became the rage, a new and fashionable parlour game, in the 1970s and the market was flooded with devices for inducing instant alpha rhythms.

The Brain's Incredible Feats
Amongst all the improbability, nothing stands out more dramatically than the human brain, in the creation of which – said Arthur Koestler - "evolution has wildly overshot the mark. (Koestler, 1978). It seems to be an instrument well in advance of our needs. Why else should it be possible for anyone to respond, just four seconds after being asked to turn 4 / 47 into a decimal, with the reply "Point 0851063829787234042553 1914." A. C. Aitken, then Professor of Mathematics at Edinburgh University, did this in just 24 seconds, then stopped to think for a moment before adding"89361702127659574468 - and that's the repeating point. It starts again then at 085. (43)

The philosopher Bertrand Russel once told how his parents used to madden him by replying to his childish questions about mind with words: "What is mind? Doesn't matter. What is matter? Never mind." Doubtless it was the wish to prove to them that such questions do matter that impelled him to become a philosopher and spend a good part of his life debating such issues. Alas, what the philosophers have to say about mind has, for me (Gordon Rattray Taylor) at least, confused the issue, not clarified it.

Wiggle Your Toes

Where do you feel things? Wiggle your toes. Do you feel them? But where do you really feel them? Not in your toes. Toes feel nothing. You feel them in your brain. Anyone who has had the misfortune of having a limb amputated can tell you how the missing limb continues to be felt in the brain. The brain has within it maps of the body that record every sensation and then projects that sensation onto the mental image of the relevant body part. But it certainly feels like I'm feeling my toes in my toes. And it is not just the toes. The entire reality, what we see and what we feel, what we smell and what we hear, is mapped in the brain and then those recorded sensations reach out to our consciousness from within the two-to-four-millimetre (about one-eighth-inch) thin wrinkled grey layer, the cerebral cortex, that rests at the top of each of our brains. There is a reality out there in the world, but what we experience-every touch and every sound, every sight, smell and taste arises in our heads. (44)

Taylor suggested that the function of the brain and nervous system and sense organs is in the main *eliminative* and not *productive*. Each person is, at each moment, capable of remembering all that has ever happened to him and of perceiving everything that is happening everywhere in the universe. The function of the brain and nervous system is to protect us from being overwhelmed by this mass of useless and largely irrelevant knowledge, by shutting out most of what we would otherwise perceive or remember at any moment, and leaving only that small selection which is likely to be practically useful. (45)

Children Perform Better with half a Brain

People missing half their brain, after surgery, function almost perfectly normally, suggesting that the mind must be functioning outside of the brain. The procedure, called a hemispherectomy, removes half of the brain from the patient's head. The operation has been performed hundreds of times for disorders that can't be controlled using any other treatments. Remarkably, even when half of the brain has been removed, the patients retain their personalities and memories. In fact, a study of children who had half their brains removed found they often were able to perform better in their school work.

A number of instances have been recorded in which an adult was found to have virtually no brain, but had functioned from childhood through adulthood as a perfectly normal person; a brain wasn't necessary for normal daily functioning or storing and recalling memories. This account is from a July 19, 2007, story on Reuters. (46)

Prodigies

Hudson discusses the mystery of calculating prodigies – usually young boys of no particular talent who can perform astonishing feats of calculation within seconds – like five-year-old Zera Colburn, who once snapped out her answer to the square root of 106,929 before the questioner had finished speaking.

The power of such prodigies seems incredible. One six-year-old boy, Benjamin Blyth, was out walking with his father when he asked what time he was born. His father told him four a.m. A few minutes later the child stated the number of seconds he had lived. When they got home, his father worked it out on paper, and told Ben he was 172,800 seconds wrong. 'No,' said the child, 'you have forgotten two leap years.'

Most calculating prodigies lose their power in their teens, when life becomes more complex and difficult, and sexual changes in the body disturb the emotions. But the inference is that our Brains have an extraordinary power that few of us ever bother to develop.

Certainly one of the greatest blocks we have in understanding life after death stems from having been told that the brain and mind are synonymous. However, a different picture emerges for those serious researchers into the nature of Man who can look beyond conventional notions. For such scientists it has become increasingly obvious that the brain and mind are not the same thing.

One of the most conclusive pieces of evidence was provided by the research of the eminent Canadian neurosurgeon, Dr. Wilder Penfield. He was considerably surprised at how large a piece of the brain could be surgically removed with little or no effect on the ability of the patient to carry on living as usual. To use a now out-of-date analogy comparing the brain with a telephone switchboard, it was almost as though several of the "operators" went out for lunch, but as long as even one was still on duty, the calls could come in and go out much as usual.

A man with an unusually tiny brain managed to live an entirely normal life despite his condition caused by a fluid build-up in his skull, French researchers reported.

Scans of the 44-year-old man's brain showed that a huge fluid-filled chamber called a ventricle took up most of the room in his skull, leaving little more than a thin sheet of actual brain tissue.

"He was a married father of two children, and worked as a civil servant," Dr. Lionel Feuillet and colleagues at the Universite de la Mediterranee in Marseille wrote in a letter to the Lancet medical journal ...... "What I find amazing to this day is how the brain can deal with something which you think should not be compatible with life," commented Dr. Max Muenke, a paediatric brain defect specialist at the National Human Genome Research Institute. (47)

Our consciousness of the world is biased. We see not with our eyes, but with our brains. What a piece of bread looks like, depends on how hungry we are. The same coin looms larger in the minds of poor children than it does in those from wealthy homes. (48)

But as the psychoanalyst H. J. H. Home Points out, today we are more likely to make the contrary mistake of explaining human purpose in mechanical terms. A massive example of this error was Marx's explanation of social behaviour in terms of historical 'forces' rather than of human motivations. To treat processes as 'things' is known as reification. To treat things as gods is deification. As Home neatly says, 'To reify is to deify.'

Prediction is a central function of the brain, and the brain constantly monitors discrepancies between intention and performance. Thus it is a cardinal error to regard it - as has so long been the case - as an input-output device. (49)

As the philosopher Michael Polanyi has pointed out. When dealing with hierarchies you cannot derive information about a a higher level from studying a lower level. Knowledge about atoms cannot reveal the soapiness of soap.

The Brain Beats the Computer Hands Down
It is not only at the intellectual level that computers are in a different ball-park from man. Computers are not motivated, they have no curiosity, and they only address a problem when instructed to do so. Computers, have no moral sense, no conscience; they are incapable of

generosity. Computers have no aesthetic feelings, no sense of wonder, and - worst of all - no sense of humour.

Lastly, they have no emotions, hence no values, attitudes or preferences. The human cortex, as it reasons, constantly refers the data to the mid-brain, which assesses the desirability of each step. Computers do not, as man does, sleep on a problem while their unconscious explores imaginatively the emotional balance sheet of various possible outcomes of what is planned. Man has a memory stocked with a huge range of personal experience, as well as 'facts', and any provisional decision is liable to be checked against such experience, consciously or unconsciously.

Weizenbaum emphasizes the danger of leaving decisions to computers in view of their vast deficiencies. A military computer may devise a strategy which will maximize the chance of victory, within the definition of victory embodied in its programme, but this could be a victory which was at an unacceptable price in broad human terms. (Presumably two of us' left alive and none of 'them' would constitute victory. Of course, a computer would be instructed to reject certain solutions, such as those involving unacceptable loss of life, but programmers are not likely to foresee all the possibilities and provide for them.)

Computers now modify their own programmes in the light of their own calculations with the result that we can never know how they reach their conclusions. We are forced to trust them - that is to trust to the wisdom, care and even the value systems of those who programmed them. It is an abdication of human responsibility which I, for one, regard as totally unacceptable even mad. (50)

The role of memory in all this is clearly crucial, but far from clearly understood. Psychology breaks the process of memory down into the four sub-functions of learning, retention, remembering, and forgetting. Biology sees it in more organic terms as a single process, an organism's unwritten record of reality. Both regard it as something which passes through the brain, leaving a memory "trace", but neither can be certain where this is housed. Large parts of the brain can be destroyed without abolishing memory of past events. Suspicion at one time fell on RNA molecules as chemical memory banks, raising the awesome possibility of memory transmission through cannibalism, but this has never been satisfactorily proven. And now the new physics revives an old idea – that memory could be stored, or at least carried, in a physical form.

Before Copiers & Printers
Before the advent of printing and general literacy, most cultural material was stored and transmitted orally and a good memory was a useful talent, perhaps even one with enough survival value for it to be favoured by natural selection. But the period during which we were advanced enough to enjoy living together, swapping tales across a campfire, and yet not advanced enough to have invented writing, was a comparatively short one in our evolution and cannot in itself account for the explosive growth of our brains. Everything we know about the evolution of the brain suggests that it was big enough and complex enough to handle feats of memory and calculation long before we found ourselves in situations where such talents might prove to be useful. Our cortical skills were undoubtedly honed and polished during the last few hundred thousand years, but it looks as though we came to the game already provided with most of the right equipment. (51)

There is an astonishing case on record of a man who was able to recall a pattern of apparently random dots with such clarity that, on being presented the following day with a second pattern, he could fuse the two in his mind. Proof that he was doing so was provided by the fact that the two pictures had been very carefully designed so that when one was superimposed precisely on the other, and only then, a square appeared in the centre. (52) This is known as visual or "eidetic" imagery and may be rare, but many of those with unusually good recall use some kind of synesthesia or sensory blending, associating numbers and names with vivid images or musical tones. 'The mixture, it seems, lowers the threshold for all the senses and widens the reducing valve enough to expose the mind to larger concerns. This provides information and produces talents that confer no obvious selective advantage on an individual or even on a species, but they do offer fascinating glimpses of levels on which such things perhaps have reason and meaning.

Does the Pineal Gland enable Telepathy?
"The pineal gland," says this Eastern writer, "is a mass of nervous substance which is found located in the brain, in a position near the centre of the skull almost directly above the extreme top of the spinal column, It is shaped like a small cone, and is of .reddish-grey colour. It lies in front of the cerebellum and is attached to the third ventricle of the brain. It derives its scientific name from its shape, which resembles a pine cone. The Oriental occultists claim that the pineal gland, with its peculiar arrangement of nerve-cell corpuscles and its tiny grains of brain sand is intimately associated with certain transmissions and reception of waves of mental vibration. Western students have been struck with the remarkable resemblance between the pineal gland and a certain part of the receiving apparatus employed in wireless telegraphy, the latter also containing small particles which bear a close resemblance to the 'brain sand' of the pineal gland. (53)

--o--

CHAPTER SIX

MAGIC, MIRACLES & THE UNBELIEVABLE

*A great man once said that if we do
not expect the unexpected, we will
never find it.
In this chapter there is a lot of
the unexpected. I, personally, never
cease to feel amazed at what goes
on in this universe we live in.*

"The world is nothing but an objectivized dream," says Yogananda, and "whatever your powerful mind believes very intensely instantly comes to pass. (54) Have such individuals discovered a way to tap just a little of the sea of cosmic energy that Bohm says fills every cubic centimetre of empty space?

A remarkable series of materializations that has received even greater confirmation than that bestowed by Haraldsson on Sai Baba was produced by Therese Neumann. In addition to her stigmata, Neumann also displayed inedia, the supernormal ability to live without food. Her inedia began in 1923 when she "transferred" the throat disease of a young priest to her own body and subsisted solely on liquids for several years. Then, in 1927, she gave up both food and water entirely.

Woman Lives without Food or Water for 35 Years

When the local bishop in Regensburg first learned of Neumann's fast, he sent a commission into her home to investigate. From July 14, 1927, to July 29, 1927, and under the supervision of a medical doctor named Seidl, four Franciscan nursing sisters scrutinized her every move. They watched her day and night, and the water she used for washing and rinsing her mouth was carefully measured and weighed. The sisters discovered several unusual things about Neumann. She never went to the bathroom (even after a period of six weeks she only had one bowel movement, and the excrement, examined by a Dr. Reismanns, contained only a small amount of mucus and bile, but no traces of food). She also showed no signs of dehydration, even though the average human expels about four hundred grams (fourteen ounces) of water daily into the air, he or she exhales a like amount through the pores. And her weight remained constant; although she lost nearly nine pounds (in blood) during the weekly opening of her stigmata, her weight returned to normal within a day or two later.

At the end of the inquiry Dr. Seidl and the sisters were completely convinced that Neumann had not eaten or drunk a thing for the entire fourteen days. The test seems conclusive, for while the human body can survive two weeks without food, it can rarely survive half that time without water. Yet this was nothing for Neumann; she did not eat or drink a thing for the next thirty-five years.

When I was a boy I read a story in one of my weekly comics. It really caught my attention. The boy in the story looked on in horror as a wall began to topple over onto his friend. Without hesitation he grabbed a stick and pointed at the wall, willing it to turn into a hay stack; and it did!

I thought "wouldn't it be great if we could make magic happen just like that." I tried it out a few times but it never worked for me.

As I became more scientific and logical in my way of thinking I realized that there was no such magic in the world. How could there be?

The World is full of Magic
I now realize just how wrong I was. This world is absolutely full of magic; I don't mean conjuring; I mean the real thing. It surrounds us everywhere. If, like me, you are not psychic then you will find it hard to believe. If, on the other hand you have been born into a psychic family then you will see natures greatest mysteries unravel.

In this chapter I look at just a few of these amazing things but, believe me, there are many, many more.

The sudden acquisition of linguistic, musical and artistic skills presents a real problem for any explanation of the paranormal. They seem to rule out any possibility of telepathy or extrasensory perception - even of the more naturalistic shaman kind I have been suggesting. Which would appear to leave us with just two other possibilities: true possession - the actual invasion by an alien entity; or reincarnation - which in the final analysis amounts to the same thing, except that the entity involved is dead.

The Ouija Board
The Ouija Board is one of the most widely used methods of "untrained" Spirit communication. The name is taken from the French and German words for yes - oui and ja. It consists of a flat board with the letters of the alphabet printed on it.

In the summer of 1913, a housewife in St. Louis got out a "Ouija board as part of a parlour game. The pointer began spelling out a message from a female personality calling herself Patience Worth, who supposedly lived in England in the seventeenth century. Over a period of twenty-five years, Patience Worth dictated poetry and novels which were published and received critical notice. The housewife, Mrs Pearl Curren, was not an educated woman. Her personality was nothing like Patience Worth's.

Patience wrote in the idiom of a bygone era, with authentic archaic spelling. She spoke casually in her fiction, of daily household articles that have long since vanished from use and memory. The case was well investigated. No hint of fraud was ever discovered. Disagreements arise only from the various explanations given as to the origin of the Patience Worth personality.

Was Patience Worth the spirit of a woman long dead? Did she have significant knowledge of the seventeenth century because she had lived in it? Or had Mrs Curren, unknown to herself, accumulated a fantastic amount of information, subconsciously, all of it pertaining to the past? If so, what was the source of the knowledge?

Many of the details given in the "Ouija" board messages were known only to scholars. If Mrs Curren's subconscious mind some-how picked up this wealth of knowledge, then this is evidence that the subconscious has at its command abilities of which the conscious mind is unaware. Even this explanation for the Patience Worth case leaves many questions unanswered. The sort of information given was not of the kind that is available ordinarily. Where did it come from? How did Mrs Curren's subconscious mind organize the material into novels and plays?

On the other hand, if Patience Worth was actually a personality who once operated within physical matter, then a different set of questions present themselves.

In either case we are left with the fact that the human personality is less limited by time and space than we suppose.

People using the Ouija Board place their fingers lightly on a pointer, which then rapidly, and without the conscious knowledge of the members present, moves to spell out a series of messages. Sales of Ouija boards in the United States peaked during World War One, and the Thirties, Forties, and Sixties witnessed national Ouija crazes during which the "Mysterious Talking Oracle" became very frequently used by students. (55)

The Ouija board is included because it is often the first method used by amateurs to try to investigate Psychic phenomena. It is scientific in the sense that people closely following the formula will get a similar result. Some will get intelligent messages - intelligent in the sense that answers are given to specific questions. Of course, the quality of responses will depend on who or what is answering.

Psychics and experienced mediums believe in the reality of spirit contact and that the responses to the Ouija board are sometimes made by human and non-human entities of different levels of refinement, but most often by the lowest entities who operate close to our own "wavelength." If contact is made with a more refined entity, the response will usually be sophisticated. If the contact is made with uncouth, very lowly-placed entities, then the information is usually the same as from a, person, on earth who is uncouth, vulgar, stupid, arrogant and blasphemes for the purpose of shocking those around them. Psychic investigator Professor Archie Roy likens using a Ouija board to the practice of picking up total strangers in a bar and inviting them home. (56)

The materialist view is that the messages come from the action of the subconscious or unconscious minds of the "players" - a form of automatism." For years the Ouija board has been sold in toy shops and game departments in the USA, and people have tended to use it for fun or for personal advantage such as trying to get winning numbers for gambling, etc. But no sceptic has been able to explain how groups of normal, decent people have elicited horrible blasphemies, curses and all kind of terrifying threats from the Ouija board in a way that they certainly did not from other methods which supposedly projected the unconscious.

The Boy with X-Ray Eyes
In 1963 a 12-year old South African named Pieter van Jaarsveld became world famous as "the boy with X-ray eyes" for his ability to detect water hidden deep underground. He used no sort of dowsing rod but claimed he was able to see water "shimmering like green moonlight" through the surface of the soil. Peter was very surprised to learn that other people could not see it equally well. I think that when we begin to realize that nature and the classic five senses are only a small part of the real magic of Supernature, more of us might begin to join in seeing things as they really are. (57)

Music
The poverty of an objectivistic account is made only too clear when we consider the mystery of music. From a scientific point of view, it is nothing but vibrations in the air, impinging on the eardrums and stimulating neural currents in the brain.

How does it come about that this banal sequence of temporal activity has the power to speak to our hearts of an eternal beauty? The whole range of subjective experience, from perceiving a patch of pink, to being enthralled by a performance of the mass in B Minor, and on to the mystic's encounter with the ineffable reality of the one, all these truly human experiences are at the centre of our encounter with reality, and they are not to be dismissed as epiphenomenal froth on the surface of a universe whose true nature is impersonal and lifeless. (58)

> The waves of sound impinging upon my ear drum and in a beautifully complex path become converted to bio-electrical pulses that are chemically stored in the cortex of my brain.

The cosmos is full of "noise," irregular jumbles of wave-lengths, but all its useful signals are regular patterns. Combinations of musical notes chosen at random jar on our nerves; we find them unpleasant. But tones with certain regular intervals between them are harmonious, we find them pleasing. A note played together with another one that has exactly double its frequency, that is, one octave higher, makes a very harmonious sound. Three notes go well together as a chord if their relative frequencies are in the proportion 4:5.6. These are purely mathematical relationships, but we know from experience that these are the ones to which man responds. Music is being played to other animals on farms and in zoos with similarly marked effects. Preferences differ from species to species, presumably because their structure and sensitivity, and therefore their resonant frequencies, differ. Research is now going on into the effect of music on plants. It has been discovered that geraniums grow faster and taller to the accompaniment of Bach's Brandenburg Concertos. If the dominant frequencies in these pieces of music are broadcast to the Plants, they have some effect, but growth is, more marked if the frequencies occur in the spatial relationship so carefully designed by the composer. Bacteria are affected in the same way, multiplying under the influence of certain frequencies and dying when subject to others. It is not a long step from this discovery to the old idea that frequent repetition of certain chants or songs could cure disease. (59)

The Magnetic Girl

Mesmer heard about a girl named Mary Novotny, daughter of a tax collector in Vienna, who suffered from general debility and cataleptic attacks - like Justinus Kerner's famous patients, Friederike Hauffe, 'the Seeress of Prevorst'. Herr Novotny was asked if he would take a large magnet - no doubt supplied by Reichenbach - into his daughter's bedroom in the middle of the night, and see if she responded to it. The results were far more striking than he had expected. Around the poles of the magnet, the girl saw a fiery glow, a kind of aurora borealis, reddish-yellow from the south pole and bluish-green from the north. Could this have been autosuggestion?

Reichenbach got his assistant to go into the next room and point the magnet at her through the wall; she immediately detected its presence. Blindfolded, she could tell when the armature was moved from the end of the magnet. And, like Caspar Hauser, Miss Novotny proved to be a kind of magnet herself - at least, her hand stuck to the magnet as if her skin was made of iron. (60)

Energy Around Standing Stones

Encouraged by their finding, the group built an even more sensitive detector designed to exclude all possibility of radio interference and stray signals from local energy sources or geological faults. And they put it into action all year round. On streets and bridges, in gardens and woods nearby, there was never anything more than weak and random background noise. But at Rollright there was a consistent pulsing which could be measured near dawn on any day, regardless of weather conditions, and which rose to an ultrasonic screech lasting for several hours on those mornings in March and October which coincide with the feasts of equinox. And there are records of equinoctial rites being held at Rollright even in historic times.

At other times, the stones seemed almost to be creating an ultrasonic barrier. "This was the weirdest thing," says Robins:

Plants Have Feelings

On a February morning in 1966 Cleve Backster made a discovery that changed his life and could have far-reaching effects on ours. Backster was at that time an interrogation specialist who left the CIA to operate a New York school for training policemen in the techniques of using the polygraph, or "lie detector." This instrument normally measures the electrical resistance of the human skin, but on that morning he extended its possibilities. Immediately after watering an office plant, he wondered if it would be possible to measure the rate at which water rose in the plant from the root to the leaf by recording the increase in leaf-moisture content on a polygraph tape. Backster placed the two psychogalvanic reflex (PGR) electrodes on either side of a leaf of Dracaena massangeana, a potted rubber plant, and balanced the leaf into the circuitry before watering the plant again. There was no marked reaction to this Stimulus, so Backster decided to try what he calls 'the threat-to-well-being principle, a well-established method of triggering emotionality in humans." In other words he decided to torture the plant. First of all he dipped one of its leaves into a cup of hot coffee, but there was no reaction, so he decided to get a match and burn the leaf properly. "At the instant of this decision, at 13 minutes and 55 seconds of chart time, there was a dramatic change in the PGR tracing pattern in the form of an abrupt and prolonged upward sweep of the recording pen. I had not moved, or touched the plant, so the timing of the PGR pen activity suggested to me that the tracing might have been triggered by the mere thought of the harm I intended to inflict on the plant."

Plants React to Dying Shrimp

Backster went on to explore the possibility of such perception in the plant by bringing some live brine shrimp into his office and dropping them one by one into boiling water. Every time he killed a shrimp the polygraph recording needle jumped violently. To eliminate the possibility of his own emotions producing this reaction, he completely automated the whole experiment so that an electronic randomizer chose odd moments to dump the shrimp into hot water when no human was in the laboratory at all. The plant continued to respond in sympathy to the death of every shrimp and failed to register any change when the machine dropped already dead shrimp into the water.

Gravity & Magnetism

But what is it that produces the force of gravity, that pulls an apple to the ground, or holds the distant moon in orbit? For a force to act at a distance, for the earth to reach out to the moon and hold it, there must be something making contact between the two bodies, otherwise how can the force be felt at a distance? We call that force gravity without really knowing what it is. Anyone who predicts that we are approaching the end of science is fooling himself The secrets of gravity may one day unlock more human potential than the sum total of the technology we possess today.

Magnets presented the same enigma. The magnet is here and the iron nail is there. Empty space lies between. Slowly at first and then with increasing speed, the nail moves toward the magnet. No problem. Everybody knows magnets attract iron. But how? What reaches out from the magnet, beckoning the iron to come hither? It's a lesson in the magic of our universe. Take two horseshoe magnets. Try to push north onto north and south onto south. Look closely at the space between the opposing poles. Nothing is seen, but the force is mightily felt as the poles constantly slip aside, avoiding one another.

When Isaac Newton was twenty-three years old and a student at Cambridge, he was forced to leave his college by the wave of bubonic plague that brought black-death to most of England in 1665. While on this enforced holiday in the country, he saw an orb-like apple fall to the earth and, in his own words, "began to think of gravitation as extending to the orb of the moon." These thoughts led to his universal theory of gravity, which says that every particle in the universe attracts every other particle with a force that depends on their masses and the distance between them. The earth attracts the moon strongly enough to hold it in orbit, and the moon is large enough and close enough to tug insistently at earth's mantle. The water on earth's surface behaves like a loose garment that can be pulled out from the body to fall back as earth turns away again.

The moon circles the earth once every 24.8 hours, rotating brazenly as she does so, to keep the same face turned always towards us, but earth shows all its sides to the satellite once every 24.8 hours. This means that the waters of earth flow out toward the moon, and therefore bring high tide to any land that lies in that direction, forty-eight minutes later each day.

Every drop of water in the ocean responds to this force, and every living marine animal and plant is made aware of the rhythm. The lives of those that inhabit the margins of the sea depend entirely on this awareness. One very small fiat-worm, for instance, has entered into partnership with a green alga, and whenever the tide goes out, it must come up from the sand to expose its greenery to the sun. Rachel Carson took some of these animals into the laboratory and there described their conditioning to the tidal rhythm in her usual effortless and poetic way: 'Twice each day Convoluta continues to live out its life in this alien place, remembering, in every fibre of its small green body the tidal rhythm of the distant sea." (61)

The Sun

Beyond earth's atmosphere, beyond even the orbit of the moon, lies space. By definition this is supposed to be empty, an interval separating things from each other, but instruments sent out to probe this space reveal that it is far from empty. The vacuum is filled with a variety of forces, many of which reach the earth and some of which affect life here. The most powerful of these forces come from the star we call our sun.

The sun is a dense mass of glowing matter a million times the volume of earth and in a permanent state of effervescence. Every second, four million tons of hydrogen are destroyed in incredible explosions that start somewhere near the core, where the temperature is 13 million degrees C, and send fountains of flame shooting thousands of miles out into space. In this continuous and unimaginable holocaust, atoms are split into streams of fast-moving electrons and protons that rush out into space as a solar wind that buffets all the planets in our system. Earth falls well inside the sun's atmosphere and is constantly exposed to the changes in its weather. Scattered over the face of the sun like acne are spots of even more violent activity that flare up from time to time. These are usually about the size of earth, and some-times the rash spreads quickly and the sun erupts in a bout of bad weather that produces magnetic storms in our atmosphere as well.

We first notice these storms when they disrupt radio and television reception and produce the fantastic draperies of the aurora borealis, but we continue to feel their effects in changes they produce in our own weather. At times of sun-spot activity there is a tendency for cyclones to form over the ocean and for anti-cyclones to develop over the land masses, producing bad weather at sea and fine conditions ashore. One of the ways in which the moon may influence weather is by deflecting the solar wind so that it hits the earth at a different angle or misses it altogether. The IMP-1 satellite of 1964 recorded fluctuations in magnetic field produced in this way. (62)

It would be possible to use sunspot activity as an aid to weather forecasting were it not for the fact that it seems to vary from day to day in a completely random fashion, but there are regular cycles of activity covering much longer periods of time. In 1801 Sir John Herschel discovered an 11-year sunspot cycle, which has since been confirmed many times and found to correlate with the thickness of annual rings in trees, the level of Lake Victoria, the number of icebergs, the occurrence of drought and famine in India, and the great vintage years for Burgundy wines. All these variables are dependent on the weather, and it seems certain that this regular pattern of change is produced by cycles in the sun. An even more sensitive measure has recently been made available by the study of thin layers of fossil mud deposited on the bottoms of old lakes. These layers are called varves, and their thickness depends on the annual rate at which glaciers melt and therefore provides an indication of climate conditions. Microscopic measurement of varves going back as much as five hundred million years shows that, even in Pre-Cambrian times, there were cycles about eleven years long. (63)

Our sensitivity to the sun extends from light rays into the longer wavelengths of radio. We see the sun, we feel its warmth, and we respond to changes it produces in the earth's magnetic field. These changes affect radio reception in a pattern that as Nelson has shown, can be predicted by the position of the planets. (64) The amount of change is small, but its effect is most marked on biochemical processes such as nerve activity. Even by drilling two holes in the trunk of a tree, one can measure variations in electrical potential that follow the movements of bodies in our solar system, so it is no surprise to find that the complex human organism is affected by the planets. (65)

Michel Cauquelin, of the Psycho physiological Laboratory at Strasbourg, was the first to quantify this "effect". His twenty years of painstaking research are summarized in his excellent book The Cosmic Clocks. In 1950 Cauquelin became interested in planetary rhythms and looked for possible correlations on earth. As our planet spins on its axis, the sun and the moon appear to move overhead, rising and setting in solar and lunar days whose length depends on our latitude and the time of year. The other planets travel across our horizon in the same way, producing Venusian and Martian days that are equally predictable. In Europe all local authorities record the exact moment of birth in official registers, so Cauquelin was able to collect this information and match it with the positions of planets computed from astronomical tables.

We Are All Effected by the Planets
Cauquelin selected 576 members of the French Academy. Of Medicine and found, to his astonishment, that an unusually large number of them were born when Mars and Saturn had just risen or reached their highest point in the sky. To check these findings, he took another sample of 508 famous physicians and got the same results. (66) There was a strong statistical correlation between the 'rise of these two planets at a child's moment of birth and his future success as a doctor.

Taken together, the two tests produce odds of ten million to one against this happening just by chance. For the first time in history a scientist had produced evidence that the planets actually influence, or indicate an influence, on our lives. This gives science a point of vital contact with the old beliefs of astrology.

So astrology claims that long experience has shown that planets have a predictable influence on character and is modified by secondary, though equally predictable, effects of stars in conjunction with the planet at that moment. Also that the combined effects of these forces on a person are determined by the position of the planet / star combination in space at the moment of the child's birth. There are ten large bodies in our solar system, twelve groups of stars, and twelve areas they can all occupy, but astrologers believe that the most important associations are those actually on the eastern horizon at the time of birth (the rising signs) and those that will be there when the sun comes up (the sun signs). This tallies with Gauquelin's finding that it was the planet rising at birth that was linked with the medical profession. So, if a cosmic force exerts a special influence just as the earth turns toward it, it seems reasonable that this would be reinforced by the sun coming into view at the same time as well. Once again there is little in the mechanics of these suggested effects that would offend a broad-minded scientist, but it is with the specific attributes of the astrological tradition that difficulties arise. There are more of both to come.

Astrology goes on to claim that a person's character (as determined by a planet) and its manifestation (as influenced by a star group) are even further modified by the relationships of the different planets to each other. When a planet stands at a certain angle to another, they are said to be 'in aspect." If the two can be seen together at the same point in the sky, they are in "conjunction" and said to exert a powerful influence on events. If one is on the eastern and the other on the western horizon, they are 180 degrees apart and in "opposition," which is said to be a negative, or bad, relationship. If one is on the horizon and the other is directly overhead, they are 0 degrees apart, in "square," and this, too, is bad. But if the angle between them is 120 degrees, they are in "trine,' which is positive and good. These are the main aspects, but angles of 30, 45, 60, 135, and 150 degrees are also significant. In practice, a variation of up to 9 degrees from these set aspect angles is regarded as permissible.

Water
Every high school student knows that water is H_2O, a chemical compound of two simple elements. And yet scientific journals are full of articles arguing the merits of various theories on the structure of water, and we still do not understand exactly how it works. There are so many anomalies: water is one of the very few substances that are more dense in the liquid than the solid state, so ice floats; water is unique in that it is most dense a few degrees above its melting point, so that heating it up to 4 degrees C from its melting point of 0 degrees C causes it to contract even further; and water can act both as an acid and as a base, so that it actually reacts chemically with itself under certain conditions.

The clue to some of water's strange behaviour lies with the hydrogen atom, which has only one electron to share with any other atom with which it combines. When it joins with oxygen to form molecules of water, each hydrogen atom is balanced between two oxygen atoms in what is called the "hydrogen bond"; but having only one electron to offer, the hydrogen atom can be attached firmly on only one side, so the bond is a weak one. Its strength is 10 per cent of that of most ordinary chemical bonds, so for water to exist at all there have to be lots of bonds to hold it together. Liquid water is so intricately laced that it is almost a continuous structure, and one worker has gone so far as to describe a glass of water as a single molecule. (67) Ice is even more regular, and forms the most perfectly bonded hydrogen structure known. Its crystalline pattern is so very precise that it seems to persist into the liquid state, and though it looks clear, water contains short-lived regions of ice crystals that form and melt many millions of times every second. It is as though liquid water remembers the form of the ice from which it came by repeating the formula over and over again to itself, ready to change back again at a moment's notice. If one could take a photograph with a short enough exposure, it would probably show ice-like areas even in a glass of hot water.

Ancient Technology
The origins of alchemy lie in early agricultural communities, when technology had not yet been segregated from other aspects of daily life and the craftsmen who made metal farming implements and the dyes for weaving, carried out their trades to the accompaniment of religious and magical rites. The Egyptians, the Greeks, and the Arabs all contributed their skills and philosophies, and some great discoveries were made. In the Baghdad Museum are some stones found in a remote part of Iraq and classified as "ritual objects,' but that have now been shown to be the cores of electric batteries invented two thousand years before Galvani. (68)

Some pieces of bronze, dredged up off the shores of Greece at Antikythera and dated sixth century B.C., turn out to be components of an early computer for calculating astronomical positions. So many of our proudest new achievements seem to have been anticipated by the alchemists and their contemporaries that one wonders what other lost skills we have yet to rediscover.

Cosmic Rays
Over a period of twenty years, Takata has been able, to show that changes in blood serum occur mainly when major sunspots are interfering with earth's magnetic field. He made tests during the eclipses of 1941, 1943, and 1948 and found that these inhibited his reaction as much as performing them in a mine shaft six hundred feet underground. (69) He also experimented on subjects in an aircraft at over thirty thousand feet and discovered that the reaction took place more strongly at heights where the atmosphere was too thin to provide effective protection

from solar radiation. Recent Soviet work lends support to the idea that our blood is directly affected by the sun. Over 120,000 tests were made on people in a Black Sea resort to measure the number of lymphocytes in their blood. These small cells normally make up be between 20 and 25 per cent of man's white blood cells, but in years of great solar activity this proportion decreases. There was a big drop during the sunspot years of 1956 and 1957, and the number of people suffering from diseases caused by a lymphocyte deficiency actually doubled during the tremendous solar explosion of February 1956.

Pyramids Defy the Laws of Science
In 1968 a team of scientists from the United States and from Ein Shams University in Cairo began a million-dollar project to X-ray the pyramid of Chephren, successor to Cheops. They hoped to find new vaults hidden in the six million tons of stone by placing detectors in a chamber at its base and measuring the amount of cosmic-ray penetration, the theory being that more rays would come through hollow areas. The recorders ran twenty-four hours a day for more than a year until, in early 1969, the latest, IBM 1130, computer was delivered to the university for analysis of the tapes. Six months later the scientists had to admit defeat: the pyramid made no sense at all. Tapes recorded with the same equipment from the same point on successive days showed totally different cosmic-ray patterns. The leader of the project, Amr Gohed, in an interview afterward said, 'This is scientifically impossible. Call it what you will, occultism, the curse of the pharaohs, sorcery, or magic, there is some force that defies the laws of science at work in the pyramid.'

The idea of shape having an influence on the functions taking place within it is not a new one. A French firm once patented a special container for making yogurt, because that particular shape enhanced the action of the microorganism involved in the process. The brewers of a Czechoslovakian beer tried to change from round to angular barrels but found that this resulted in deterioration in the quality of their beer despite the fact that the method of processing remained unchanged. A German researcher has shown that mice with identical wounds heal more quickly if they are kept in spherical cages. Architects in Canada report a sudden improvement in schizophrenic patients living in trapezoidal hospital wards. (70)

Pyramids Preserve Human Tissues

The pyramids on the west bank of the Nile were built by the pharaohs as royal tombs and date from about 3000 B.C. The most celebrated are those at Giza, built during the fourth dynasty, of which the largest is the one that housed the pharaoh Khufu better known as Cheops. This is now called the Great Pyramid. Some years ago it was visited by a French-man named Bovis, who took refuge from the midday sun in the pharaoh's chamber, which is situated in the centre of the pyramid, exactly one third of the way up from the base. He found it unusually humid there, but what really surprised him were the garbage cans that contained, among the usual tourist litter, the bodies of a cat and some small desert animals that had wandered into the pyramid and died there. Despite the humidity, none of them bad decayed but just dried out like mummies. He began to wonder whether the pharaohs had really been so carefully embalmed by their subjects after all, or whether there was something about the pyramids themselves that preserved bodies in a mummified condition.

Bovis made an accurate scale model of the Cheops pyramid and placed it, like the original, with the base lines facing precisely north-south and east-west. Inside the model, one third of the way up, he put a dead cat. It became mummified, and he concluded that the pyramid promoted rapid dehydration. Reports of this discovery attracted the attention of Karel Drbal, a radio engineer in Prague, who repeated the experiment with several dead animals and concluded, "There is a relation between the shape of the space inside the pyramid and the physical, chemical, and biological processes going on inside that space. By using suitable forms and shapes, we should be able to make processes occur faster or delay them. (71)

The Pyramid Razor Blade Sharpener
Drbal remembered an old superstition which claimed that a razor left in the light of the moon became blunted. He tried putting one under his model pyramid, but nothing happened, so he went on shaving with it until it was blunt, and then put it back in the pyramid. It became sharp again. Getting a good razor blade is still difficult in many Eastern European countries, so Drbal tried to patent and market his discovery. The patent office in Prague refused to consider it until their chief scientist had tried building a model himself and found that it worked. So the Cheops Pyramid Razor Blade Sharpener was registered in 1959 under the Czechoslovakian Re-public Patent No. 91304, and a factory soon began to turn out miniature cardboard pyramids. Today they make them in Styrofoam.

The edge of a razor blade has a crystal structure. Crystals are almost alive, in that they grow by reproducing themselves. When a blade becomes blunted, some of the crystals on the edge, where they are only one layer thick are rubbed off. Theoretically, there is no reason why they should not re-place themselves in time. We know that sunlight has a field that points in all directions, but sunlight reflected from an object such as the moon is partly polarized, vibrating mostly in one direction. This could conceivably destroy the edge of a blade left under the moon, but it does not explain the reverse action of the pyramid. We can only guess that the Great Pyramid and its little imitations act as lenses that focus energy or as resonators that collect energy, which encourages crystal growth. The pyramid shape itself is very much like that of a crystal of magnetite, so perhaps it builds up a magnetic field. I do not know the answer, but I do know that it works. My record so far with Wilkinson Sword blades is four months of continuous daily use. I have a feeling that the manufacturers are not going to like this idea.

Mysticism & Magic
It was the belief of those who were Mystics, and experience repeatedly gave it confirmation, that it was only by transcending the mind, or with the mind emptied of all content and made calm like a lagoon of still blue water, could a glimpse of Eternity be mirrored. When the modifications of the thinking principle had been stifled or transcended, when the constant whirling which is a characteristic of the normal mind has been quelled, and a serene tranquillity substituted. Only then could there occur that vision of spirituality, and a depth of imaginings of the highest and all-embracing kind.

The technique of Mysticism divides itself naturally into two major divisions. The one is Magic, with which this treatise will deal; the other is Yoga. Now it is necessary to register a vehement protest against those critics who, in opposition to Mysticism (by which term some such process as Yoga or Contemplation is understood) posit Magic as a thing completely apart, unspiritual and of this earth. This classification I hold to be contrary to the implications of both systems and quite inaccurate, as I shall hereafter try to show. Yoga and Magic, are both different phases comprehended in the one term Mysticism. However often abused and misused as a word, Mysticism is throughout this book used because it is the correct term for that Mystical or ecstatic relationship of the Self to the Universe. It expresses the relation of the individual to a more comprehensive consciousness. He discovers his adjustment to larger, more harmonious ends. If this definition is inconsistent with our views then it is obvious that Magic, also devised to accomplish that same necessary relationship, may not satisfactorily be placed against the other.

Nothing has hitherto been issued to act as a definitive statement of what Magic really is. This work does not pretend to deal in any way with love-charms, philtres and potions, nor with amulets preventing one's neighbour's cow from giving milk, robbing him of his wife, or to ascertain the whereabouts of gold and hidden treasure. Such vile and stupid practices rightly deserve that much-abused term "Black Magic."

This study has nothing to do with Black Magic. But if any man is anxious to discover the eternal font wherefrom the flame of Godhead springs, let such a man turn eagerly to Magic. In its technique, may be found the means to the fulfilment of the loftiest dreams of the soul.

Communication with the Afterlife
To my surprise, very few people are aware of the dramatic leap which has occurred in communicating with the afterlife using high technology. Whilst there are highly credible books by unimpeachable sources on Electronic Voice Phenomena, or EVP as it is known, the mass media rarely report it. Yet these most important findings reveal objective communication between those who live physically here on this earth with those who died and are now living in a different dimension

For more than 50 years experimenters all over the world have been tape-recording "paranormal voices" - voices which cannot be heard when a tape-recorder is playing but which can be heard when the tape is played back. Many of the very short messages claim to be from loved ones who have passed on. These are not just random noises or words; they use the experimenter's name and they answer questions.

There are thousands of researchers around the world who have been researching this most fascinating psychic phenomenon. At the time of writing, the Internet search engine Google had more than 76,700,000 listings for EVP (up from 50,000 in 2002). It is particularly relevant to my argument since it follows strict scientific procedures and experiments have been duplicated under laboratory conditions by all kinds of researchers in many different countries.

Persistent investigators get a powerful shock when they decide to investigate Electronic Voice Phenomena because by using the proper method of tape recording and following a specific procedure they are likely to hear voices of loved ones or friends who have died.

The group is now in the process of conducting a number of additional experiments, including using more sophisticated electronic equipment to analyze the voices. This is especially important because I have since attended meetings where two entities claiming to be world celebrities - Louis Armstrong and Mahatma Gandhi - materialized.

We continue to proceed with caution and go to the forensic audio equipment to do full correlation tests. So far, the conduct of the entities is consistent with what we know about them. Full results will be published in a future book.

Materializations
Evidence for materialization is substantive not only in England and the United States but in other countries such as Brazil, where materializations took place in daylight in the presence of hundreds of hard-core sceptics.

Ash and Hewitt give many examples of well documented materializations and dematerializations. Materialization is consistent with the argument that life continues after physical death.

A round hundred of scientists, all profoundly sceptical, and some openly hostile, declared themselves, without exception, completely convinced after having worked under the direction of Dr. Schrenck-Notzing with his medium Willy Schneider. I myself took part in twenty-five of these experiments, and have convinced myself that telekinesis and materialization are facts. This conviction was shared by all the other scientific witnesses. They are all in accord that the hypothesis of fraud is quite untenable. (Dr. Gustave Geley)

> The point is, if you want real conviction
> of life after death, physical mediumship
> is the answer.
>
> (Leslie Flint)

I am absolutely convinced that phenomenal activity took place, that materialized entities conversed with us and that the entity that called himself Arthur Conan Doyle did in fact shake my hand.

Sai Baba

For starters, Sai Baba can materialize specific objects on request. Once when Haraldsson was having a conversation with him about spiritual and ethical issues, Sai Baba said that daily life and spiritual life should "grow together like a double rudrakshas". When Haraldsson asked what a double rudrakshas was, neither Sai Baba nor the interpreter knew of the term. Sai Baba knew the English equivalent of the term. Sai Baba tried to continue with the discussion, but Haraldsson remained insistent. Then suddenly, with a sign of impatience, Sai Baba closed his fist and waved his hand for a second or two. As he opened it, he turned to me and said: 'This is it.' In his palm was an acorn-like object. This was two rudrakshas grown together like a twin orange or a twin apple," says Haraldsson.

When Haraldsson indicated that he wanted to keep the double-seed as a memento, Sai Baba agreed, but first asked to see it again. "He enclosed the rudraksha in both his hands, blew on it, and opened his hands toward me. The double rudraksha was now covered, on the top and bottom, by two golden shields held together by a short golden chain. On the top was a golden cross with a small ruby affixed to it, and a tiny opening so that it could hang on a chain around the neck. (72) Haraldsson later discovered that double rudrakshas were extremely rare botanical anomalies. Several Indian botanists he consulted said they had never even seen one, and when he finally found a small, malformed specimen in a shop in Madras, the shopkeeper wanted the Indian equivalent of almost three hundred dollars for it. A London goldsmith confirmed that the gold in the ornamentation had a purity of at least twenty two carats.

Such gifts are not rare. Sai Baba frequently hands out costly rings, jewels, and objects made of gold to the throngs who visit him daily and who venerate him as a saint. He also materializes vast quantities of food, and when the various delicacies he produces fall from his hands they are sizzling hot, so hot that people sometimes cannot even hold them. He can make sweet syrups and fragrant oils pour from his hands (and even his feet), and when he is finished there is no trace of the sticky substance on his skin. He can produce exotic objects such as grains of rice with tiny, perfectly carved pictures of Krishna on them, out-of-season fruits (a near impossibility in an area of the country that has no electricity or refrigeration), and anomalous fruits, such as apples that, when peeled, turn out to be an apple on one side and another fruit on the other.

Equally astonishing are his productions of sacred ash. Every time he walks among the crowds that visit him, prodigious amounts of it pour from his hands. He scatters it everywhere, into offered containers and outstretched hands, over heads, and in long serpentine trail, on the ground. In a single transit of the grounds around his ashram he can produce enough of it to fill several drums. On one of his visits Haraldsson, along with Dr. Karlis Osis, the director of research for the American Society for

Psychical Research, actually saw some of the ash in the process of materializing. As Haraldsson reports, "His palm was open and turned downwards, and he waved his hand in a few quick, small circles. As he did, a grey substance appeared in the air just below his palm. Dr. Osis, who sat slightly closer, observed that this material first appeared entirely in the form of granules (that crumbled into ash when touched) and might have disintegrated earlier if Sai Baba had produced them by a sleight of hand that was undetectable to us. (73)

Internal Vision
In some shamanic cultures internal vision is one of the prerequisites for becoming a shaman. Among the Araucanian Indians of Chile and the Argentine pampas, a newly initiated shaman is taught to pray specifically for the faculty. This is because the shaman's major role in Araucanian culture is to diagnose and heal illness, for which internal vision is considered essential. (74) Australian shamans refer to the ability as the "strong eye," or "seeing with the heart. (75) The Jivaro Indians of the forested eastern slopes of the Ecuadorian Andes acquire the ability by drinking an extract of a jungle vine called ayahuasca, a plant containing a hallucinogenic substance believed to bestow psychic abilities on the imbiber. According to Michael Harner, an anthropologist at the New School for Social Research in New York who specializes in shamanic studies, ayahuasca permits the Jivaro shaman "to see into the body of the patient as though it were glass. (76)

Indeed, the ability to "see" an illness-whether it involves actually looking inside the body or seeing the malady represented as a kind of metaphorical hologram, such as a three-dimensional image of a demonic and repulsive creature inside or near the body, is universal in shamanic traditions. But whatever the culture in which internal vision is reported, its implications are the same. The body is an energy construct and ultimately may be no more substantive than the energy field in which it is embedded.

The Indian Rope Trick

I am fascinated by the things which sometimes happen to people in crowds. I have tried for many years now, all over India, to catch a performance of the famous "rope trick" - even advertising in the Bombay Times, with the offer of a substantial reward for a successful performance. So far in vain. But there is at least one account by two psychologists who, with several hundred other people, saw a fakir throw a coil of rope into the air, watched a small boy climb the rope and disappear. They describe how dismembered parts of the boy came tumbling horribly down to the ground, how the fakir gathered these up in a basket, climbed the rope himself and came back down smiling, with the intact child. Others in the crowd are said to have agreed with most of the details of what happened, but a film record which begins with the rope being thrown into the air, shows nothing but the fakir and his assistant standing motionless beside it throughout the rest of the performance. The rope did not stay in the air and the boy never climbed it. The crowd, it seems, was party to a collective delusion. (77)

Yanomamo Indians

Working with ethhnobotanists in South America, I am constantly amazed not only by the depth of tribal Indian knowledge of their environment, but by the way this has accrued in a comparatively short time. Most estimates of human habitation of the Amazon Basin suggest that it goes back 10 thousand, perhaps 15 thousand years - no more than 500 generations. Scarcely long enough, it would seem, to uncover some secrets by trial and error alone. Yet there are herbal cures now in use by people like the Yanomamo which require a dozen intricate steps in preparation, the omission of any one of which not only renders the potion useless, but lethal. And it is hard to see how this complex procedure came to be applied to this one plant, selected from a forest containing hundreds of thousands of others, by trial and error alone. When you ask the Indians about it, they simply say "The forest told us what to do."

Conibo Indians

Well, perhaps it did. Anthropologists are learning to take what people tell them at face value. One of the bravest of the new breed is Michael Harner of the School for Social Research in New York, who not only listens, but gets involved. While living with the Conibo in the Peruvian Amazon, he was told that he would never understand them unless he took a sacred drink made from ayahuasca, the "soul vine". He did and had complex visions of crocodilian demons, soul boats and bird-headed people. The experience was vivid and disturbing, with intriguing parallels to descriptions in the biblical Book of Revelation. Harner was interested, but doubtful of the value of such hallucination in helping him to understand the Conibo. He assumed that the imagery was drawn from his own cultural background, until he talked to an old sorcerer about it. To his astonishment, this Amazonian shaman told him exactly what he had seen in the vision. "I was stunned. What I had experienced was already familiar to this barefoot, blind shaman. Known to him from his own explorations of the same hidden world into which I had ventured. From that moment on, I decided to learn everything I could about shamanism. (78)

I'm not Psychic

As I have said elsewhere, I myself am not psychic. However I do have to admit to experiencing some unusual things from time to time. The first occurred in December 2009.

I have the habit of throwing my dirty clothes over the bannister into the hall below so that I can launder them later.

On this occasion I dropped a beanie hat and a jersey over into the hall but, when I went down into the hall later to pick them up, they weren't there. I looked all over the house for them but all to no avail. Next day I did the same but still no sign of them.

> The following morning I looked down over the bannister into the hall and there they were, just where I dropped them two days before.

The second case was in November 2014 and, again, it involved a beanie hat (perhaps there's something about beanie hats!). Anyhow, on this occasion I returned from my early morning walk and discovered that my beanie hat was missing. I thought that maybe I'd dropped it while out walking so for the next two days I kept my eyes open for it. Two weeks past and I had given up hope altogether, then as I started my early morning walk on 25 November, I put my hand in my pocket and there it was again in the place I normally keep it when walking!

> Well, that's about the extent of my psychic experiences. Nothing quite as magical as a disappearing grove of kenari trees, and it was without witnesses – but they definitely happened. I have a friend who said that he *mislays* things too. I didn't mislay them. I hunted high and low for them on both occasions. They had definitely disappeared.

Shamans

The woman's name was Tia, but unlike Alin's, hers did not seem to be an expression of an unconscious psychic gift. Instead it was consciously controlled and stemmed from Tia's natural connection to forces that lie dormant in most of us. Tia was, in short, a shaman in the making. Watson witnessed many examples of her gifts. He saw her perform miraculous healings, and once, when she was engaged in a power struggle with the local Moslem religious leader, he saw her use the power of her mind to set the minaret of the local mosque on fire.

The Disappearing Grove of Kenari Trees

But he witnessed one of Tia's most awesome displays when he accidentally stumbled upon her talking with a little girl in a shady grove of Kenari trees. Even at a distance, Watson could tell from Tia's gestures that she was trying to communicate something important to the child. Although he could not hear their conversation, he could tell from her air of frustration that she was not succeeding. Finally, she appeared to get an idea and started an eerie dance.

Entranced, Watson continued to watch as she gestured toward the trees, and although she scarcely seemed to move, there was something hypnotic about her subtle gesticulations. Then she did something that both shocked and dismayed Watson. She caused the entire grove of trees suddenly to blink out of existence. As Watson states, "One moment Tia danced in a grove of shady Kenari, the next she was standing alone in the hard, bright light of the sun."

A few seconds later she caused the grove to reappear, and from the way the little girl leapt to her feet and rushed around touching the trees, Watson was certain that she had shared the experience also. But Tia was not finished. She caused the grove to blink on and off several times as both she and the little girl linked hands, dancing and giggling at the wonder of it all. Watson simply walked away, his head reeling. (79)

Watson witnesses another Miracle

In my conversation with my professor, I admitted that I was intrigued by Don Juan's assertion that two mutually exclusive realities could each be real and felt that the notion could explain many paranormal events. Moments after discussing this incident we left the restaurant and, because it was a clear summer night, we decided to stroll. As we continued to converse I became aware of a small group of people walking ahead of us. They were speaking an unrecognizable foreign language, and from their boisterous behaviour it appeared that they were drunk. In addition, one of the women was carrying a green umbrella, which was strange because the sky was totally cloudless and there had been no forecast of rain.

Not wanting to collide with the group, we dropped back a little, and as we did, the woman suddenly began swinging the umbrella in a wild and erratic manner. She traced out huge arcs in the air, and several times as she spun around, the tip of the umbrella nearly grazed us. We slowed our pace even more, but it became increasingly apparent that her performance was designed to attract our attention. Finally, after she had our gaze firmly fixed on what she was doing, she held the umbrella with both hands over her head and then threw it dramatically at our feet.

We both stared at it dumbly, wondering why she had done such a thing, when suddenly something remarkable began to happen. The umbrella did something that I can only-describe as "flickering" like a lantern flame about to go out. It emitted an, odd, crackling sound like the sound of cellophane being crumpled, and in a dazzling array of sparkling, multi-coloured light, its ends curled up, its colour changed, and it reshaped itself into a gnarled, brown-grey stick. I was so stunned I didn't say anything for several seconds. My professor spoke first and said in a quiet, shocked voice that she had thought the object had been an umbrella. I asked her if she had seen something extraordinary happen, and she nodded. We both wrote down what we thought had transpired and our accounts matched exactly. The only vague difference in our descriptions was that my professor said the umbrella had "sizzled" when it transformed into a stick, a sound not too terribly dissimilar from the crackly sound of cellophane being crumpled. (Lyall Watson, The Holographic Universe page156).

Dowsing
Dowsing is something which is still disbelieved by many scientists (It's that same old principle at work: "If you can't explain how something works then just pretend that it doesn't exist). However, it DOES work. I have come across it a number of times and have been impressed by its effectiveness on every occasion. I will just give you a couple of examples:

Some years ago, when I was an engineer at the Sheet Works of Pilkington Brothers, St. Helens, a group of senior engineers were called together at the corner of Watson Street to see a demonstration of equipment for the detection of underground services. We all stood there chatting, waiting for the demonstrator to arrive. Eventually he turned up carrying a long thin wooden box with a hinged lid. Ah! A magnetic, or maybe microwave device we thought.

He bent down and raised the lid of the box. It was obviously not an electronic device of any kind. It looked like a set of polished chrome handles and chrome rod attachments. At this point there was some tittering amongst the engineers and someone said "this should be good!"

He started to put all the bits and pieces together so that he had two handles with pivoted rods coming out the top. The left handle had a collection of things suspended on rubber bands between two chrome rings. It was looking even more like 'a one man band'.

He took up his position at the centre of the road and began to walk slowly forward with the rods pointing straight ahead of him. At this point there was laughter among the engineers. However, as he moved forward the metal rods suddenly swung and crossed one another.

"We've got something here," he said.

"How do you know what it is?" someone asked.

The man grabbed hold of a number of the suspended items, some glass, some stone, and so on, and pressed them against the left handle.

"That will eliminate those materials," he said.
He moved forward again and again the rods swung and crossed over.

"It must be an electric cable," he said.

At that point I unfolded some drawings which I had under my arm and laid one on the road (I was the Works Electrical Engineer) and sure enough, a cable crossed the road at that point.

"That's correct," I said. "Can you tell us anything more about it?"

He stepped back and traversed the area a couple of more times – from each direction.

"Yes, it's about 5 feet down."

At this point the laughing had stopped and people were taking a lot more interest.

The man moved on again down the centre of the road until the rods again responded. Once again he fiddled with the materials on the left handle and eventually said, "it's is a fairly big pipe carrying water."

At this point George Pye (Works Mechanical Engineer) produced a drawing and confirmed that he was correct.

The man continued and produced more details. Eventually, we reached a point on Watson Street where railway lines crossed from one part of the factory on the right hand side of the road, to the factory on the left hand side.

He turned left and moved forward until the rods responded again. At that point someone pointed upwards.

"How do you know it's not something up there?" someone asked looking up at a collection of services carried on a steel gantry.

The man laid the rods down on the ground, fiddled around in his pocket, and brought out a small wire cross which he attached to his lapel.

"This will eliminate everything up there," he said. "It doesn't have to be a cross. It could be a circle or a square. As long as it's symmetrical it will work OK."

It was mind boggling and we all wanted to laugh but we had all grown to trust this guy.

He went on to find a lot more stuff and it was all correct. We went on to buy some equipment and it was used all over the factory.

That day a lot of logically thinking engineers learned that there is a lot more to life than just nuts and bolts.

My second story takes place some years later when my wife and I were living in Tabuk in Saudi Arabia and I was working as the Engineer over the Military City.

It was a dangerous thing to dig in the ground without knowing what was there. You might hit a military communications cable or a High Voltage cable – or maybe something even more devastating. The financial penalty, for making such a mistake, was enormous, so you had to make sure that it never happened.

In the Water Department they had a Filipino engineer who used to use a bent coat hanger to locate stuff under the ground. I used to watch him work and I was always impressed. He always got it right.

He didn't have any bits of stuff hanging on rubber bands so I asked him "how do you know if it's a cable or a pipe and not just a stream running underground?"

Oh, it's easy," he replied. "If I want to find a stream then that's just what I think about and this," he nodded at the coat hanger, "will only respond to running water."

Well, up to that point I thought I knew all about dowsing but this business about using his mind really blew my mind as well.

When I got home that evening I couldn't wait to get on the Web and check out about dowsing. Sure enough, many dowsers were saying the same thing. They just had to think about what they had to detect.

It still blows my mind. I've tried, without success, to figure out how it works. Much better brains than mine have tried to figure it out but have failed to do so.

Yes. dowsing *IS* weird.

That's the end of my personal stories but there is one other thing I must mention about dowsing that is even weirder. (Hold your breath).

Dowsing on a Map

There are dowsers who can locate things while thousands of miles away from the location. They use a map (it doesn't need to have contours) and they, usually, use a pendulum. In that way they locate ancient artefacts, burial grounds, hidden water and oil, and more.

All the big oil companies employ at least one dowser for that purpose and say that they couldn't work without them. The dowsers save them a lot of money.

Yes. It's definitely weird

The history of divination is long and its success widespread. People keep discovering things that would seem to be beyond their grasp.

Dowsers, working on the basis of "no find, no fee", regularly locate sources of water where geological experts have failed to do so; and provide accurate information about depth, yield and purity. Every major pipeline company in the United States has one on its payroll, and there is at least one in the permanent employ of the Canadian Ministry of Agriculture. UNESCO has also engaged a dowser to pursue official investigations for them. Marine divisions in Vietnam using bent coat-hangers to detect concealed Vietcong tunnels. Soviet scientists have made good use of dowsing techniques to pinpoint structures below ground at the Volokamsky Monastery near Moscow, and for geological exploration from the air over Siberia.

They report a saving of 30 per cent in the amount of drilling needed to find and mine gold deposits in the Northern Caucasus. Even Alfred Wegener, the German geologist who first proposed the theory of "continental drift", was a dowser - once tracking a fault line with a pendulum from the back of a yak in the Urals.

Willow wands, hazel twigs, whalebone, copper wire, steel rods, pitchforks, walking sticks, amber beads on silken threads are pressed into service all over the world - and apparently succeed in doing everything from sexing fertilized eggs to diagnosing cancer. The problem, as far as science is concerned, is that controlled tests under laboratory conditions are seldom as successful. In experiments at the Military Engineering Experimental Establishment of the British Ministry of Defence, twenty dowsers failed to find buried metallic or plastic mines, and were unable to determine whether or not water was flowing through buried pipes. But it is difficult to ignore "on the job" results by professionals going about their trade. The pharmaceutical company Hoffmann-La Roche always include a dowsing survey when setting up new factories anywhere in the world. Their spokesman explains: "We use methods which are profitable, whether they are scientifically explainable or not. The dowsing method pays off. (80)

The system works. And the difficulty of proof and lack of an identifiable force, prompt comparisons with many other elusive paranormal phenomena. Dowsers, on the whole, are a down-to-earth sort of people who are anxious not to be linked with the psychic world. "Anyone can dowse," insists veteran British dowser Tom Graves. "It's just a skill which, like any other, can be learnt with practice, awareness and a working knowledge of its basic principles and mechanics." These he sets out very clearly in the best practical guide to the subject, noting in discussion of mechanical aids that dowsing is an essentially mental skill. The instruments I've described are tools to tell you what your hands are doing, and not much more. (81)

We are all sensitive to the physical forces around us, and it seems that there are ways of enhancing this sensitivity. One has been in use for at least five thousand years. Bas-reliefs from early Egypt show figures in strange headgear carrying, at arm's length in front of them, a forked stick; and Emperor Kwang Su of China is depicted in a statue dated 2200 B.C. carrying an identical object. Both, it seems, were in search of water.

Many animals have an extraordinary sensitivity to water, and some, such as the elephant, succeed in finding it underground. In times of drought, elephants often perform vital community services by using their tusks and pile driving feet to expose hidden water sources. It is possible that they can smell the water percolating through the soil or that they have come to have a fairly elementary knowledge of geology, always digging at the lowest point on the outside curve of a dry river bed, where water is most likely to collect. But there are instances in which neither of these solutions is tenable, and we are left with the possibility that some other sense is being used. Like the surface of the earth, two thirds of most animals is water. One of the preconditions for resonance is that there should be similar, or at least compatible, structures in sender and receiver, so if the energy is broadcast by a water source, it could probably find a response in the body of most mammals. Our brains are 78 per cent water, which makes them even more liquid than blood, so the resonance might take place there, but the response seems to be most manifest in the long muscles of our bodies.

The classical method of water divining, or dowsing, is to cut a forked twig from a shade tree such as willow, hazel, or peach and to hold it out in front of the body parallel to the ground. In this position the muscles of the arm are under some tension; it is claimed that as the dowser approaches water, this tension somehow extends into the twig and induces it to move. The patterns of movement depend very much on the individual. Some say that an upward thrust of the dowsing rod indicates the upstream side of a water flow and the pattern of gyration indicates depth, but others disagree completely. There is a tremendous variation in technique among dowsers. Instruments in use include metal rods, coat hangers, whalebone, copper wire, walking sticks, pitchforks, Bakelite strips, surgical scissors, pendulums, and even, it is said, a German sausage. For each dowsing aid there are as many different ways of holding it and interpreting the way it moves. Just one thing takes all this extraordinary pantomime out of the area of sheer farce, the dowsers enjoy a very high rate of success.

Every major water and pipeline company in the United States has a dowser on its payroll. The 'Canadian Ministry of Agriculture employs a permanent dowser. UNESCO has engaged a Dutch dowser and geologist to pursue official investigations for them. Engineers from the US. First and Third Marine divisions in Vietnam have been trained to use dowsing rods to locate booby traps and sunken mortar shells. The Czechoslovakian Army has a permanent corps of dowsers in a special unit. The geology departments of Moscow State and Leningrad universities have launched a full-scale investigation into dowsing, not to find out if it works, but to discover how it works. There is obviously something in it.

Psychometry
A psychiatrist at the University of Cape Town buried a purse wrapped in brown paper and covered the site with a flat brown stone with a smaller grey one on top of it. Nobody saw him do it. He then drove for two hours to the home of a Tembu diviner, who danced himself into a trance and described the purse, its contents and its hiding place in accurate detail. (82)

A merchant in Africa equipped eight hunters, sent them out in search of elephant and arranged to meet them at a chosen spot on a certain day. None turned up, so he went to a local seer, who promised to "open the gate of distance and travel through it". In trance, this wizard told of the death of one man by fever, and of another trampled by an elephant. He described the success of a third, who was returning with eight tusks, and the fortunes of each of the other five who, he informed the merchant, were still 200 miles away and would not return for another three months. He was right in every detail. (83)

Norman Emerson, Professor of Archaeology at the University of Toronto, regularly uses what he calls "intuitive archaeology" on field expeditions. He has discovered a truck driver called George McMullen, who has no formal education and never reads anthropological literature, but seems to be able to "read" artefacts in the same way as Stefan Ossowiecki - providing information on the Iroquois Indians, which Emerson knows to be accurate. Taken to a potential site, McMullen "almost quivers and comes alive like a sensitive bird dog scenting his prey". He walks rapidly over the area to orient himself and then begins to describe the people who lived there - their age, their dress, their way of life and the whereabouts of their buildings. He once walked over a patch of bare ground, pacing out the perimeter of what he claimed was an Iroquois long house, while Emerson followed behind him placing survey pegs in the earth. Six weeks later, the entire structure was excavated exactly where McMullen said it would be. (84)

The strongest evidence suggestive of mental meditation in dowsing and psychometry is the ability of some diviners to work, not on site in the field or with an actual object, but on maps many miles away.

Norman Emerson in Canada once used psychics to dowse maps of the long Montreal River in Ontario and in one day they pin-pointed thirty-two Indian sites, which turned out to be good ones, much to the chagrin of his colleagues who had spent five years on an unsuccessful field survey of the same area. In this instance, it is possible that Emerson's own knowledge and expectations had something to do with the result, but there are numbers of examples in the literature of dowsers working without any possible access to information on areas they know nothing about. Canadian archaeologists William Ross and William Noble of McMasters University, have both had conspicuous success in field excavations as a result of preliminary surveys made by simply holding a flint arrowhead over a map of an otherwise unexplored area, months before setting out to dig. (85)

This knowledge-from-a-distance is as difficult to deal with in scientific terms as the action-at-a-distance of poltergeists. Neither seems to provide any possibility of electromagnetic explanation and both, as a result, have been summarily dismissed. Which is understandable, but remains irrational, because the evidence is substantial and widespread.

> This technique, of using a pendulum to acquire information not only about an object's location but also of its character, has become known as "radiesthesia"-meaning sensitivity to radiations. It is used, among other things, for sex detection. The Japanese have always been expert in the difficult art of determining the sex of day-old chicks, but now they are able to do it even before the eggs hatch, with the aid of nothing more than a bead on the end of a piece of silk thread. Eggs pass by the expert on a conveyor belt with their long axes north-south. The bead is held over the line and swings along the same axis if the egg is sterile, gyrates in a clockwise circle for a cock chick, and anti-clockwise for a hen. The factories claim a success rate of 99 per cent for this system. There are practitioners in England who apparently can sex humans in the same way when provided only with a drop of blood or saliva on a piece of blotting paper. They have been used several times to assist police forensic laboratories in murder investigations.

Acupuncture

Meek writes that he was travelling in the People's Republic of China. In the museum in Soochow I stood before a large bronze figure of a man-taller than my six-foot-three frame-and learned how two hundred years ago the medical students were trained to insert acupuncture needles at the proper locations. A very small hole had been drilled through the hollow bronze casting at the precise location of each acupuncture point. The bronze figure was then covered with a thick wax and filled with water. A student instructed to insert a needle for a particular malady would know he had not hit the right place unless he was greeted by a spurt of water.

Traveling on to Nanking, I got dramatic proof of the efficacy of acupuncture when used as an anesthetic. A small group of which I was a member visited the Nanking General Hospital. The general administrator, after giving us a talk on their use of acupuncture, took us on a tour of the out-patient and recovery wards and four operating rooms. Wearing surgical gowns and face masks, we proceeded to watch four operations, all major, in which acupuncture was the only anesthetic. I will describe one of these to give you a better understanding of the reality of these energies which I am discussing and about which our, modern science knows very little.

The patient, a 40-year-old man, was being operated on for an ulcerated stomach condition which had not responded to treatment. A few hours before the operation he was given orally a very mild tranquilizer to ease the perfectly normal fear of the dangers which might lie ahead once he was wheeled out of his room and into the operating room.

Upon arrival in the operating room, a nurse inserted three small needles into the periphery of the patient's left ear. Each needle had a small wire extending to a nearby instrument-about the size of a small tape recorder. This instrument supplied a six-volt direct current to each needle. These three needles provided the only anesthetizing effect.

Extending up from the patient's throat area was a cloth screen about one foot square which prevented the patient from observing the actions of the surgeons. However, we could see the patient's face as well as all the actions of the surgeons. With the hospital administrator serving as translator, we were able to converse with the patient at all stages of the operation.

The two surgeons, standing on each side of the operating table, made the incision. Gradually they progressed to the point where they took the patient's stomach out and lifted it up so that they could carefully inspect it. The condition they found apparently warranted their decision that it was necessary to remove fully sixty percent of the stomach. This they did. Then they completed the many details and closed the incision. At no time did the patient experience discomfort. He apparently had no knowledge of what was going on.

One of our group was an American surgeon in his sixties. Knowing nothing about the subtle and invisible energy systems and related energy fields of the human body, he was totally mystified. I observed him standing aside and through his face mask mutter, "Incredible. Absolutely incredible! There is just no anatomical basis for this nonsense." How right he was! None of the present day medical texts on anatomy discusses the invisible -but very real -energy systems such as the acupuncture meridians.

If Tiller is right that the universe is an enormous holodeck, the ability to materialize a gold ring or cause a grove of kenari trees to flick on and off is no longer so strange. Even the umbrella incident (see earlier) can be viewed as a temporary aberration in the holographic simulation we call ordinary reality. Although my professor and I were unaware that we possessed such an ability, it may be that the emotional fervour of our discussion about Castaneda caused our unconscious minds to change the hologram of reality to better reflect what we were believing at the moment. Given Ullman's assertion that our psyche is constantly trying to teach us things we are unaware of in our waking state, our unconscious may even be programmed to produce occasionally such miracles in order to offer us glimpses of reality's true nature, to show that the world we create for ourselves is ultimately as creatively infinite as the reality of our dreams. (86)

--o--

CHAPTER SEVEN

MIND OVER MATTER

*How can the Mind affect machines?
How can the Mind influence things
at a distance? Read on, it really **is**
Mind blowing.*

Luck
My daughter has a talent. She doesn't work at it. It just happens to be there.

> We were recently stopping at the Luxor Hotel in Las Vegas. Linzi settled down to playing on three - sort of - one armed bandit machines. She quickly discovered that it was the left hand machine that was for her.

She put a coin in the machine and pulled the handle and $600 tumbled out. She did it again and $500 tumbled out. Then again and $700 dropped out!!

> I had a feeling that the machines cringed as she walked past, and who could blame them?

I have spoken to her recently since she visited Las Vegas again. On this occasion she won $1,000 on the roulette table and she was made a VIP Host!!!

And yet again, I spoke with her 12th February 2015 when I was checking through the proof of this book.

100

She'd been to Reno and won $1000, and then a further $900 next morning and it paid for their holiday!!

Luck is not a "chance" thing; it comes from a state of mind. People (like Linzi) just "get on a roll."

In theory, games such as roulette and dice depend only on chance, but if people believed this, gambling would soon die a natural death. Those who take part in horse racing, football, and poker clearly exercise a great deal of skill, and those who bet on the ability of their favourites also have to show some skill in assessment. But many of the most popular games of chance' survive purely because the gambler believes that he can somehow control their outcome. He believes that by manipulating the objects involved, either directly or from a distance, he can exert an influence that will be to his benefit. He calls this influence luck, but it looks very much like Psychokinesis.

Grof says that he has already described that UFO's (unidentified flying objects), popularly known as "flying saucers" are a subjective experiences and that seeing physical or metaphysical space-crafts, being in contact with their crews or gadgets, and even personally meeting the aliens are common in non-ordinary states of consciousness. In this context, I will narrow the discussion to those cases where subjective reports are combined with some physical evidence. There is reason to believe that the conclusions drawn from the US Air Force projects Grudge and Blue Book were politically motivated. The same seems to be true for a special committee of the University of Colorado that attributed virtually all physical evidence to natural causes - balloons, meteors, birds, reflections of light, and others.

Richard Taylor recently asked subjects in his laboratory to guess the sequence of colours in a shuffled pack of playing cards. After the first run, those with high scores were separated from the others, and in following tests the "lucky" ones continued to do much better than the "unlucky" group.

Taylor cautiously concluded that "this data provides some empirical support for the popular notion of luck" (87).

Similar evidence led the Director of the Netherlands Foundation for Industrial Psychology to say, "There are clear indications that some people have a certain flare for attracting good fortune. (88) These are valid comments, but both just miss the point that becomes clear as soon as one takes Taylor's test just one stage further. If a group of subjects are selected at random following the first run, regardless of their score, and told that they have done exceptionally well and are very lucky, this group continues to score significantly better than the others. Luck, it seems, is a state of mind.

(Read about my daughter in Chapter 6).

All casinos know that certain individuals keep on winning slowly and consistently, and now the staff of a gambling magazine have produced a book that gives detailed instructions on how to join that fortunate few. They have examined the methods of laboratory investigation into Psychokinesis and adapted them to the casino environment. Included in their advice is the importance of cultivating the proper attitude for winning, which they describe as "confident, relaxed, and almost playful. (89) We are still a long way from a situation where gambling houses are put right out of business by an invasion of parapsychologists, but there are signs that a few people are beginning to learn how to tip the odds in their favour.

Unidentified Flying Objects (UFO's)

As in the case of Para psychological phenomena, many of the UFO reports came from people who were emotionally stable, well-educated and trained, intelligent, and articulate. There are good reasons to assume that the UFO phenomena are mental events, in which psychological and physical manifestations can be combined in various proportions. This characteristic would make it very difficult to study them in the context of mechanistic science with its sharp division into material or psychological phenomena. A detailed discussion of the UFO material (historical and modern) which is fraught with many controversies, would be clearly beyond the scope of this discussion. I will refer interested readers to Carl Custav Jung's fascinating book Flying Saucers: *A Modern Myth of Things Seen in the Skies* (Jung 1964) and to the writings of Jacques Vallee, who has dedicated many years of his life to intense and systematic study of the UFO phenomenon (Vall'e'e1965). (90)

> Science may not be the only force that offers us passage to the land of non-where. In his book *Heading toward Omega* Ring points out that there is compelling evidence that NDEs are on the increase. As we have seen, in tribal cultures individuals who have NDEs are often so transformed that they become shamans. Modern NDEers become spiritually transformed as well, mutating from their pre-NDE personalities into more loving, compassionate, and even more psychic individuals. From this Ring concludes that perhaps what we are witnessing is "the shamanizing of modern humanity. But if this is so, why are NDEs increasing? Ring believes that the answer is as simple as it is profound; what we are witnessing is "an evolutionary thrust toward higher consciousness for all humanity."

And NDEs may not be the only transformative phenomenon bubbling up from the collective human psyche. Grosso believes that the increase in Marsian visions during the last century has evolutionary implications as well. Similarly, numerous researchers, including Raschke and Vallee, feel that the explosion of UFO sightings in the last several decades has evolutionary significance. Several investigators, including Ring, have pointed out that UFO encounters actually resemble shamanic initiations and may be further evidence of the shamanizing of modern humanity. Strieber agrees. "I think it's rather obvious that, whether the [UFO] phenomenon is being done by somebody or [is happening] naturally, what we're dealing with is an exponential leap from one species to another. I would suspect that what we're looking at is the process of evolution in action. (91)

There is evidence that some UFOs may also be some kind of hologram like phenomenon. When people first started reporting sightings of what appeared to the spacecraft from other planets in the late 1940s, researchers who delved deeply enough into the reports to realize that at least some of them had to be taken seriously and assumed that they were exactly what they appeared to be, glimpses of intelligently guided crafts from more advanced and probably extraterrestrial civilizations. However, as encounters with UFOs become more widespread -- especially those involving contact with UFO occupants. As data accumulates, it becomes increasingly apparent to many researchers that these so-called spacecraft are not extra-terrestrial in origin.

Some of the features of the phenomenon that indicate they are not extraterrestrial include the following: First, there are too many sightings; literally thousands of encounters with UFOs and their occupants have been documented, so many that it is difficult to believe they could all be actual visits from other planets. Second, UFO occupants often do not possess traits one would expect in a truly extraterrestrial life form; too many of them are described as humanoid beings who breathe our air, display no fear of contracting earthly viruses, are well adapted to the earth's gravity and the sun's electromagnetic emissions, display recognizable emotions in their faces, and talk our language, all of which are possible but unlikely traits in truly extraterrestrial visitors.

Third, they do not behave as extraterrestrial visitors. Instead of making the proverbial landing on the White House lawn, they appear to farmers and stranded motorists. They chase jets but don't attack. They dart around in the sky allowing dozens and sometimes hundreds of witnesses to see them, but they show no interest in making any formal contact. And often, when they contact individuals their behaviour still seems illogical. For instance, one of the most commonly reported type of contact is that which involves some sort of medical examination. And yet, arguably, a civilization that possesses the technological capability to travel almost incomprehensible tracts of outer space would most assuredly possess the scientific wherewithal to obtain such information without any physical contact at all or, at the very least, without having to abduct the scores of people who appear to be legitimate victims of this mysterious phenomenon.

Finally, and most curious of all, UFOs do not even behave as physical objects do. They have been watched on radar screens to make instant ninety-degree-angle turns while traveling at enormous speeds, an antic that would rip a physical object apart. They can change size, instantly vanish into nothingness, appear out of nowhere, change colour, and even change shape (traits that are also displayed by their occupants). In short, their behaviour is not at all what one would expect from a physical object, but of something quite different, something with which we have become more than a little familiar in this book. As astrophysicist Dr. Jacques Vallee, one of the world's most respected UFO researchers and the model for the character LaCombe in the film Close Encounters of the Third Kind, stated recently, "It is the behaviour of an image, or a holographic projection. (92)

As the nonphysical and hologram like qualities of UFOs become increasingly apparent to researchers, some have concluded that rather than being from other star systems, UFOs are actually visitors from other dimensions, or levels of reality (it is important to note that not all researchers agree with this point of view, and some remain convinced that UFOs are extra-terrestrial in origin). However, this explanation still does not adequately explain many of the other bizarre aspects of the phenomenon, such as why UFOs aren't making formal contact, why they behave so absurdly, and so on. Indeed, the inadequacy of the extra dimensional explanation, at least in the terms in which it was initially couched, only becomes more glaring as still further unusual aspects of the UFO phenomenon come into focus. One of the more baffling of these is growing evidence that UFO encounters are less of an objective experience and more of a subjective, or psychological, one. For instance, the well-known "interrupted journey" of Betty and Barney Hill, one of the most thoroughly documented UFO abduction cases on record, seems as if it were an actual alien contact in all ways except one: the commander of the UFO was dressed in a Nazi uniform, a fact that does not make sense if the Hills' abductors were truly visitors from an alien civilization, but it does if the event was psychological in nature and more akin to a dream or hallucination, experiences that often contain obvious symbols and disconcerting flaws in logic. (93)

Mental Concentration can affect Machines

Jahn and Dunne found that by mental concentration alone, human beings are able to affect the way that certain kinds of machines operate. This is an astounding finding and one that cannot be accounted for in terms of our standard picture of reality.

Talbot says: "I am lucky. I have always known there was more to the world than is generally accepted. I grew up in a psychic family, and from an early age I experienced first-hand many of the phenomena that will be talked about in this book *(The Holographic Universe).* Occasionally and when it is relevant to the topic being discussed, I will relate some of my own experiences. Although they can only be viewed as anecdotal evidence, but for me they have provided the most compelling proof that we live in a universe we are only just beginning to fathom."

The Human Mind can effect Machines

Jahn and Dunne think their findings may explain the propensity some individuals seem to have for jinxing machinery and equipment to malfunction. One such individual was physicist Wolfgang Pauli, whose talents in this area are so legendary that physicists have jokingly dubbed it the "Pauli Effect." It is said that Pauli's mere presence in a laboratory would cause a glass apparatus to explode, a sensitive measuring device to crack in half, and in one particularly famous incident a physicist wrote Pauli to say that at least he could not blame Pauli for the recent and mysterious disintegration of a complicated piece of equipment since Pauli had not been present, only to find that Pauli had been passing by the laboratory in a train at the precise moment of the mishap! Jahn and Dunne think the famous "Gremlin effect," the tendency of carefully tested pieces of equipment to undergo inexplicable malfunctions at the most absurdly inopportune moments, often reported by pilots, aircrew, and military operators, may also be an example of unconscious PK activity.

It is important to note that this kind of Psychokinesis would not be due to a causal process, that is, a cause-and-effect relationship involving any of the known forces in physics. Instead, it would be the result of a kind of non-local "resonance of meanings," or a kind of non-local interaction similar to, but not the same as, the non-local interconnection that allows a pair of twin photons to manifest the same angle of polarization. (For technical reason: Bohm believes mere quantum non-locality cannot account for either PK or telepathy, and only a deeper form of non-locality, a kind of "super" non-locality, would offer such an explanation).

In 1967 a Kiev film company produced a costly professional film about a middle-aged Leningrad housewife. (94) She is shown sitting at a table in a physiology laboratory after being medically examined and X-rayed to ensure that nothing is hidden on or in her body. She puts out her hands, with the fingers spread, about six inches above a compass in the centre of the table and tenses her muscles. She stares intently at the compass, lines etched deeply into her face showing the strain of a body under acute tension. Minutes pass and sweat breaks out on her brow as she continues the struggle, and then, slowly, the compass needle quivers and moves to point in a new direction. She starts to move her hands in a circular motion and the needle turns with them, until it is rotating like the second hand on a watch. The field produced by the body can, under certain conditions, it seems, be stronger even than the field of earth itself.

While the demonstration was taking place, her EEG showed intense emotional excitement. There was great activity in the deeper levels of the reticular formation, which co-ordinates and filters information in the brain. The cardiogram showed an irregular action of the heart with that confusion between the chambers that is characteristic of great alarm. Her pulse soared to 240 beats a minute, four times its normal level, and high percentages of blood sugar were recorded together with other endocrinal disturbances all characteristic of a stress reaction. The test lasted thirty minutes, and during this time Nelya lost over two pounds in weight. At the end of the day she was very weak and temporarily blind. Her ability to taste was impaired, she had pains in her arms and legs, she felt dizzy, and she was unable to sleep for several days.

Our Thoughts Effect Water Crystals
Dr. Masaru Emoto has conducted thousands of experiments with water crystals showing that the mind's attitudes affect how water crystallizes when frozen. In one experiment, for example, Dr. Emoto put water from the same source into two bottles. He wrote the words "You fool" on a label and taped it

to one of the bottles. He wrote the words "Thank you" on a second label and taped that label to the second bottle.

Dr. Emoto then froze water from each bottle and photographed the crystals that were formed using a microscope and camera. The result was that the crystals formed from water taken from the bottle with "You fool" on it were grotesque and misshapen. The crystals formed from water taken from the bottle with "Thank you" written on it were beautiful and symmetrical, like snowflakes.

We must assume it wasn't the printed words that influenced the water; it was the minds of the people who wrote and read the words. We know that because the symbols on the labels are just ink stains on a flat surface with no meaning except to people; the writer's and reader's minds created meaning from the ink marks.

These experiments have now been performed many times using different sources of water and different treatments. In all circumstances, when a loving, compassionate, gentle attitude or melodious sound is focused on the water, beautiful crystals form when the water is frozen. When harsh, demeaning, hateful, dehumanizing attitudes or cacophonous sounds are focused on the water, the frozen crystals are misshapen and grotesque.

When tap water is frozen, it doesn't form clear crystals; the forms are disorganized. But when the same water is prayed for, the water crystallizes into beautiful, delicate crystals.

When a sample from a Japanese city reservoir's water (Fujiwara Dam) was frozen, it showed misshapen crystals, but when a prayer was offered before the reservoir, samples of its water formed beautiful crystals when frozen.

The data from these studies show that our minds are influencing the physical realm, but we have no idea how wide ranging and pervasive this influence is. We can see the effects only in computer measured random white noise and numbers, water crystals, rates of healing, and growth of cells. However, we must assume that the effects aren't limited to the small number of things we measure; there is no reason not to believe that our collective minds are influencing every living and non-living thing in the same way, with lasting effects, just as spaces are conditioned to be more conducive to healing.

Poltergeists (see also Chapter 15)

Watson has no difficulty accepting the possibility that some people, some of the time, are able to influence things in their environment - particularly if such action serves some useful end. Poltergeist activity in the home of a disturbed child really doesn't surprise me. I can cope with the notion that a dilute form of this talent could be revealed by bringing statistical searchlights to bear on laboratory situations which have little biological significance, but at least catch the interest or challenge the ego of a subject. I suspect, however, that this talent is probably already near vanishing point in even the best laboratory studies and I have enormous problems with the exercise of such borderline ability, from a distance and by a sleeping subject. I don't dispute the results. They seem to reveal the existence of some marginal effect, but I can't help wondering just what is being measured. (95)

Radioactive Decay

Perhaps the best clue has come during the last decade from the work of Helmut Schmidt, a physicist now on the staff of a Foundation in North Carolina, who uses the most fundamental of all random systems. As radioactive substances decay, particles or rays are emitted from them at rates which are uninfluenced by temperature, pressure, electricity, magnetism or chemical change. The rate of emission is totally unpredictable and there is no way it can be fraudulently controlled. Schmidt connected such a substance to an electronic switch, producing a random event generator that ran a variety of displays, ranging from simple lights that turned on or off `to complex video games - and then asked his subjects to try to influence the outcome. Several did so with conspicuous success. (96)

Jinxing of Machines

Watson once worked for an untroubled week with a German television team filming healers in action in the Philippines, only to have the lights fail during the crucial few-minute treatment of a patient with a known case history who had been specially flown in for the programme. There is an almost wilful elusiveness about phenomena under close scrutiny that often leaves workers with little more than lame excuses, and leads to a lot of ribald and knowing comment from their critics. I don't know why the difficulties exist, and can only suggest that it has something to do with our own unwillingness to take conscious responsibility for talents which can be frightening and are bound to set us apart from our friends.

Almost all the laboratory experiments which enjoy any success do so as a result of some dilution or lightening of the protocol to permit those involved to relax and treat it as a game. But, as critics have been quick to point out, these procedures also make it easier for deception to be introduced. It seems almost impossible to squeeze what are essentially spontaneous talents into the clinical confines of fraud-free control. Which is why I continue to travel on my own, without cameras or recorders, simply soaking up situations and trying to get some feel for what is going on. I am intrigued, though, by a new mini-lab which could combine the rigors of the laboratory with the necessary spontaneity of the real world.

Sealed Mini- Lab

Veteran American parapsychologist William Cox has designed what he calls a "mini-lab", which consists of a glass tank or dome that is lidded, locked and sealed.

Inside are a variety of target objects, each connected to a switching device that activates lights and a camera if it is disturbed in any way. With such a contraption installed in the basement of a family home in Missouri, Cox claims to have obtained film of rings linking and unlinking, of objects leaving sealed envelopes, of clocks running backwards and pens caught in the act of writing their own notes. (Psychokinesis – Reference 132) (Isaacs). Julian Isaacs in England has begun similar work with modified mini-labs of his own design under video surveillance, and reports unaided object movement and metal-bending. (97)

Nelya Mikhailova
Of all these special people, none is more talented or consistent than Nelya Mikhailova. She was born just ten years after the Russian Revolution, and at the age of fourteen she was fighting in the front lines of the Red Army. She was injured by artillery fire near the end of the war and spent a long time recovering in the hospital. It was during this period that she began to develop her strange abilities. "I was very angry and upset one day,' she recalls. 'I was walking toward a cupboard when suddenly a pitcher moved to the edge of the shelf, fell, and smashed to bits. (98) After that all kinds of changes began to take place around her. Objects moved of their own volition, doors opened and closed, lights went on and off. But, unlike most people plagued by poltergeist activities, Nelya realized that she was somehow responsible and that she could control the energy. She could summon and focus it at will.

One of the first to study her talents was Edward Naumov, a biologist from Moscow State University. In a test in his laboratory, he scattered a box of matches on a table and she circled her hands over them, shaking with the strain, until the whole group of matches moved like a log run across to the edge of the table and fell off one by one to the floor. To rule out drafts of air, threads, or wire, Naumov put another batch of matches under a plexiglass cover, but Nelya still made them shuttle from side to side (99). Five cigarettes were then placed under the jar, and Nelya showed that she could be selective, picking out only one of them and making it move. Afterward the cigarettes were shredded to make sure that nothing was hidden inside.

Two famous Soviet writers have examined her, admittedly in uncontrolled conditions, but their accounts give some idea of the scope of her talents. Lev Kolodny visited her apartment for an interview and was startled to see the top of his pen being pursued across the table by a glass tumbler. "Both objects moved to the edge of the table as if they were in harness. The tablecloth wasn't moving, the other glasses besides mine were still sitting there. Could she be somehow blowing on them to make them move? There was no draft of air and Mikhailova wasn't breathing heavily. Why didn't a jar in their path also move? I ran my hands through the space between Mikhailova and the table. No threads or wires. If she was using magnets, they wouldn't work on glass. (100)

Vadim Marin, who was dining out with Nelya, reports, "A piece of bread lay on the table some distance from her. Mikhailova, concentrating, looked at it attentively. A minute passed, then another ... and the piece of bread began to move. It moved by jerks. Toward the edge of the table, it moved more smoothly and rapidly. Mikhailova bent her head down, opened her mouth, and, just as in the fairy-tale, the bread itself (excuse me but I have no other words for it) jumped into her mouth! (101)

Lovers Minds are Linked
Very interestingly, when the EEC electrodes were attached to a young couple who were deeply in love, the brain patterns showed them to be closely synchronized constantly, throughout the experiment, even when there were no stimuli. Their minds were linked continually. The couple also reported that-they had a sense of a deep 'oneness' with one-another.

As further proof that the subjects minds were linked, he found that when a receiver showed reactions to the sender's shocks in one experiment, the receiver usually showed them in other types of experiments with that sender as well

Time provides an additional clue in the brain / mind puzzle. We drift in a river of time. There's no possibility of swimming up-stream, of going back in time. Destroy every clock, every item that feels the passage of time. The flow of time continues unabated. Time is an intrinsic, ubiquitous quality of our universe, irrespective of whether or not we measure its passage. Might consciousness also be an intrinsic, all-present part of nature, of the universe? In that case every particle would have some aspect of consciousness within it. The more complex the entity, the greater would he its awareness of the consciousness housed within.

Bohm believes that an electron is not only mind-like but is a highly complex entity, a far cry from the standard view that an electron is a simple, structure-less point. The active use of information by electrons, and indeed by all subatomic particles, indicates that the ability to respond to meaning is a characteristic not only of consciousness but of all matter. It is this intrinsic commonality, says Bohm. That offers a possible explanation for PK. He states, "On this basis, Psychokinesis could arise if the mental processes of the material systems in which this Psychokinesis was to be brought about were the same as the person causing the action." (102)

If quantum physics is correct, and it has an excellent track record of being on the mark, then this suggestion is not so very far from mainstream thought. Every particle, every body, each aspect of existence appears to be an expression of information, information that via our brains or our minds, we interpret as the physical world. Physicist Freeman Dyson, upon his acceptance of the Templeton

Prize, stated the idea this way: "Atoms are weird stuff, behaving like active agents rather than inert substances. They make unpredictable choices between alternative possibilities according to the laws of quantum mechanics. It appears that mind, as manifested by the capacity to make choices, is to some extent inherent in every atom.

Earth's Magnetism

Earth is a permanent magnet with its field stretched between north and south magnetic poles. When a conductive body like a shark cuts across this field by swimming west to east, it acts in the same way as a copper wheel, inducing an electric current that flows through the fish, setting up a subtle field available to the ampullae of Lorenzini. In other words, a shark can by its own motion, acquire an electromagnetic compass wherever it may be, and learn to orient itself, not only with respect to this handy personal probe, but also to much larger and more stable fields such as those induced by ocean currents that interfere with Earth's field in the same way. The fact that many animals do precisely this, is only just beginning to be appreciated.

In 1961, Robert Becker began to look at the effects on humans of disturbances in Earth's field caused by magnetic storms in the sun. He compared the admission of over 28,000 patients to psychiatric hospitals with sixty-seven severe magnetic storms recorded during the previous four years, and found a strong correlation. Significantly more people were admitted just after magnetic upheavals. He watched schizophrenics already in hospital and found marked changes in behaviour just when low energy cosmic ray flares were disrupting Earth's field. He found high levels of stress, abnormal endocrine activity and slowed reaction times during sunspot activity. And concluded that our body's direct current electrical control system is tuned by natural rhythms and is responsive to changes that take place at surprisingly low levels. A conclusion strongly supported by recent work on biological cycles, particularly that of Rutger Wever in West

Germany, who has found that people kept from all contact with Earth's field in an artificially shielded environment, become thoroughly desynchronized.

The nice thing about poltergeists is that they are so accessible. Anyone prepared to take the time and trouble to track down reports can, sooner or later, see or hear one for themselves. They suffer from all the shortcomings of any investigation outside the laboratory - it is hard to establish adequate controls or to be absolutely certain that no fraud could possibly be involved; but they have the merit of being largely spontaneous, of taking place in situations that reflect real biological need, and they often display a degree of very human whimsy.

In 1967 electrical mayhem broke out in a lawyer's office in the Bavarian town of Rosenheim. Lights went on and off, bulbs became unscrewed, fuses blew, photocopiers spewed out their fluids, telephones rang for no reason and made calls that were never dialled. Hans Bender of the University of Freiburg came in to investigate and soon noticed that the events seemed to follow a new employee, a nineteen-year-old girl called Annemarie, beginning as soon as she arrived for work each morning. Lights hanging from the ceiling swung behind her as she walked down the corridors and exploding bulbs showered her with glass. Bender discovered that she had a feeling of resentment towards her employer and he not only decided that she was unconsciously working off this grudge in an electrical frenzy, but determined to find out how.

He called in two physicists from the Max Planck Institute who at first suspected voltage surges in the power supply, but the phenomena continued even after they had isolated the office from the mains and put it on to a controlled and independent generator. They did a series of experiments which, in turn, ruled out the possibility of magnetic fields, ultrasonics, infrasonics, electrostatics, strong vibrations or the presence of any fraudulent mechanism on the premises. All the observers saw drawers popping out of filing cabinets, they filmed paintings swinging and turning to face the wall, and heard untraceable loud sounds - and they witnessed the end of all the phenomena when Annemarie was finally discharged. They were forced in the end to conclude that the events defied any explanation they could offer in terms of conventional physics, but faced with a telephone that, untouched by human hand, kept on dialling Germany's speaking clock, had to admit that some of the events at least "seemed to be carried out under intelligent control". (103)

Random Number Generators
Other studies of the influence of minds on random-number generators have measured whether an event that affects large numbers of people can influence changes in the numbers being produced, even though people aren't trying to influence the machines. That would show that the entire environment, across large geographical areas, is being influenced when many minds are thinking and feeling something. (104)

In the studies, random-number generators around the world were examined after events that affected great numbers of people to see whether the numbers began to show some order during the events. During widely televised events that have captured the attention of many people, such as Princess Diana's death and the 9/11 tragedies, the combined outputs of sixty random-number generators around the world showed changes at the exact moments of the announcements of the events, changes that could not be due to chance.

The Mind Affects the World Around Us
Dean Radin describes the results in The Conscious Universe. He uses "RNG" to stand for "random-number generators." "Order" in the numbers means the machines were being affected in some way because they were not generating entirely random numbers.

.... around the time that the TV pre shows began, at 9:00AM Pacific Time, an unexpected degree of order appeared in all the RNGS. This soon declined back to random behavior until about l0:00 AM, which is when the verdict was supposed to be announced. A few minutes later, the order in all five RNG's suddenly peaked to its highest point in the two hours of recorded data precisely when the court clerk read the verdict. (105)

What happened was that millions of minds were united in their sentiments. We know they affected the random-number generators because we have recorded factual data from computers evaluating the numbers. But more importantly, that means the collective minds affected trees and mountains and buildings and people. Influences on other things just can't be measured, but must be there as well. In other words, when an event of great significance occurs, many minds react to it together and that collective mind then affects inanimate objects such as computers.

It shows that we are all one with each other and with the material realm!!

William A. Tiller, Ph.D., Stanford University Professor Emeritus in physics, performed experiments to discover whether conscious intention influences the material world. In carefully controlled experiments, people were asked to focus on specific things in the material world, trying to influence their composition. The focused attention of subjects had these effects on the physical world of matter and energy:

● The acidity (pH) of water was intentionally raised or lowered by one pH unit.
● The activity of a human liver enzyme was increased by 15% to 30%.

● The larval growth rate of a fly was increased by 25%.

(The results measured were highly significant; the possibility of occurrence by chance was less than one in 1000).

Tiller's experiments had one other finding that showed how the mind affects physical reality. The spaces in which the experiments were conducted seemed to become increasingly conducive to enhancing the experimentation the more they were used. People's minds were able to influence things in the space more strongly and more quickly as time went on; the space was conditioned by the minds of the experimenters, they were increasingly more conducive to having effects. As Tiller put it, in those spaces, the laws of physics no longer seem to apply. (106)

Mysterious Passenger Lift
During demolition of the old Palace Hotel at Southport in 1969, the contractors were alarmed when a four ton lift began to move up and down by itself, despite the fact that the entire power supply had been cut off weeks before. The Electricity Board were called in to investigate and reported: "There isn't an amp going into the place", but just as they were leaving the lobby, the lift doors slammed shut and it shot up to the second floor. To rule out hoaxers, they set the brake on the lift and removed the emergency winding handle, but the next evening the lift performed on cue for a BBC television team. The activity seemed to be connected with one young member of the demolition squad, and only ended when the cables were cut and he and the rest of his team had beaten the irrepressible machine to death with 28-pound hammers. (107)

Such antics may be incomprehensible, but they do not come as a complete surprise to anyone who has ever given a motor car a personal name, coaxed a new one into reluctant life on a cold morning, or nursed an ageing one through its umpteenth nervous breakdown. There is something about some machines that gives them what amounts almost to an individual personality, which can be gentle and cooperative or simply bloody-minded. Most of us, at some time or another, have had cause to curse a recalcitrant lawnmower or outboard engine that seems to run perfectly well for everybody else; and it is easy to succumb to the temptation to give the thing a good kick. Which can help to make one feel a little better, but just how do you go about really insulting a machine? That may sound like a daft question, but with the invention of the silicon chip, it becomes one of real relevance. (108)

Computers can become Psychotic
A computer is an autonomous machine. One that operates for long periods of time without input, worrying over the details in some internal model. The big ones have big worries and the really powerful ones have become so complex that nobody understands them. They are now so thoroughly unpredictable that some, like the monster coordinating the defence network of the United States, is now officially described as "psychotic (109)

It has on several occasions already, without any appropriate input, decided that the country was under attack by the Soviet Union - and had to be restrained from retaliating in kind. Given the dangers inherent in such malfunction, it is hardly surprising that research has begun into all possible sources of error. Many seem to be an internal, part of the computer's own complex "psychology", but some are apparently external and yet unconnected with programming.

Just a few years ago, the subject was part of transistor folklore, but all the big manufacturers and many computer users have been aware for some time, at least at an operational level, that there are individuals who have an inimical effect on the machinery. These people are usually singled out and quietly transferred to the modern equivalent of the mill canteen, but attempts are now being made to try to identify the kind of influence involved.

Robert Morris, the first incumbent of the prestigious Koestler Chair in Edinburgh, gives as his current focus of interest, "the investigation of psychic functioning in anomalous interactions between people and equipment". A concern which cannot be unrelated to the fact that he comes direct from employment as Senior Research Scientist in the School of Computer and Information Science in New York State. (110)

It begins to look as though metal bending and silicon-psychosis have much in common and cannot safely or simply be dismissed as conjuring tricks.

White Noise influenced by Peoples Worry
Since 1998, about 50 computers around the world have been constantly recording and analysing white noise generated from devices much like the television set when there is no signal. If the noise suddenly hade some organization to it that wasn't random, we would say it was affected by something. The effect wouldn't be audible to the human ear but the computer could identify it and let the researchers know that something just happened.

The Twin Towers
The 50 or so computers measuring white noise since 1998 have shown very remarkable findings. At the time of the terrorist attacks on the World Trade Centre, white noise from the computers around the world showed that something dramatic had happened. (Von Beungner)
    More interestingly the computers measuring changes in the white noise showed that the global consciousness had been alert at 4 a.m., five hours before the first aeroplane crashed at 8-45 and six and a half hours before the second plane crashed at 10-30. That would have been around the time the hijackers started to

put their plan into action. The events had not occurred and whether these men were going to be successful in their plan could not have been known in any ordinary sense, but our collective minds knew what was going to happen, and our shock registered on inanimate devices around the world. (111)

The same effects on the white noise have resulted during dozens of other such incidents that affected the minds of many people, such as floods, bombings, tsunamis, house-votes, acquittals of figures, earthquakes, and plane crashes. The randomness of the white noise changes with each event. The chances that these reactions in inanimate machines occurred coincidentally at those times are less than a million to one. The data on the other events are available from the Princeton University Website.

The minds of millions of people were affecting inanimate computers in the physical world, meaning they were also affecting all organic and inorganic things. We just don't know to what extent.

Snow, like Loys, turned to the holographic model for the answer, and like Loys, believes that there are several potential features, or holoverses, forming in the gathering mist of fate. But like other past-life researchers he also believes we create our own destiny, both individually and collectively, and thus the four scenarios are really a glimpse into the various potential futures the human race is creating for itself en masse.

Consequently, Snow recommends that instead of building bomb shelters or moving to areas that won't be destroyed by the "coming Earth changes" predicted by some psychics, we should spend time believing and visualizing a positive future. He cites the Planetary Commission, the ad hoc collection of millions of individuals around the world who have agreed to spend the hour of 12:00 to 1:00

P.M., Greenwich mean time, each December thirty-first united in prayer and meditation on world peace and healing – as a step in the right direction. "If we are continually shaping our future physical reality by today's collective thoughts and actions, then the time to wake up to the alternative we have created is now, " states Snow. "The choices between the kind of Earth represented by each of the Types are clear. Which do we want for our grandchildren? Which do we want perhaps to return to ourselves someday?" (112)

Our senses are less restrictive, but no less selective. When you walk into a room that contains a grandfather clock, the tick-tock seems very loud. Your brain-waves, heart-beat and skin resistance all fluctuate in time with the noisy mechanism. But after a while, you no longer find it quite so intrusive and eventually cease to hear it at all. You tune it out, your skin resistance remains undisturbed and, if measurements are taken from your auditory nerve, these show that news of the clock is no longer even being sent on from the ear to the brain. (113) The clock becomes a constant part of the environment, one without further news value. But if the clockwork rhythm changes or stops altogether, then attention returns to it immediately. Something has happened which might be significant and needs to be considered.

Neurophysiologist Karl Pribram of Stanford University describes this as the "Bowery Effect", after an elevated railroad of that name which once ran along Third Avenue in New York. It was travelled, at the same time late each night, by a particularly noisy train involved in maintenance work. People in the neighbourhood were delighted when the track was demolished, but for months after the line closed, the local police station was besieged by reports of "something strange", possibly thieves or burglars, making noises in the night. It turned out that all the calls came in at precisely the time of the former late-night train - from residents now "hearing" the absence of a once familiar sound." (114)

--o--

CHAPTER EIGHT

MIND OVER BODY

> *Be positive about yourself and about your health. As you will see in this chapter your frame of mind can remove cancers and other debilitating diseases. There seems to be no end to what the mind is capable of.*

When we lived in Riyadh, the capital of Saudi Arabia, we knew a lot of people who worked in hospitals there. We were told by one of them that Saudi men were having an operation to insert an air bladder into their penis and another operation to insert a pumping device, under the skin behind the scrotum.

> At first I thought that it was a joke but then others reported the same thing and, subsequently, an advertisement appeared in one of the local newspapers showing the device and how it operated. Apparently. It was inserted under local anaesthetic and, once installed, the pump under the scrotum could be hand operated to give the man a (pretend) erection. It even described how to stop the erection by bending the erect penis at an angle of about 90 degrees. I bet that brought tears to the eyes!!

The whole thing was quite hilarious and a group of us, men and women alike, used to describe all kinds of imagined situations. We only had to be out together and I would start stamping my right foot up and down on the ground. There would be laughter as they knew I was using an (imaginary) foot pump to inflate my penis.

Viagra Saves the Day
But, as always, technology moves on and it was less than 10 years before Viagra appeared and did away with the need for a foot pump or any other kind of pump. Well, at least, it gave us all a good laugh while it lasted.

I am surprised, thinking about it now, that some people can perform such amazing feats of 'mind over body', while some of us fail (as I did for a while) to even get an erection.

Some of those feats of 'mind over body' are quite unbelievable and include the elimination of cancer and other terrible afflictions – but that's another story for elsewhere in this book.

Each of us possesses the ability, at least at some level, to influence our health and control our physical form in ways that are nothing short of dazzling. We are all potential wonder workers, dormant yogis, and it is clear from the evidence that it would behove us both as individuals and as a species to devote a good deal more effort into exploring and harnessing these talents.

The Healing of Bones
With fifty thousand patients so far treated with electricity to mend intractable bone fractures; with countless others now being fitted with simple electric jewellery that succeeds from outside the body in stabilizing heart-beat and disturbances in brain-wave rhythms that may produce epileptic fits; with coils and implants healing ulcers, severe burns and painful tendonitis - it is no surprise that

electromagnetic medicine is coming of age and we begin to wonder what effects natural and artificial fields might have on the behaviour and physiology of whole organisms. If we are essentially electric, then what does it mean to us to live in an increasingly electric environment? (115)

There is evidence that PK abilities can also be used to heal bones. Several examples of such healing have been reported by Dr. Rex Gardner, a physician at Sunderland District General Hospital in England. One interesting aspect of a 1983 article in the British Medical Journal is that Gardner, an avid investigator of miracles, presented contemporary miraculous healings side by side with examples of virtually identical healings collected by seventh-century English historian and theologian the Venerable Bede. (116)

A present-day healing involved a group of Lutheran nuns living in Darmstadt, Germany. The nuns were building a chapel when one of the sisters broke through a freshly cemented floor and fell onto a, wooden beam below. She was rushed to the hospital where X rays revealed that she had a compound pelvic fracture. Instead of relying on standard medical techniques, the nuns held an all-night prayer vigil, despite the doctors' insistence that the sister should remain in traction for many weeks, the nuns took her home two days later and continued to pray and perform a laying on of hands. To their surprise, immediately following the laying on of hands, the sister stood up, free of the excruciating pain. The fracture had apparently healed. It took her only two weeks to achieve a full recovery, whereon she returned to the hospital and presented herself to her astonished doctor. (117)

Healers

Healers have been known to have a positive effect on people who are ill, both when in the same room and from great distances. The intentions of healers to connect with those who are the focus of the healing (receivers) were studied by measuring whether the receivers had changes in MRIs of their brains at the moments the healers focused on them. Jean Achterberg, Ph.D., professor of psychology at Southwestern Medical School and the Saybrook Institute, studied 11 pairs of healers and receivers of the healing intentions. Before beginning the MRIs of the receivers' brains, each healer was asked to try to connect with the receiver in any way they used in their own healing traditions: sending energy, prayer, having good intentions, or thinking of the receiver and wishing the highest good for him or her.

The receiver was in the MRI machine and completely isolated from the healers and the experimenters. The healers were asked to send their prayers or thoughts for two minutes at irregular times determined by tosses of a coin. The, study is considered "blind" because the receivers in the MRI did not know when the distant intentions were being sent.

The results of the study were highly significant. MRI scans of the brains of 9 of the 11 receivers showed major significant changes in brain function each moment the healers began praying or thinking about them, even though they did not know when they were receiving the attention. Their brains, according to Dr. Achterberg "lit up" like Christmas trees. (118)

Historical and anthropological literature abounds in reports about various forms of spiritual healing and hexing performed by special individuals or entire groups and about complex rituals carried out for that purpose. Studies conducted by medical anthropologists have shown that the therapeutic results of the healing procedures and ceremonies of such systems as santeria, palerismo, or umbanda in groups of Latin American immigrants are in many cases superior to those achieved by Western psychiatry and medicine. Whether this applies only to emotional and psychosomatic disorders or extends to some categories of medical problems remains to be found. Research of psychedelic substances has shown that many shamans have at their disposal tools which are much more effective than the verbal techniques of Western psychotherapists. Sophisticated researchers with good academic credentials, such as Walter Pahnke, Andrija Puharich, or Stanley Krippner, were deeply impressed by the phenomena surrounding the work of the spiritist psychic surgeon Arrigo in Brazil or of Tony Agpoa and others in the Philippines. (119)

While studying healers living in the rice fields of a northern part of the Philippines, we were fortunate enough to capture on film a red-orange stream of healing energy. Josefina Sisson is just starting to treat the eye of a patient who has come from the out-back area of Australia. This momentary blast of healing energy was invisible to the members of the five-man team of specialists we had with us, but it was detected and recorded by the emulsions on the photographic film.

Multiple Personalities
Even More noteworthy are the biological changes that take place in a multiple's body when they switch personalities. Frequently a medical condition possessed by one personality will mysteriously vanish when another personality takes over. Dr. Bennett Braun of the International Society for the Study of Multiple Personality, in Chicago, has documented a case in which all of a patient's sub-personalities were allergic to orange juice, except one. If the man drank orange juice when one of his allergic personalities was in control, he would break out in a terrible rash. But if he switched to his non allergic personality, 'the rash would instantly start to fade and he could drink orange juice freely. (120).

Dr. Francine Howland, a Yale psychiatrist who specializes in treating multiples, relates an even more striking incident concerning one multiple's reaction to a wasp sting. On the occasion in question, the man showed up for his scheduled appointment with Howland with his eye completely swollen shut from a wasp sting Realizing he needed medical attention, Howland called an ophthalmologist. Unfortunately, the soonest the ophthalmologist could see the man was an hour later, and because the man was in severe pain, Howland decided to try something. As it turned out, one of the man's alternates was an "anesthetic personality" who felt absolutely no pain. Howland had the anesthetic personality take control of the body, and the pain ended. But something else also happened. By the time the man arrived at his appointment with the ophthalmologist, the swelling was gone and his eye had returned to normal. Seeing no need to treat him, the ophthalmologist sent him home.

After a while, however, the anesthetic personality relinquished control of the body, and the man's original personality returned, along with all the pain and swelling of the wasp sting. The next day he went back to the ophthalmologist to at last be treated. Neither Howland nor her patient had told the ophthalmologist that the man was a multiple, and after treating him, the ophthalmologist telephoned Howland. "He thought time was playing tricks on him." Howland laughed. "He just wanted to make sure that I had actually called him the day before and he had not imagined it." (121)

Placebos
Another medical phenomenon that Provides us with a tantalizing glimpse of the control the mind has over the body is the Placebo Effect. A placebo is any medical treatment that has no specific action in the body but is given either to humour a patient or as a control in a

double-blind experiment, that is, a study in which one group of individuals is given a real treatment and another group is given a fake treatment. In such experiments neither the researchers nor the individuals being tested know which group they are in so that the effect of the real treatment can be assessed more accurately. Sugar pills are often used as Placebos in drug studies. So is saline solution (distilled water with salt in it) although placebos need not always be drugs. Many believe that any medical benefit derived from crystals, copper bracelets, and other non-traditional remedies is also due to the placebo effect. (122)

Even surgery has been used as a placebo. In the 1950s, angina pectoris, recurrent pain in the chest and left arm due to decreased blood flow to the heart, was commonly treated with surgery. Then some resourceful doctors decided to conduct an experiment. Rather than perform the customary surgery, which involved tying off the mammary artery, they cut patients open and then simply sewed them back up again. The patients who received the sham surgery reported just as much relief as the patients who had the full surgery. The full surgery, as it turned out, was only producing a placebo effect.'" None-the-less, the success of the sham surgery indicates that somewhere deep in all of us we have the ability to control angina pectoris.

And that is not all. In the last half century the placebo effect has been extensively researched in hundreds of different studies around the world. We now know that on average 35 percent of all people who receive a given placebo will experience a significant effect, although this number can vary greatly from situation to situation. In addition to angina pectoris, conditions that have proved responsive to placebo treatment include migraine headaches, allergies, fever, the common cold, acne, asthma, warts, various kinds of pain, nausea and seasickness, peptic ulcers, psychiatric syndromes such as depression and anxiety, rheumatoid and degenerative arthritis, diabetes, radiation sickness, Parkinsonism, multiple sclerosis, and cancer.

Clearly these range from the not so serious to the life threatening but placebo effects on oven the mildest conditions may involve physiological changes that are near miraculous. Take, for example, the lowly wart. Warts are a small tumorous growth on the skin caused by a virus. They are also extremely easy to cure through the use of placebos, as is evidenced by the nearly endless folk rituals that are used by various cultures to get rid of them. Lewis Thomas, president emeritus of Memorial Sloan-Kettering Cancer Centre in New York, tells of one physician who regularly rid his patients of warts simply by painting a harmless purple dye on them. Thomas feels that explaining this small miracle by saying it's just the unconscious mind at work doesn't begin to do the placebo effect justice. "If my unconscious can figure out how to manipulate the mechanisms needed for getting around that virus, and for deploying all the various cells in the- correct order for tissue rejection, then all I have to say is that my unconscious is a lot further along than I am. (123)

Understanding the role such factors play in a placebo's effectiveness is important, for it shows how our ability to control the body holographic is moulded by our beliefs. Our minds have the power to get rid of warts, to clear our bronchial tubes, and to mimic the painkilling ability of morphine, but because we are unaware that we possess the power, we must be fooled into using it. This might almost be comic if it were not for the tragedies that often result from our ignorance of our own power. (124)

Is Disease all in the Mind?
That all diseases might have their origin in the mind does not disturb Siegel. He sees it rather as a sign of tremendous hope, an indicator that if one has the power to create sickness, one also has the power to create wellness.

The connection between image and illness is so potent, imagery can even he used to predict a patient's prospects for survival. In another landmark experiment, Simonton, his wife, psychologist Stephanie Matthews-Simonton, Achterberg, and psychologist G. Frank Lawlis performed a battery of blood tests on 126 patients with advanced cancer. Then they subjected the patients to an equally extensive array of psychological tests, including exercises in which the patients were asked to draw images of themselves, their cancers, their treatment, and their immune systems. The blood tests offered some information about the patients' condition, but provided no major revelations. However, the results, of the psychological tests, particularly the drawings, were encyclopaedias of information about the status of the patient's health. Indeed, simply by analysing patients' drawings, Achterberg later achieved a 95% rate of accuracy by predicting who would die within a few months and who would beat their illness to go into remission.

Positive Thought Cures Cancer
No incident better illustrates this than a now famous case reported by psychologist Bruno Klopfer. Klopfer was treating a man named Wright who had advanced cancer of the lymph nodes. All standard treatments had been exhausted, and Wright appeared to have little time left. His neck, armpits, chest, abdomen, and groin were filled with tumours the size of oranges, and his spleen and liver were so enlarged that two quarts of milky fluid had to be drained out of his chest every day.

But Wright did not want to die. He had heard about an exciting new drug called Krebiozen, and he begged his doctor to let him try it. At first his doctor refused because the drug was only being tried on people with a life expectancy of at least three months. But Wright was so unrelenting in his entreaties, his doctor finally gave in. He gave Wright an injection of Krebiozen on Friday, but in his heart of heart he did not expect Wright to last the weekend. Then the doctor went home.

To his surprise, on the following Monday he found Wright out of bed, and walking around. Klopfer reported that his tumours had "melted like snowballs on a hot stove" and were half their original size. This was a far more rapid decrease in size than oven the strongest X-ray treatments could have accomplished. Ten days after Wright's first Krebiozen treatment, he left the hospital and was, as far as, his doctors could tell, cancer free. When he had entered the hospital he had needed an oxygen mask to breathe, but when he left he was well enough to fly his own plane at 12,000 feet with no discomfort.

Wright remained well for about two months, but then articles began to appear asserting that Krebiozen actually had no effect on cancer of the lymph nodes. Wright, who was rigidly logical and scientific in his thinking, became very depressed, suffered a relapse, and was readmitted to the hospital. This time his physician decided to try an experiment. He told Wright that Krebiozen was every bit as effective as it had seemed, but that some of the initial supplies of the drug had deteriorated during shipping. He explained, however, that he had a new highly concentrated version of the drug and could treat Wright with this. Of course the physician did not have a new version of the drug and intended to inject Wright with plain water. To create the proper atmosphere he even went through an elaborate procedure before injecting Wright with the placebo.

Again the results were dramatic. Tumour masses melted, chest fluid vanished, and Wright was quickly back on his feet and feeling great. He remained symptom-free for another two months, but then the American Medical Association announced that a nationwide study of Krebiozen had found the drug worthless in the treatment of cancer. This time

Wright's faith was completely shattered. His cancer blossomed anew and he died two days later. (125)

Then to Frank's great good fortune, Dr. O. Carl Simonton, a radiologist and medical director of the Cancer Counselling and Research Centre in Dallas, Texas, was asked to participate in the treatment. Simonton suggested that Frank himself could influence the course of his own disease. Simonton then taught Frank a number of relaxation and mental imagery techniques he and his colleagues had developed. From that point on, three times a day, Frank pictured the radiation he received as consisting of millions of tiny bullets of energy bombarding his cells. He also visualized his cancer cells as weaker and more confused than his normal cells, and thus unable to repair the damage they suffered. Then he visualized his body's white blood cells, the soldiers of the immune system, coming in, swarming over the dead and dying cancer cells, and carrying them to his liver and kidneys to be flushed out of his body.

The results were dramatic and far exceeded what usually happened in such cases when patients were treated solely by radiation. (126)

People can control Their own Blood Cells
Achterberg found that the physiological effects produced through the use of imagery are not only powerful, but can also be extremely specific. For example, the term white blood cell actually refers to a number of different kinds of cell. In one study, Achterberg decided to see if she could train individuals to increase the number of only one particular type of white blood cell in their body. To do this she taught one group of college students how to image a cell known as a neutrophil, the major constituent of the white blood cell population. She trained a second group to image T cells, a more specialized kind of white blood cell. At the end of the study the group that learned the neutrophil imagery had a significant increase in the

number of neutrophils in their body, but no change in the number of T cells. The group that learned to image T cells had a significant increase in the number of that kind of cell, but the number of neutrophils in their body remained the same.

Think Your Cancer Away

Achterberg says that belief is also critical to a person's health. As she points out, virtually everyone who has had contact with the medical world knows at least one story of a patient who was sent home to die, but because they "believed" otherwise, they astounded their doctors by completely recovering. In her fascinating book *Imagery in Healing* she describes several of her own encounters with such cases. In one, a woman was comatose on admission, paralyzed, and diagnosed with a massive brain tumour. She underwent surgery to "de-bulk" her tumour (remove as much as is safely possible), but because she was considered close to death, she was sent home without receiving either radiation or chemotherapy.

Instead of promptly dying, the woman became stronger by the day. As her biofeedback therapist, Achterberg was able to monitor the woman's progress, and by the end of sixteen months the woman showed no evidence of cancer. Why? Although the woman was intelligent in a worldly sense, she was only moderately educated and did not really know the meaning of the word tumour --- or the death sentence it imparted. Hence, she did not believe she was going to die and overcame her cancer with the same confidence and determination she'd used to overcome every other illness in her life, says Achterberg. When Achterberg saw her last, the woman no longer had any traces of paralysis, had thrown away her leg braces and her cane, and had even been out dancing a couple of times. (127)

The most astonishing thing about these feedback devices is that many of them actually work. Even the simplest can make it possible for anyone to know when alpha or theta rhythms are present, which knowledge helps to sustain such brain activity, which in turn helps people to relax. None of this, of course, is a guarantee of any kind of enlightenment. Eastern adepts use meditation as a means and not as an end in itself, but the craze has at least produced a shift in emphasis in large parts of our culture. A move away from individual, linear and analytic processes; towards more communal, holistic and intuitive ways of seeing the world.

Hypnotism (see also Chapter 19)
Back in 1948, some experiments in using hypnotism to enlarge the bosom had been reported, and in 1974 one J. E. Williams reported some success. Soon after, R. D. Willard, who was working at the Institute of Behaviour and Mind Sciences, decided to test these claims scientifically. He rounded up twenty-two volunteers, of all ages from nineteen to fifty-four. Their breasts were carefully measured by an independent physician: height, diameter and circumference. They were told to imagine warm water flowing over their breasts, the breasts becoming warm; if this did not work, they were to imagine a heat-lamp playing on them. They would begin to feel their breasts pulsating. These suggestions were made under light trance. They were given tape-recorded instructions, with the aid of which they were to repeat this routine daily. There were periodic check-ups. At the end of twelve weeks, twenty-eight per cent of the women had reached the size of breast they aimed at, and ceased to practice. Eighty-five per cent had achieved some enlargement, and forty-six per cent had to buy a bigger bra. The average increase was about two-thirds of an inch vertically, over an inch horizontally, and I.37 inches in circumference. Some women managed almost twice these gains. A cynic might wonder if they had simply put on weight in general, but in fact forty-two per cent of them lost two pounds or more. Moreover, fourteen of the volunteers had had

children and wanted firmer breasts. All of these achieved some improvement in that respect. And, as a final bonus, those women whose breasts had been unequal in size ended up with symmetrically equal ones. (128)

Even professional hypnotists were somewhat surprised at the ease with which these results were achieved, and two psychologists at the University of Houston attempted to repeat the results. It occurred to them that, as breasts vary in size with the menstrual cycle, a false impression might have been created by making initial measurements and final measurements at different points in the cycle. They also wanted to know if the gains in size were retained after the treatment was concluded. They made repeated measurements of their subjects and found that the growth was progressive with time, and thus not a function of the menstrual cycle; and that, while there was some loss of size after the treatment ceased, more than eighty per cent of the gain was still retained three months later.

Faith Healing
Bernard Grad of McGill University has done pioneer work in this field. His subject was a faith healer who claimed to be able to cure disease by the biblical method of 'laying on of hands.' In a preliminary test involving three hundred mice with identical injuries, those held by the healer for fifteen minutes a day did in fact heal more quickly than those held by other people. (129) Grad tried to expose this ability to more critical analysis by narrowing down its effect in an ingenious experiment with barley seeds. The seeds were treated with salt and baked in an oven for long enough to injure but not kill them. Then twenty seeds were planted in each of twenty-four flower pots and watered each day. The water to be used was taken straight from a tap into two sealed glass bottles, and each day the healer held one of these in his hands for thirty minutes. An experimental procedure was designed so that no person knew which plants were being given the treated

water, but after two weeks it was found that those given the benefit of the healer's hand on their water supply were not only more numerous but also taller and gave a higher yield. (130)

Grad tested the treated water and found no major changes, but a later analysis showed that there was a slight spreading between the hydrogen and oxygen atoms. The change in what we know to be an unstable molecule was apparently triggered by the action of an individual human field. Following this clue, Grad tried to assess the property involved in this healing response. He had water for a second barley-seed test treated by three different people. One was a psychiatrically normal man, one was a woman with a strong depressive neurosis, and the third was a man with psychotic delusional depression. The water treated by the normal man produced seeds that showed no difference from control ones, but the growth of all seedlings that received water handled by the depressed patients was greatly retarded. (131)

--o--

CHAPTER NINE

HEALTH

> *I have already tried to demonstrate what your mind is possible of doing with everyday things so it should come as no surprise that your mind can play a big part in the state of your health. If you have heart problems, diabetes, or many of the other maladies that beset us then please take note. It does good to be aware, too, of what the placebo can do; its 'pretence' can work marvels. And then there is your Aura. In it, any good Medium can read your health like a book.*

When the members of the Society for Psychical Research set to work to collect evidence in connection with what they termed supernormal phenomena, the first thing that impressed them was the frequency of records of the apparent action of the human consciousness at a distance from the place where the physical form was at the time being located. The second point which became rapidly apparent was that these phenomena took place, as far as could be judged, quite indifferently whether the consciousness of the communicator (or agent as he was called) was still the tenant of his physical form or whether it had passed out of it never to return. Most frequently such phenomena were observed to occur about the time of death when it was impossible to state with certainty whether the communicator was actually still alive or had just passed over. It was, however, noted that these occurrences were by no means uncommon when the communicating individual was asleep or in trance and when the thoughts of the person in question were strongly directed to the spot where his (or her) apparition was seen. (132)

Ancient writings speak of still another type of energy as being involved in human life and have called it by names such as prana, od, odic force, ki, baraka, etc. This subtle energy from the cosmos enters the body through whirling energy vortexes known as chakras. Only recently has an American scientist, Itzhak Bentov of Boston, Massachusetts, and the Japanese scientist, Dr. Motoyama, invented equipment which can prove that these normally invisible energy centers actually do exist. (133)

The human energy field is not always bluish white, but can possess various colors. According to talented psychics, these colors, their muddiness or intensity, and their location in the aura are related to a person's mental state, emotional state, activity, health, and assorted other factors. I can only see colours occasionally and sometimes can interpret their meaning, but again my abilities in this area are not terribly advanced.

Barbara Brennan
One person who does have advanced abilities is therapist and healer Barbara Brennan. Brennan began her career as an atmospherics physicist working for NASA at the Goddard Space Flight Center, and later left to become a counselor. Her first inkling that she was psychic came when she was a child and discovered she could walk blindfolded through the woods and avoid the trees simply by sensing their energy fields with her hands. Several years after she became a counselor, she began seeing halos of colored light around people's heads. After

overcoming her initial shock and scepticism, she set about to develop the ability and eventually discovered she had an extraordinary natural talent as a healer.

Brennan not only sees the chakras, layers, and other fine structures of the human energy field with exceptional clarity, but can make startlingly accurate medical diagnoses based on what she sees. After looking at one woman's energy field, Brennan told her there was something abnormal about her uterus. The woman then told Brennan that her doctor had discovered the same problem, and it had already caused her to have one miscarriage. In fact, several physicians had recommended a hysterectomy and that was why she was seeking Brennan's counsel. Brennan told her that if she took a month off and took care of herself, her problem would clear up. Brennan's advice turned out to be correct, and a month later the woman's physician confirmed that her uterus had returned to normal. A year later the woman gave birth to a healthy baby boy.

In another case Brennan was able to see that a man had problems performing sexually because he had broken his coccyx (tailbone) when he was twelve. The still out-of-place coccyx was applying undue pressure to his spinal column, and this in turn was causing his sexual dysfunction.

There seems to be little Brennan cannot pick up by looking at the human energy field. She says that in its early stages cancer looks gray-blue in the aura, and as it progresses, it turns to black. Eventually, white spots appear in the black, and if the white spots sparkle and begin to look as if they are erupting from a volcano, it means the cancer has metastasized. Drugs such as alcohol, marijuana, and cocaine are also detrimental to the brilliant, healthy colors of the aura and create what Brennan calls "etheric mucus." In one instance she was able to tell a startled client which nostril he habitually used to snort cocaine because the field over that side of his face was always gray with the sticky etheric mucus. (134)

One of Hunt's most startling findings is that certain talents and abilities seem to her related to the presence of specific frequencies in a person's energy field. She has found that when the main focus of a person's consciousness is on the material world, the frequencies of their energy field tend to be in the lower range and are not too far removed from the 250 cps of the body's biological frequencies. In addition to these, people who are psychic or who have healing abilities, also have frequencies of roughly 400 to 800 cps in their field. People who can go into trance and apparently channel other information sources through them, skip these "psychic" frequencies entirely and operate in a narrow band between 800 and 900 cps. "They don't have any psychic breadth at all," states Hunt.-"They're up there in their own field. It's narrow. It's pinpointed, and they literally are almost out of it. (135)

People who have frequencies above 900 cps are what Hunt calls mystical personalities. Whereas psychics and trance mediums are often just conduits of information, mystics possess the wisdom to know what to do with the information. Says Hunt. They are aware of the cosmic interrelatedness of all things and are in touch with every level of human experience. They are anchored in ordinary reality, but often have both psychic and trance abilities. However, their frequencies also extend way beyond the bands associated with these capabilities. Using a modified electromyogram (an electromyogram can normally detect frequencies only up to 20,000 cps) Hunt has encountered individuals who have frequencies as high as 200 cps in their energy fields. This is intriguing, for mystical traditions have often referred to highly spiritual individuals as possessing a "higher vibration" than normal people. If Hunt's findings are correct, they seem to add credence to this assertion.

The Human Double (see also Chapter 10)
The accumulation of evidence pointed to the fact that where certain persons of what might be termed a psychic temperament, their likeness, was frequently observed at a distance from the spot where their bodies were situated, when there was nothing apparently abnormal in their physical state. They might in short be in what is colloquially termed a brown study or perhaps in an after-dinner nap. The Reverend Charles Tweedale gives a number of instances in which his form was seen by his family at his own home when he was some distance away, his relations mistaking it constantly for his actual physical self, so realistic did it appear. It becomes therefore clear that such phenomena, though most frequently observed at the time of death, are by no means necessarily related to any such occurrence. They need not even imply any serious illness of the person concerned. The concentration of the thoughts of the individual might be sufficient in itself to evoke the double in the mind and indeed to the actual physical vision of the friend who was the subject of the thought projected. The question then naturally arose: How could the visible picture of the communicator (if we may so term him) become apparent to the percipient? Could his mere thought acting on the consciousness of the percipient evoke his image in physical form before the percipient's eyes? Was it merely a matter of a "brain wave" arousing a suggestion in the percipient's mind which took bodily form as a mental image of the communicator? Or was it some part of the communicator's real self that projected itself and thus became visible to the percipient?

The Aura
Reports that 'the field pulsates are going to bring great gladness to the hearts of spirit mediums everywhere, who have always insisted that their sensitivity was due to "vibrations". Many including the famous New York clairvoyant Eileen Garrett, have reported seeing spirals of

energy leaving a newly dead body. (136) And now Sergoyev's claim that his detectors sprang into action near the body of a man whose heart and brain waves had stopped, and was therefore chemically dead, but who still seemed to be releasing electrical energy. The idea of an energy cloud, or 'aura," surrounding the body goes back many centuries. Old pictures of holy men show them standing in a luminous surround long before Christians invented the halo. This haze with the mythical properties was first investigated by Walter Kilner of St. Thomas' Hospital in London, who found in 1911 that, by looking through colored-glass screens, he could see a radiant fringe about six inches wide around most bodies. (137) He claimed that this aura changed shape and color according to the well-being of the person wearing it, and he used it as an aid to medical diagnosis.

As a physicist, Brennan is keenly interested in describing the human energy field in scientific terms and believes Pribram's assertion that there is a frequency domain beyond our field of normal perception is the best scientific model we have so far for understanding the phenomenon. "From the point of view of the holographic universe, these events [the aura and the healing forces required to manipulate its energies] emerge from frequencies that transcend time and space; they don't have to be transmitted. They are potentially simultaneous and everywhere," she says." (138)

That the human energy field exists everywhere and is non-local until it is plucked out of the frequency domain by human perception is evidenced in Brennan's discovery that she can read a person's aura even when the person is many miles distant. The longest-distance aura reading she has done so far was during a telephone conversation between New York City and Italy. She discusses this, as well as many other aspects of her remarkable abilities, in her recent and fascinating book *Hands of Light*.

It is worth noting that we really don't know what any field is. As Bohm has said, "What is an electric field? We don't know. When we discover a new kind of field it seems mysterious. Then we name it, get used to dealing with it and describing its properties, and it no longer seems mysterious. But we still do not know what an electric or a gravitational field really is. As we saw in an earlier chapter, we don't even know what electrons are. We can only describe how they behave. This suggests that the human energy field will also ultimately be defined in terms of how it behaves, and research such as Hunt's will only further our understanding. (139)

Multiple Personalities (see also Chapter Eight)
We are deeply attached to the inevitability of things. If we have bad vision, we believe we will have bad vision for life and if we suffer from diabetes, we do not for a moment think our condition might vanish with a change in mood or thought. But the phenomenon of multiple personality challenges this belief and offers further evidence of just how much our psychological states can affect the body's biology. If the psyche of an individual with MPD is a kind of multiple image hologram then it appears that the body is one as well, and can switch from one biological state to another as rapidly as the flutter of a deck of cards.

The systems of control that must be in place to account for such capacities is mind-boggling and makes our ability to will away a wart look pale. Allergic reaction to a wasp sting is a complex and multi-faceted process and involves the organized activity of antibodies, the production of histamine, the dilation and rupture of blood vessels, the excessive release of immune substances, and so on. What unknown pathways of influence enable the mind of a multiple to freeze all these processes in their tracks? Or what allows them to suspend the effects of alcohol and other drugs in the blood, or turn diabetes on and off? At the moment we don't know and must console our-selves with one simple fact. Once a multiple has undergone therapy and in some way becomes whole again, he or she can still make these switches at Will. (140)

This suggests that somewhere in our psyches we all have the ability to control these things. And still this is not all we can do.

Becker was encouraged by Russian evidence that regeneration in plants and animals was accompanied by a "current of injury" -an electric potential that could be measured at the 'site of the wound. He suspected that the electricity might be more than a symptom of the injury and decided to see whether induced changes in such currents had any effect on the healing process. Or at least that was his intention until he discovered that American science was not as open-minded as its Soviet equivalent. "The Russians are willing to follow hunches," says Becker, "their researchers are encouraged to try the most outlandish experiments, ones that our science just knows cannot work. Furthermore, Soviet journals publish them - even if they do not work. The response of his research board in Syracuse, New York, was hostile. "The notion that electricity has anything to do with living things was totally discredited some time ago," they pronounced. "It has absolutely no validity. The whole idea was based on its appeal to quacks and the gullible public. We will not stand idly by and see this medical school associated with such a charlatanistic, unscientific project. (141)

Handwriting & Health
There is a definite connection between handwriting and health. Some analysts claim that they can detect specific sicknesses from the script. It is true that loss of co-ordination due to something like Parkinson's disease would certainly produce gross deformation in writing. The American Medical Association reports, 'There are definite organic diseases that grapho-diagnostics can help to diagnose from their earliest beginnings. (142) They list anemia, blood poisoning,

tumours, and various bone diseases among these, but add that old age can produce substantially the same signs. A few skilled geriatricians believe that it is possible to use handwriting as a sort of X-Ray to distinguish between actual mental unbalance and normal senility. The general disruption of handwriting patterns that occurs in both emotional and physical disorders is clearly recognizable and almost impossible to disguise.

Like the serious astrologer or chirologist, a good graphologist is concerned with details. Before making an assessment, he collects several samples of script produced at different times, preferably with different pens, and never works with material specifically written for analysis. He examines the slant and weight of the writing; looks at margins, spacing, rhythm, and legibility; watches punctuation and the way in which t is crossed and i and j are dotted; studies the shape of loops and the way in which strokes begin and end. With all these characters, repetition is considered to be important; the more often a trait is recorded in the script, the stronger it is thought to be. The relative frequency is also measured, so patterns that indicate contrasting traits can be reconciled. If only a limited amount of script is available for analysis, graphologists can get most information from the signature of the subject. This is something that is written so often and with such specific reference to self that it becomes a stylized representation of the writer as unique as a fingerprint. Hence its use for purposes of identification. (143)

Stress

But while the existence of hysterical and stress disorders is pretty generally recognized, doctors have been sceptical of the idea that psychosomatic factors might be at work in infectious disease or even in degenerative disease like cancer. There was general incredulity when, twenty-five years ago, Dr. D. M. Kissen showed that emotional factors were involved in tuberculosis. Stomach ulcers and skin conditions were one thing; TB was another! Tuberculosis seemed to them essentially a physical illness, the cause of which was understood. But, as always with infectious disease, the question is: why does one person fight off infection and another succumb? To say a disease is infectious does little to explain it. As Professor Rene Dubos, one of medicine's wise old men, has remarked: 'If the infectious theory of disease were true, there would be nobody here to believe it.' The truth is, the body's system of immune defences normally protects us from infection. We fall ill whenever the system is not fully effective, and this, it seems impossible to deny, can be brought about by mental states.

Subsequently Kissen showed that emotional factors were present in cancer too, but this was too much for the orthodox to swallow and his work was ignored. Very recently the idea has been mooted again in the light of accumulating evidence.

I should add that the term 'stress' does not necessarily mean extreme pressure, such as Clifford Troke was exposed to; any demand for readjustment seems to create a significant measure of stress. A careful study by the American doctor Thomas H. Holmes shows this. With the assistance of a young physicist, Richard Rahe, he devised a scale for measuring the number of changes in a person's life. Had he moved his home? Had he changed jobs or been promoted? Had his parents divorced, remarried, died? Had he divorced or remarried? And so on. They found that people who had experienced marked changes in the preceding year were much more likely to fall ill. Later the scale was tested on a variety of groups, from unemployed blacks to naval personnel. The naval study was particularly valuable, since full sickness records were available, while the men, living on ships at sea, were all exposed to similar risks of infection, on similar diets, and so on. They found that the ten per cent who had experienced most change were almost twice as likely to have been ill than the ten per cent who had experienced least change. While Holmes and Rahe stressed 'illness' in their analysis, it is obvious that all changes impose stresses, and demand adaptations

Our Attitudes
Another way belief manifests in our lives is through our attitudes. Studies have shown that the attitude an expectant mother has toward her baby, and pregnancy in general, has a direct correlation with the complications she will experience during childbirth, as well as with the medical problems her newborn infant will have after it is born. (144)

Indeed, in the past decade an avalanche of studies has poured in demonstrating the effect our attitudes have on a host of medical conditions. People who score high on tests designed to measure hostility and aggression are seven times more likely to die from heart problems than people who receive low scores. (145)

Here are six, brief but interesting
findings along with their references:

● Married women have stronger immune systems than separated or divorced women, and happily married women have even stronger immune systems. (146)

● People with AIDS who display a fighting spirit live longer than AIDS-infected individuals who have a passive attitude (147)

● People with cancer also live longer if they maintain a fighting Spirit. (148)

● Pessimists get more colds than optimists (149)

● Stress lowers the immune response. (150)

●People who have just lost their spouse have an increased incidence of illness and disease. (151)

and so on.

Kirlian Photography
In 1939 the electrician Semyon Kirlian was called to a university laboratory to repair an instrument used in electro-therapy. He noticed that when a patient received treatment with the machine, there was a tiny flash of light between the electrodes. He tried to take photographs with this light and discovered that it was possible to do this without a camera by inserting a plate directly between the high-frequency spark and his hand. On being developed, the photo-graphic plate produced a glowing image of his outstretched fingers. Other living objects also made pictures studded with dots and flares, but with inert objects there was no image at all. Kirlian built his own machine to generate high-frequency electrical fields with an oscillation of two hundred thousand sparks per second between two electrodes. He also designed an optical viewer (now the subject of fourteen Soviet patents) to make it possible to watch the process directly without films or emulsion. (152). It was a view of his own finger under this instrument that provoked that pyrotechnic description from the academician.

One of those to make the pilgrimage to see the Kirlians in Krasnodar was Mikhail Gaikin, a surgeon from Leningrad. After looking at the cavalcade of lights in his own hands, he began to wonder about their origin. The strongest flares shone right out of the skin like searchlights, but their positions corresponded with no major nerve endings in the body, and the pattern of their distribution showed no correspondence with arteries or veins. Then he remembered his experiences on the Zabaikal front in 1945 and the lessons he had learned from a Chinese doctor in the art of acupuncture. Acting on his hunch, he sent the Kirlians a standard acupuncture chart of seven hundred important points on the skin, and they tallied exactly with charts that the Kirlians had prepared under their high-frequency machine.

Every living thing placed in the high-frequency discharge produces these patterns. A whole hand can look like the Milky Way, sparkling and twinkling against a glowing background of gold and blue. A freshly picked leaf shines with an internal light that streams out through its pores in beams that gradually flick out one by one as it dies. Leaves taken from plants of the same species show similar jeweled patterns, but if one of the plants is diseased, the pattern in its leaf is entirely different. Similarly the patterns produced by the same fingertip change with the mood and health of the man to whom it belongs. Kirlian says, 'In living things, we see the signals of the inner state of the organism reflected in the brightness, dimness and color of the flares. The inner life activities of the human being are written in these 'light hieroglyphs. We've created an apparatus to write the hieroglyphs, but to read them we're going to need help. (153)

You may have read in Time or The Reader's Digest about the Brazilian healer Jose P. de Freitas, popularly known as Arigo. Two paragraphs in the *Time* story of October 16, 1972 give the overall picture:

"Even before he died last year in an automobile accident at the age of 49, the peasant known as Arigo had become a legend in his native Brazil. Claiming to be guided by the wise voice of a long-dead physician whom he had never known personally. The uneducated healer saw as many as 300 patients a day, diagnosing and treating them in minutes. He treated almost every known ailment, and most of his patients not only survived but actually improved or recovered.

'A few years ago, reports on the exploits of such miracle workers would have drawn little more than derision from the scientifically-trained. Now, however, many medical researchers are showing new open-mindedness toward so-called psychic healing and other methods not taught in medical schools."

As a boy, Arigo had no education except for two years at a parochial school from which he was dismissed because, in his own words, he was too stupid to continue. His subsequent career involved hard labour, either in the fields or mines, and later, a clerical job in a social security office. Nobody ever saw Arigo read a book, or even attempt to read one, as was discovered in an extensive sociological study of his background. For all practical purposes, Arigo could be considered an illiterate. Thus, it was necessary to consider very seriously the hypothesis that there indeed may have been a voice presenting itself in his head. The important question is: What was its source?

Arigo the healer was able to make a complete diagnosis by merely looking at a patient. A team of medical doctors and scientists from the United States took 3,000 pounds of medical diagnostic equipment with them to Brazil for the Arigo research. Andrija Puharich, M.D., the team leader, arranged to have a diagnosis made of each of about 450 patients, taken at random from the lines that formed daily to obtain Arigo's services. When comparing the teams diagnosed, Arigo called out in Portuguese in the time it took patients to walk the few steps from the head of the line to stand before him, it was concluded that there was good agreement in 92 percent of the cases. Puharich later confided in me, "George, we will probably never find out, but there exists the sneaking suspicion in my mind that Arigo may have been right in the other 8 percent!"

Equally beyond medical comprehension was the fact that Arigo was one of the few healers who prescribed every known modern molecular medicine. In two cases, he dictated a prescription for medicine that had just been put on the market in Europe but which had not yet been imported into Brazil.

Arigo often treated a few hundred patients a day. Patients who seemingly suffered the full range of human ailments. Usually Arigo would complete his handling of the patients in one to four minutes each. (154)

The Man in the Ear

A French physician and acupuncturist named Paul Nogier published a book called Treatise of Auriculoherapy, in which he announced his discovery that in addition to the major acupuncture system, there are two smaller acupuncture systems on both cars. He dubbed these acupuncture micro systems and noted that when one played a kind of connect-the-dots game with them, they formed anatomical map of a miniature human inverted like a foetus. Unbeknownst to Nogier, the Chinese had discovered the "little man in the ear" nearly 4,000 years earlier, but a map of the Chinese ear system wasn't published until after Nogier had already laid claim to the idea.

The little man in the ear is not just a charming aside in the history of acupuncture. Dr. Terry Oleson, a psychobiologist at the Pain Management Clinic at the University of California at Los Angeles School of Medicine, has discovered that the ear micro system can he used to diagnose accurately what's going on in the body. For instance, Oleson has discovered that increased electrical activity in the ear, generally indicates a pathological condition (either past or present) in the corresponding area of the body. In one study, forty patients were examined to determine areas of their body where they experienced chronic pain. Following the examination, each patient was draped in a sheet to conceal any visible problems. Then an acupuncturist with no knowledge of the results examined only their ears. When the results were tallied it was discovered that the ear examinations were in agreement with the established medical diagnosis 75.2 percent of the time.

Meanwhile, in the United States, a neurologist had made another fascinating discovery. Albert Abrams was treating a patient with a small cancer on his lip, and ended a routine general examination with percussion - tapping the abdomen and listening to the quality of the sound. He found a spot that made a dull sound, instead of the expected hollow note of a healthy stomach – but could only get the discordant response when his patient was standing up and facing west. This made little sense to Abrams, but it intrigued him.

He brought in a medical student in robust good health and tried percussing the unfortunate young man in every possible position and compass direction, with nothing but the normal hollow sound. But then he gave the student a small glass container with a sample of cancerous tissue and asked him to hold this against his face. As soon as he did, Abrams got the same dull percussive note as he had noticed with his cancer patient. Now he was excited.

Abrams broadened his inquiry by bringing in samples of tissue from patients suffering from tuberculosis, pneumonia and malaria- and found that each produced the dead sound in different parts of his subject's abdomen. He had discovered, he decided, a new system of diagnosis.

The diseased tissues, Abrams reasoned, must be transmitting some kind of "radiation" which could be measured. So he built himself an old-fashioned variable resistance box and soon found that the effects of each sample could be cancelled out by introducing a different resistance into the circuit consisting of tissue -machine - human abdomen. Cancerous tissue, for instance, was neutralized by a resistance of precisely 50 ohms. The next step was the discovery that it was not necessary to have a whole tissue sample - it was possible to identify diseases purely by the reaction of his apparatus to one drop of a patient's blood. With this discovery, Abrams had his famous "black box" - and a fierce scientific and medical controversy.

The problem is that there is no known radiation coming from a sample of dried blood that could influence such a machine, and though Abrams got impressive results with his equipment, few other people could do so. He was dismissed as a quack and died discredited in 1924. (155)

A few years later, an American chiropractor took the next necessary step and replaced the cumbersome abdomen-of-a-medical-student-facing-due-west that Abrams used as his detector, with a simple rubber diaphragm. Ruth Drown also took another great stride by claiming that her modified apparatus not only diagnosed disease at a distance, but could treat it as well by the use of "radio therapy" to restore the energetic harmony of patients who did no more than provide a sample of blood or a lock of hair. The medical authorities were predictably outraged and in 1951 Drown was arrested. She was accused of fraud and jailed. Her equipment and her records were destroyed and she died of a stroke days after her eventual release at the age of seventy-two. (156)

During the last forty years, everything has changed. The technological boom which began after World War 2 has left us awash in a sea of strange energies. Every digital watch, flashlight and portable radio produces a direct current magnetic field. The stopping and starting of each electric train turns the power rail into a gigantic antenna that radiates low frequency waves for over a hundred miles. High voltage power lines, of which there are half a million miles in the United States alone, produce powerful fields that are concentrated by metal objects nearby, and pass through switching stations that also emit radio frequencies. Low frequency radio waves emanate from navigation beacons and military net-works. The medium frequencies are loaded with AM transmitters, and the high and very high frequency channels bristle with police and taxi traffic, the numerous spy satellites and the ceaseless babel of millions of CB radios. And in addition, we are bombarded at home and at work, every hour of the day and night, by errant microwaves from antitheft devices, metal detectors, automatic door openers, walkie-talkies, cordless telephones, vulcanizers, heat sealers and ovens."

We are, without permission but with our tacit approval, the subjects of a giant electrical experiment. Nor is there any end in sight. The density of radio waves around us now is 100 million times the natural level reaching us from the Sun, and by 1990 it will have doubled again. When superconducting cables are introduced, the field strength around power lines will be increased by another twenty times. And electric cars and vehicles moved by magnetic levitation will add entirely new sources of electro pollution to the stew with which we are already assailed. Meanwhile, the first results of the experiment are starting to come in and there is, it seems, no place to hide.

Since 1982, a high incidence of leukaemia has been reported in three independent studies of people exposed to high electromagnetic frequencies - those who work as radio operators, electronic technicians, power linemen, aluminium smelters and electrical engineers in California, England and Wales. An increased susceptibility to cancer has been found in children whose homes lie near high voltage power lines. Helicopter pilots, who may be exposed to more radiation than the rest of us, are producing an unusually large number of club-footed children. Pregnant women operating video display terminals in the United States, Canada and England appear to suffer miscarriages, have stillbirths or give birth to deformed children far more often than the population as a whole. And large numbers of people in highly electrical environments everywhere complain of headaches, loss of appetite and frequent fatigue. The trickle of such reports grows to a flood, provoking some consumer resistance and predictable disclaimers from the power companies and other vested interests. But perhaps the most disconcerting aspect of electromagnetic smog is that those, like Robert Becker, who know most about the biological effects, are least concerned about the more obvious sources of contamination. It is the low-intensity radiations that worry them - the ones closest in strength to Earth's own subtle signals. These are the ones, according to a Soviet scientist, that "alter visual, acoustic and tactile sensations, changing physiological functions and affecting emotional states" (157).

Mobile Phones

On May 31, 2011, the World Health Organization (WHO)/International Agency for Research on Cancer (IARC) issued a report admitting cell phones might indeed cause cancer, classifying radiofrequency electromagnetic fields as "possibly carcinogenic to humans" (Class 2B) The classification came in part in response to research showing wireless telephones increase the risk for brain cancer.

Dr. Devra Davis, one of the most well-respected and credentialed researchers on the dangers of cell phones, and founder and president of Environmental Health Trust shares information about the risks of cell phone use that you might not be aware of.

A cell phone is a two-way microwave-radiating device that has been associated with brain tumours and salivary gland tumours, weakened sperm production and cell membranes, hearing loss and tinnitus, among other issues

The telecom industry is a global multi-trillion dollar industry that influences government policies through persistent lobbying efforts, sizeable political donations, and manipulation of science.

A recent Government Accountability Office Report: "Exposure and Testing Requirements for Mobile Phones Should be Reassessed," has added pressure on the Federal Communications Commission to strengthen cell phone testing, as has a letter from the American Academy of Paediatrics urging that children are especially vulnerable to damage from cell phone radiation, and should not use them without special protections, if at all, (or only for very limited amounts).

Adults should not keep a cell phone in a pocket or on the body, and should use an air-tube headset or the speakerphone feature as much as possible, remembering that 'distance is your friend.'

On 26 February 2015 I (John Burrows) read a new article on the Internet. It said that one Russian father discovered a unique property of the magnetic material he was using to educate his son. When placed beside a cell phone, the metallic ore began to twist and mutate, almost as if alive. Credit: YouTube / АБАКАКА (1:49). The article had a video showing the fine wire ore twisting and turning when the phone was transmitting. It was quite frightening, and it made me wonder what it would do to the tiny filaments in the brain which are more than a million times smaller. It doesn't bear thinking about.

--o--

CHAPTER TEN

THE HUMAN DOUBLE

Yesterday, upon the stair,
I met a man who wasn't there.
He wasn't there again today,
I wish that man would go away.

The view, as I understand, of the orthodox Theosophist, is that the astral body takes the place of the etheric envelope within a brief period after the etheric cord is finally broken, and when in consequence there can be no further return to the earth plane, at least in the individual's present physical form.

Now it would seem to me to be rather dangerous to dogmatize on a point with regard to which we have, as it would appear, very little positive knowledge, but I would suggest that a few general observations on this somewhat obscure matter might tend to clear the ground, and at least avoid misunderstanding as regards statements made in the present volume, and the use employed in it of certain expressions in this connection. In the first place, it may do well to observe that the idea of individual existence, apart from some vehicle through which the consciousness may operate, is contrary to reason. Individuality signifies limitation, and without a body of some sort, material, etheric or other, there can be no such thing as limitation, and in consequence no such thing as individual consciousness, apart from the universal consciousness or life stream. In conformity with this view

Mr. William Kingsland confirms this in his learned and philosophical work on Rational Mysticism (Chapter X).

Survival of Bodily Death

"It is quite evident that if we are to believe in any conscious entities or beings whatsoever in the Universe, whether of a Cosmic or of a more limited nature. Or if we are to believe in any manner in our own conscious survival of bodily death, then such individual survival, or such entities or beings, must have some substantial vehicle or body through which Life and Consciousness continue to function and manifest. "

> Mr. Kingsland goes on to point out, taking our own case as human beings as an instance, that such a body cannot spring into existence as the result of the death of the physical body. It must exist now as the energizing principle of the body, and the apparent death of the individual must be due to the withdrawal of this etheric envelope or subtle body without the aid of which the physical form can no longer function on the physical plane. (158)

There must be always some appreciable inter-blending of the physical and the etheric and the disintegration of the body at death must of necessity be a very gradual process. Hence the theosophical theory of "shells" which are left behind when the consciousness escapes from its physical envelope and of the powers and properties of which I think a good deal too much has been made in certain quarters. This is doubtless a matter of conjecture, but we should bear in mind the fact that the dissolution of the soul and the body at death is hastened in cases where cremation is employed and is normally protracted through a considerable period. The lights seen at times in church-yards and cemeteries, especially by clairvoyants, are the visual evidence of the process of disintegration involved. To explain the phenomena of materialization on the basis of shells or remnants that have been discarded in the process of physical death appears to me to be entirely erroneous, as also is the theory that the etheric body as a whole follows the physical form in its process of dissolution. (159)

Useful Message from the Afterlife

It appears that an officer had died in the town of Montpelier and, as happens not infrequently in France, he had put away his possessions, including title deeds, etc., in a secret hiding-place which his heirs were unable to discover. One of them, faced with this difficulty, decided to consult the Parisian clairvoyants. Mlle. C., after asking for the most minute details, including the name of the street, number of the house, description of the rooms, etc., entered into her trance condition, and made what is termed in the record a mental journey to Montpelier. After some hesitation (according to her own account) she reached the town and street notified, stopped at the number mentioned, went upstairs, identified the rooms described and, entering one of them, raised the curtains of the bed on which the officer had died and, noting a hiding-place in the wall, looked into it and discovered there the missing title deeds, together with a 100-franc gold piece, which the uncle had treasured and had previously shown to his nephews. The nephew, acting on the clairvoyant's instruction, went to Montpelier and found the deeds and the 100-franc piece in the spot where Mlle. C. had stated that they were.

The Cure of Saint-Sulpice (the Abbe Meretan) is quoted as the authority for another story bearing witness to this Parisian clairvoyant's powers. It appears that he had in his parish a poor sempstress who had made an expensive dress to the order of a society lady, a Baroness X, and had herself delivered it at the lady's house on the day arranged. The lady in question complained, however, that she had not received her dress, and when the sempstress assured her that she had delivered it in person, called her a liar and a thief

Very reluctantly the sempstress betook herself to Mlle. C., and confided to her about her trouble. The latter, after ascertaining full particulars as to the lady's house and the appearance of the box in which the dress had been placed, went into her trance condition (her second state, as she called it), took herself to the house in question and, after ransacking every corner, discovered the box put away in a closet apparently by a maid who had forgotten to deliver it. The sempstress thereupon went to the Baroness's and asked to be allowed to search the closet in question, where the dress was duly found. (160)

Human Double in Houses of Parliament

The "double" has even invaded the Houses of Parliament. Sir Carne Rasch, when ill in bed, was seen in the House of Commons not only by Sir Gilbert Parker, but also by Sir Arthur Hayter. Sir Gilbert said, about this experience, "When Rasch accepted my nod with what looked very like a glare, and met my kindly inquiry with silence I was a little surprised, and when he suddenly and silently vanished I put my hand to my head in utter bewilderment and asked myself if it were possible that poor Rasch, whose illness had been reported in the papers, had actually died."

Sir Arthur Hayter also was positive that he saw Sir Carne Rasch on the same occasion. He stated that he was struck by his extreme pallor, and also that he occupied a seat remote from his usual place.

On another occasion another member of the House, Dr. Mark Macdonnell, was seen by fellow members on two consecutive days, and actually recorded his vote in the division lobby, though as a matter of fact he had not left his room, being laid up at the time. These occurrences taking place under such circumstances of publicity naturally led to comment in the daily Press. (161)

A Curious Story

Another very curious story is that of Herr Becker, who was professor of mathematics at Rostock. This gentleman fell into an argument with some friends of his in reference to a disputed point in theology. In order to substantiate his case he went into his library to fetch a book to which he desired to refer, and on arriving there to his astonishment saw his own double sitting at the table in the seat which he was accustomed to occupy. He approached the figure, which appeared to be reading, and looking over its shoulder he noticed that the book open before it was the Bible, and that with one of the fingers of its right hand it pointed to the passage, "Set thine house in order for thou shalt die.

He thereupon returned to the company present, relating what he had seen and, in spite of their arguments, expressed his conviction that he was about to die, which he did on the following day at six o'clock in the evening.

A similar case is related by Stilling which had, however, no tragic consequences. A government officer at Weimar, he tells us, of the name of Triplin, on going to his office to fetch some document of importance, noticed his own double sitting there in the chair with the deed in question in front of him. Feeling considerable alarm, he retired hastily, but afterwards, summoning his maidservant, he requested her to go to his room and fetch the paper which she would find on the table. The maid went accordingly, and also seeing her master's double, came to the conclusion that he had not waited for her to perform her errand, but had gone off and arrived before her. No explanation of this curious incident -was ever forthcoming. (162)

Emile Sagee

Numerous other instances might be cited, in which a person's double is seen in one place, while he or she is in the physical body elsewhere. Generally the double is seen by others, but as will have been noted in the foregoing records, it is also liable to be seen by the person whose double it is. One of the most remarkable tales in this connection is that of Mademoiselle Emile Sagee, published in an issue of -*Light* in-the year 1883.

It appears that there existed in Livonia in the year 1845 and many years after, about thirty-six miles from Riga and four or five miles from the small town of Volmar, a school for young girls of noble birth which bore the name of the "Pensionnat de Neuwelcke". The head of this establishment was, at the date in question, a certain M. Buch.

The number of girls, almost all members of the Livonian nobility, was at that time forty-two. Among them was the second daughter of a certain Baron Guldenstubbe, a girl of thirteen years of age.

One of the school mistresses there was a French-woman. a Mademoiselle Emile Sagee, who was born at Dijon, but belonged to a Northern type, a blonde with a pink-and-white complexion, bright blue eyes, and chestnut hair. She was somewhat over middle height, amiable and cheerful in disposition, but of a shy and nervous temperament. Her health was good on the whole, and in the year and a half during which she remained at Neuwelcke she had only one or two slight indispositions. She was intelligent, thoroughly well educated, and gave every satisfaction to the directors in the matter of her teaching. She was at this time thirty-two years of age.

A few weeks after her arrival at the establishment strange rumours began to be spread among the pupils with regard to her. When one girl observed that she had seen her in one part of the house, it was a common occurrence for another to deny this and declare that she had met her elsewhere at the very same moment. In the first instance these disputes were simply putdown to some mistake, but when the same thing happened over and over again, the pupils began to think it very odd, and in due course spoke of the matter to the other mistresses. The professors who gave lessons at the establishment, when they learnt of the story, pooh-poohed the whole matter, and declared that such a thing was contrary to common sense.

But matters soon came to a head, and assumed a character which left no room for two opinions. One day, when Emile Sagee was giving a lesson to thirteen of her pupils, among whom was Mademoiselle de Gulldenstubbe and when, in order to make her explanation plainer, she was writing out the passage under discussion on a blackboard, the girls saw all of a sudden, to their intense alarm, two Mademoiselle Sagees, standing side by side. They resembled one another in every particular, and made the same identical gestures. Only the real Mademoiselle Sagee had a piece of chalk in her hand, and wrote with it on the blackboard while her double had not, and merely imitated the movements she made in writing.

Hence arose a great sensation in the establishment in as much as the young girls without a single exception had seen the second figure and were absolutely agreed as to the description they gave of the phenomenon. A short time after, one of the pupils, a certain Mademoiselle Antoinette de Wrangel, obtained permission to go to a neighbouring fate with some of her girl friends. Mademoiselle Sagee, with her usual good nature, offered to help her with her toilette, and was fastening her dress behind. Turning round during this operation the young girl glanced into the looking-glass, where she saw reflected two Mademoiselle Sagees. So scared was she at this sudden apparition that she fainted away.

Months elapsed, and these phenomena continued to take place. Mademoiselle Sagee was seen at dinner with her double standing up behind her, imitating her movements as she ate her food. The pupils and the maids who waited at table were all witnesses of these occurrences.

On one occasion, all the pupils, to the number of forty-two, were together in one room and occupied with embroidery work. The room was on the ground floor of the principal building, with four large windows or, rather, glass doors, commanding a view of the garden belonging to the establishment. The pupils seated around the table were able, from where they sat, to see what took place in the garden, and noticed Mademoiselle Sagee occupied in picking flowers not far from the house. At the upper end of the table was another mistress, charged with looking after the girls and seated in an arm-chair. After a time this mistress got up and left the room. Very shortly after the pupils, looking round, noticed the form of Mademoiselle Sagee occupying the arm-chair, while at the same time they observed her duplicate still engaged in picking flowers, but moving about more slowly, like one in a dream or brown study. By this time the girls were more or less accustomed to these strange occurrences, and two of the most forward of them walked up to the armchair and touched the apparition, which seemed to offer a faint resistance like a piece of muslin or crape. One of them even walked across a part of the phantom figure. Shortly afterwards the form disappeared altogether, while Mademoiselle Sagee resumed her occupation in the garden with her customary vivacity.

Several of the pupils subsequently asked their mistress if she had experienced any particular sensation on the occasion, to which she replied that she had merely reflected to herself on noticing the empty armchair that it was a matter for regret that the other mistress had gone off and left her class to their own devices, as she thought that they would be wasting their time.

These phenomena continued during a period of eighteen months; that is to say, all the time that Mademoiselle Sagee retained her engagement at Neuwelcke. There were, however, intervals, of several weeks during which nothing of the kind took place. It was noticed that the phenomena occurred most often when she was specially preoccupied, and that in the clearness and apparent substantiality of her double her own form showed signs of weakness and exhaustion and vice versa. She herself did not appear to be aware of what was taking place, and never perceived her own alter ego.

Naturally, there was much talk of these extra-ordinary occurrences, and when there was no longer any doubt as to their reality the parents of the pupils took exception to leaving their daughters in a school in which such strange phenomena were taking place, and many of the girls, after leaving school for their holidays, failed to return. At the end of eighteen months the scholars had dwindled from forty-two to twelve.

Unwilling as the directors were to dismiss a mistress who performed her duties in so exemplary a fashion, they felt that they had no option but to give her notice. "Alas!" she exclaimed, on their decision being intimated to her, "this is the nineteenth time. It is indeed too cruel!"

In short, from the commencement of her career as schoolmistress at the age of sixteen, she had occupied no less than eighteen previous posts, and the reason for her leaving had been always the same. As the heads of the establishments to which she had gone had never found any fault in her they had always given her excellent testimonials, but when the phenomena were noticed she was always forced, in the long run, to go elsewhere.

We have two Auntie Emilies

After leaving Neuwelcke, she withdrew for some time to the house of a sister-in-law, who had a number of young children. Mademoiselle de Guldenstubbe paid her a visit while she was living there, and found that the children were quite accustomed to the occurrences of which she was the victim, and used to say that they had two Aunt Emile's. Mademoiselle Guldenstubbe remained at the academy the whole time that Mademoiselle Sagee was a mistress there, and full details and names were supplied by her with permission to publish them. It is to be noted in the above very curious case that the witnesses to the incidents in question consisted of the whole of the pupils, the mistresses, the maids, and the directors themselves, and that all of these were absolutely convinced of the reality of the phenomena. It is also worth noting that Mademoiselle Sagees double possessed, at least on occasion, a certain physical consistency, and was actually seen reflected in the looking-glass. As we shall see later on, in the experiences narrated by Mr. Oliver Fox, there was no such reflection to be observed. It would indeed appear that this depends upon the greater or less substantiality of the phantom form and, it may be observed, there are a number of other instances on record of the reflection of an apparition being visible. (163)

The first of these experiences was recounted by a young man of about thirty years of age, an engraver by profession, who originally saw the light in a French work by Dr. Gibier entitled *Analyses de Choses*. The narrator tells of his own adventures outside his physical body, adventures unsought by himself, and befalling him in the most unforeseen and unexpected manner.

"A short time ago," he informed Dr. Gibier, "on returning home one evening about ten O'clock, I was seized with an extraordinary feeling of lassitude which I was quite unable to account for. As, however, I had made up my mind not to go to bed immediately. I lit my lamp and placed it on the table by the side of my bed. I then helped myself to a cigar which I lit at the flame of the lamp, and after drawing two or three whiffs stretched myself on a couch. Just as I had rested my head on the cushions of the sofa I realized that the surrounding objects in the room gave an impression to my mind of turning round. I underwent a sensation of giddiness, and the next thing I became aware of was that I was transported into the middle of the room. On looking round in order to get my bearings my astonishment increased: I saw myself stretched on the sofa quite comfortably and not at all stiffly, but with my left hand raised above me and holding the lighted cigar, my elbow resting on the cushion."

The engraver's first idea was that he had fallen asleep and was experiencing an unusually vivid dream, though at the same time he was conscious that his dream, if it was a dream, was unlike any other dream that he had ever had in his life. In addition to this he had a feeling, common enough as we shall see later on with astral projectors, that never before in his life had he been so closely in touch with reality. Arriving at length at the conclusion that he was not actually dreaming, there came upon him with a shock the thought that he was dead. He had heard conversations about the spirit world, and it occurred to him that he must be a disembodied spirit himself, and he reflected regretfully on the many things that he had left undone in his lifetime. Next, inspired by curiosity, he approached his own body, and was surprised to find it still breathing. He realized that he could see into the interior of his anatomy, and noticed that his heart was beating feebly indeed, but with regularity. Feeling now somewhat reassured, he began to look around and wonder how long this state of things was likely to last. He ceased to pay attention to the body he had left on the sofa, and proceeded to examine the lamp, which was burning steadily, but which, he feared, owing to its being placed so near to his bed, it might set fire to the curtains. As this thought struck him he touched the extinguisher with a view to putting out the light but, to his great surprise, however much he pressed the lever, it produced not the slightest effect.

He thereupon examined his (spirit) body and received the impression that it was clothed in white. Next, he stood in front of the mirror above his mantel-piece, but instead of seeing his own image reflected in it, his vision appeared to him to extend indefinitely, and first the wall and thereafter the backs of the pictures in his next door neighbour's room, and then the furniture there as well became visible to his sight.

Double Visits Neighbour's House

Here we may note a very curious observation on his part. "I remarked," he says, "the absence of light in my neighbour's apartments, but this caused me no difficulty. I found I could perceive quite plainly what appeared to be a ray of light emitted from my epigastrium which illuminated the objects in the room. It then occurred to him that he would transplant himself, as it were, into the room itself. "I had hardly conceived the wish," he observes, "when I found myself there. How I did it I do not know, but it seemed to me that I passed through the wall as easily as my sight had penetrated it."

It was the first time that he had ever been in the next door apartments, and his neighbour was, as he knew, at the time absent in Paris. He then inspected the rooms with a view to recalling their contents, and took special note of the titles of the books on the shelves of the library.

"I had," he says, "only to will in order to find myself wherever I wanted to be." Realizing this, he went on his travels and penetrated, as he believed, as far as Italy, but his recollection of this part of his adventure was confused as he had no longer control or mastery of his thoughts.

Eventually he woke in his own body about five o' clock in the morning, cold and stiff, and found himself lying on the couch and holding his unfinished cigar between his fingers. The lamp had gone out, and its chimney was black. No further mischief had been done. He then went to bed shivering with cold, and was for some time unable to go to sleep.

Eventually, however, exhaustion produced the desired effect, and when he woke again it was broad daylight.

Having taken his neighbour's caretaker into his confidence, he persuaded him to show him over the rooms he had visited in his etheric form. "Entering them in company with him," he observes, "I recognized the pictures and the furniture which I had seen the night before, as well as the titles of the books which I had specially noted." (164)

Among the experiences which are entitled to a niche in this record is one narrated by the celebrated medium, Daniel D. Home, in *Incidents in my Life.* Here we have an experience which seems to have taken place in a condition between sleeping and waking. "I remember," says the author, "with vivid distinctness," asking myself whether I was asleep or not, when to my amazement I heard a voice which seemed so natural that my heart bounded with joy, as I recognized it as that of one who while on earth was far too pure for such a world as ours, and who, in passing to that brighter home, had promised to watch over and protect me." She told Home that the vision he was about to have was a vision of death, but that he would not die. "Your spirit," she added, "must again return to the body in a few hours." In this experience Home says that he "saw the whole of his nervous system as it were composed of thousands of electrical scintillations". "Gradually," he continues, "I saw that the extremities were less luminous and the finer membranes surrounding the brain became as it were glowing and I felt that thought and action were no longer connected with the earthly tenement but that they were in a spirit body, in every respect similar to the body which I knew to have been mine and which I knew to have been mine now saw lying motionless before me in the bed. The only link which held the two forms together seemed to be a silvery like light which proceeded from the brain, and as if it were in response to my earlier waking thoughts the same voice, only that it was now more musical than before, said: 'Death is but a second birth, corresponding in every respect to the natural birth, and should the uniting link now be severed, you could never again enter the body. As I told you, however, this will not be.' " After this it appeared to Home that he awoke from a dream of darkness to a sense of light, but "so glorious a light that never did earthly sun shed such rays", and about him were those for whose loss he had sorrowed, for although he doubted not that they existed, nevertheless their earthly presence was not visible. He was now taken on a journey by a spirit guide.

"I found" (he says) "I was wafted upward until I saw the earth as a vision, far, far below us. Soon I found that we had drawn nearer and were just hovering over a cottage that I had never seen: and I also saw the inmates, but had never met them in life. The walls of the cottage were not the least obstructive to my sight, they only appeared as if constructed of a dense body of air yet perfectly transparent, and the same might be said of every article of furniture. I perceived that the inmates were asleep and I saw the various spirits who were watching over the sleepers. One of these was endeavouring to impress his son where to find a lost relic of him which the son much prized and the loss of which had greatly upset him. And I saw that the son awoke and thought it was an idle dream and three times this impression was repeated by the spirit, and I knew that when morning came the young man would go, out of curiosity, where he had been impressed to go and that he would there find what he sought."

Daniel D. Home states that his vision lasted in all eleven hours but that it appeared to him to be only a few minutes, and that like so many other visitors to the astral plane, he was most reluctant to return again to earth. (165)

Your Physical Body is like a House
The physical body is like a house. You can stay in it or you can come out of it, and what is more you can return to it if you have not cut yourself off from it so completely that

return has become an impossibility. We may go one step further and say that another tenant under certain circumstances may come in and take possession of it when it is found to be vacant. It may not exactly fit the new tenant but houses can be altered and adapted to the use of newcomers. They can even be improved by the new occupants. (166)

Another Strange Story
Another case may be noted, instancing once more the activities of the etheric body while the physical form is asleep. It is a well known record but appropriate to the point in question and may therefore bear repetition. The narrator is the Hon. P. H. Newnham.

"In the month of March, 1856 (he wrote), I was at Oxford; it was my first year and I was living in furnished rooms. I was subject to violent headaches, especially at night. One evening, at about eight o'clock, I had a more violent headache than usual. At about nine it became unbearable. I went to my bedroom and threw myself on my bed without undressing and soon fell asleep.

"I then experienced a dream of singular clearness and intensity. All the details are as vivid in my memory as at the moment that I was dreaming. I dreamt that I was with the family of the lady who afterwards became my wife. All the young people had gone to bed and I remained chatting as I stood before the mantelpiece. Then I took my candle and went to bed. When I reached the hall I saw that my fiancé had remained downstairs, that she had only just reached the top of the staircase. I sprang up the stairs four steps at a time, and, surprising her as she reached the last step, I from behind passed my arm round her waist. I held my candle in my left hand whilst I mounted the stairs but in my dream that did not inconvenience me at all. I then awoke and almost immediately a clock in the house struck ten.

"The impression which the dream produced on me was so strong that I wrote to my fiancé the following morning an account of it. I received a letter from the lady which was not in answer to mine, but which had crossed it in the post. It contained the following remarks: 'Did you particularly think of me last night at ten o'clock? As I went upstairs to bed I heard distinctly your footsteps behind me and I felt your arms round my waist.' "   P. H. NEWNHAM

One of the most extraordinary and best authenticated instances of the appearance of a double who was not only seen but had a conversation with a photographer at Newcastle is narrated by the late W. T. Stead - who took the trouble to interview the photographer in question and verify all the facts of the case. (It is in his collection of records of the uncanny entitled *Real Ghost Stories*).

Mr. Dickinson (the photographer in question), told Mr. Stead how he arrived at his place of business (43 Grainger Street) on January 3rd, 1891, at a few minutes before 8 AM. The lad who usually brought the keys was ill and he had come earlier on that account. The first person to call was a gentleman who wished to know if his photographs were finished.

He was a stranger to Mr. Dickinson. He was wearing a hat and overcoat and came up to the counter in the ordinary way. He did not seem very well, otherwise there was nothing unusual in his appearance. He said to Mr. Dickinson: "Are my photographs ready?" Mr. Dickinson asked his name and he said it was Thompson. He explained that his photograph was taken on December 6th and that the prints had been promised before this date. Having ascertained that it was a cash order Mr. Dickinson looked the matter up in his book, and after finding the order read it out to his visitor as follows:

Sat. Dec. 6th, '90,
Mr. J. S. Thompson,
154, William Street,
Hebburn Quay.
7/- pd.
(6 Cabinets)

Mr. Thompson (as he claimed to be) remarked:
"That is right."

"In my book," stated Mr. Dickinson, I found a date given on which the negative was ready to be put into the printer's hands and this being seventeen days before I had no hesitation in saying : 'Well, if you call later on you will get some.' "

Mr. Thompson replied that he had been travelling all night and could not call again. The photographer called after him as he got up and went out: "Can I post what may be done ? " but got no answer. He, however, turned again to the book, looked at the number and wrote on a slip of paper "No. 7976 Thompson, Post."

At nine o'clock Miss Simon, the clerk and reception-room attendant, came in and Mr. Dickinson handed the slip of paper to her saying that Thompson had called for his photographs and seemed disappointed that they were not ready.

Miss Simon expressed surprise, observing: "Why, an old man called about these photographs yesterday and I told him that they could not be ready this week owing to bad weather and that we were nearly three weeks behind with our work."

The photographer observed that it was quite time Mr. Thompson's were ready. Miss Simon replied that they were not yet printed off and pointing to a pile of negatives, said. "Thompson's is among that lot."

In due course she produced the negative asked for and Mr. Dickinson took it in his hands and looking at it carefully remarked: "Yes, that is it; that is the chap who called this morning."

On the Monday morning following (January 5th) Mr. Dickinson was at his office as usual and thinking of his interview, determined to put the matter of J. S. Thompson's photograph through at once.

Thompson's had been put back among the other negatives waiting to be printed and Miss Simon produced the lot (each negative being in a paper bag by itself), and they proceeded to look through them together.

"Before we got half-way through" (said Mr. Dickinson), "I came across one which I knew was very urgent and turned away to look up the date of it when crash went part of the negatives on the floor. This accident seemed so serious that I was almost afraid to pick up the fallen negatives, but on doing so I was greatly relieved to find that only one was broken, but judge of my horror to find that that one was Thompson's!"

Mr. Dickinson thereupon wrote to Mr. Thompson asking him to give another sitting and offering to recoup him for his trouble and loss of time.

On Friday, January 9th, Miss Simon, speaking from the lower office communicating with Mr. Dickinson's, said that the gentleman had called about the negative. "What negative?" inquired the photographer. "Well," she replied, "the one we broke." "Mr. Thompson's," he answered. "I am very busy and cannot come down. Send him up to me to be taken at once." "But he is dead I said", "Miss Simon."

Without another word Mr. Dickinson hastened down to the office, where he saw an elderly gentleman who seemed in great trouble. We must narrate the interview in his own words.

"Surely," I said I to him, "you don't mean to say that this man is dead?"

"It is only too true," he replied.

> "Well, it must have been dreadfully sudden," I said sympathetically, "because I saw him only last Saturday."

The old gentleman shook his head sadly, and said: "You are mistaken, for he died last Saturday.

> "Oh, no," I returned, "I am not mistaken, for I recognized him by the negative.

However the father (for that was his relationship to my sitter), insisted that I was mistaken and that it was he who called on the Friday and not his son, and he said. "I saw that young lady" (pointing to Miss Simon), "and she told me that the photographs would not be ready that week."

> "That is quite right," said Miss Simon, "but Mr. Dickinson also saw a gentleman on the Saturday morning, and when I showed Mr. Dickinson the negative he said: "Yes, that's the man who called. I told Mr. Dickinson then of your having called on the Friday."

It was elicited from Mr. Thompson, (Senior), that no one was authorized to call, nor had they any friend or relatives who would know of the portraits being ordered, neither was there anyone likely to impersonate the man who had sat for his portrait.

It appears that Mr. Thompson, junior, died on Saturday, January 3rd, at about 2.30 p.m. At the time Mr. Dickinson saw him he would have been unconscious and remained so till his death. The father informed Mr. Dickinson in conversation afterwards that his son on the Friday had been delirious and had cried out for his photographs so frequently that they had tried to get them and that was why he had called on the Friday night. He said that it was physically impossible for his son to have left the house. (169)

As previously reported, Mademoiselle Emilie Sagee was a highly regarded teacher. She specialized in languages and succeeded, in the complex environment of nineteenth-century Livonia, in reconciling the Russian, German, Polish and Swedish heritage of her pupils by giving them all a solid grounding in international literature. And yet, in 1845 at the age of just thirty-two, she was sacked from her nineteenth teaching post.

The directors of the school for young ladies near Riga were reluctant to let her go, but the parents insisted and began to withdraw their daughters. The problem was that the girls could sometimes see two Emilies, standing side by side at the blackboard or eating the same school dinner. On occasion, the extra Emilie would get bored with imitation and just sit quietly in a corner, but often she wandered further afield. She was frequently seen strolling through the school grounds at the same time as the devoted original, quite unaware of the bilocation, carried on with the lesson in front of her fascinated class. (170)

Doppelgangers
It is rare for doppelgangers to be so persistent or quite so evident, but traditions which describe their existence are wide-spread. One recent survey of over sixty different cultures, showed that all but three of these accepted the idea that some part of the personality is independent and can

travel beyond the bounds of the body. The African Azande, for instance, believe that everyone has two kinds of soul, one of which leaves the body when we. are asleep. This *mbisimo*, it is said, travels widely, meets up with others of its kind and has all manner of adventures. It keeps these, however, to itself. We have no memory of them on waking. The Burmese call their travelling companion "butterfly" and believe it to be fragile and easily hurt. The Bacairi people of South America say that we have an *andadura* or shadow, which "takes off its shirt" as we fall asleep. It abandons the body and its experiences form the subject matter of our dreams. Some of these we remember and all of them, suggest the Bacairi, ought to be taken seriously as sources of information about the real world. (171)

--o--

CHAPTER ELEVEN

OUT OF BODY EXPERIENCES & REMOTE VIEWING

*How wonderful it would be
to travel instantly, here
there and everywhere, to
see those hidden places
and read those secret
things, you were never
meant to see.*

Out of body experiences and remote viewing seem to have a lot in common. In both instances there is no doubt that the consciousness, somehow, has travelled to that remote location. In some cases though, the OBE'r has appeared to a (secret) psychic hidden at the remote location, and in such a case it would appear that the etheric, or spirit, body has actually made the journey.

The Past & Future
Another holographic aspect of Out of Body Experiences is the blurring of the division between past and future that sometimes occurs during such experiences. For example, Osis and Mitchell discovered that when Dr. Alex Tanous, a well-known psychic and talented OB traveller from Maine, flew in and attempted to describe objects placed on a table, he had a tendency to describe items that were placed there days later!

Travelling out of body also has other fascinating aspects. Subjects can feel themselves change into other biological species or even inanimate objects

According to Grof, there seemed to be no limits to what his LSD subjects could tap into. They seemed capable of knowing what it was like to be every animal, and even plant, on the tree of evolution. They could experience what it was like to be a blood cell, an atom, or thermonuclear process inside the sun, the consciousness of the planet and even the consciousness of the entire cosmos. More than that they had the ability to transcend space and time, and occasionally they related uncannily accurate precognitive information.

Travel to other Universes
On occasions subjects also travelled to what appeared to be other universes and other levels of reality. In one particularly unnerving session a young man suffering from depression found himself in what seemed to be another dimension. It had an eerie luminescence, and although he could not see anyone he sensed that it was crowded with discarnate beings. Suddenly he sensed a presence very close to him, and to his surprise it began to communicate with him telepathically. It asked him to please contact a couple who lived in the Moravian city of Kromeriz and let them know that their son Ladislav was well taken care of and doing all right. It then gave him the couple's name, street address, and telephone number.

The information meant nothing to either Grof or the young man and seemed totally unrelated to the young man's problems and treatment. Still, Grof could not put it out of his mind. "After some hesitation and with mixed feelings, I finally decided to do what certainly would have made me the target of my colleague's jokes, had they found out," says Grof. "I went to the telephone, dialed the number in Kromeriz, and asked if I could speak with Ladislav. To my astonishment, the woman on the other side of the line started to cry. When she calmed down, she told me with a broken voice: 'Our son is not with us any more; he passed away, we lost him three weeks ago." (172)

Grof stated: "When I became sufficiently open-minded to make attempts to verify these statements, I discovered to my great surprise that they were often accurate. I found out that in many instances the persons the subject denoted as protagonists, experienced, at exactly the same time, a dramatic shift of attitude in the direction that was predicted. This transformation happened in a way that could not be interpreted by linear time. The individuals involved were often hundreds or thousands of miles away and did not know anything about the subject's experience. They had a deep experience which transformed them and they received some information that entirely changed their perception of the subject. The timings of these happenings were often remarkable; in some instances they were minutes apart.

This aspect of past life experiences suggesting non-local connections in the universe seems to bear some similarity to the phenomena described by Bell's theorem in modern physics," (Bell 1966, Capra 1982). (173)

Astral Love
Wondering why he had been carried off to the house in question, he looked about him trying to discover the explanation. In so doing he noted that he was in a room in which were four people, one of them was a girl of about seventeen. After relaxing his conscious mind to give the astral forces full play he found himself moving, without effort on his part, to a position directly in front of the lady, who, he observes, "was sewing upon a black dress". Still he could see no reason for his presence among these strangers, so after taking a look round and noticing that the room he had been in was an apartment in a farm-house, he willed himself back into his physical body.

Six weeks passed and Mr. Muldoon had almost forgotten his astral experience when one afternoon he noticed a girl get out of a car and enter one of the neighbouring houses. He recognized her as the girl he had seen at the farm-house. His curiosity was naturally aroused and he decided to wait about until she should come out again. Eventually she did so and with some self-assurance he went up and spoke to her. "Excuse me," he asked, "would you tell me where you live?" Not unnaturally he got a snub." That was no business of his," he was told. Nothing daunted, however, he told her of their former meeting and described her home to her with convincing accuracy. She was naturally intrigued by this curious narrative and, gradually thawing, consented to make his acquaintance.

"One thing led to another," he writes, "I began to like her. I have seen her many times since, have seen her home (exactly as it was in the conscious projection), which is fifteen miles as the crow flies from my own home). (174)

Emanuel Swedenborg
In the case of the Swedish seer (Emmanuel Swedenborg) there was, indeed, no question of hypnotism. His clairvoyant powers appear never to have been in dispute, whatever views have been taken of his religious opinions. Here we have an instance in which the whole circumstances of a fire which occurred at Stockholm were witnessed by him at a distance of no less than three hundred miles, just as if he had been present there during the whole time in his physical form.

It was towards the end of the month of September, in the year 1756, and Swedenborg had only some two hours previously landed at Gottenberg, where he had been invited to stay at the house of a friend of the name of Castel, along with a number of other guests. About six o'clock in the evening he went out of the house and returned somewhat later looking pale and much upset. On being asked what troubled him, he observed that he had become conscious at that moment of a terrible fire raging in Stockholm on the Sudermalm, and he affirmed that at that very moment the fire was increasing in violence, and was causing him the greatest anxiety, more especially as the house of one of his friends had already been destroyed by the flames, and his own house was also in danger.

He thereupon went out again, but on returning at eight o'clock exclaimed, "God be praised, the fire is extinguished at the third door from my own house!" This statement caused the greatest excitement among the company present, and being repeated in the town, reached the ears of the Governor that same evening. The next day, being a Sunday, the Governor sent for Swedenborg, who on account of his extraordinary talents enjoyed a reputation second to none in Sweden, and put questions to him relative to the statement that he was alleged to have made. Swedenborg then described to the Governor the exact nature and extent of the conflagration, how it had begun, and the time during which it had continued. The story spread in all directions, as many of the citizens of Gottenberg were in great concern on account of their friends in the city, as well as for their property.

It was not till Monday evening that official news arrived at the hands of a courier, who had been despatched by the merchants of Stockholm during the fire. The account he brought confirmed Swedenborg's statements in every particular. A further courier despatched by the king arrived at the Governor's house on the Tuesday morning, giving fuller details of the ravages of the conflagration and the losses it had occasioned, and further stating that the fire was got under control at 8 p.m. (175)

> The greatest illusion is that man has
> limitations. (Robert A. Monroe)

While out-of-body experiences have been reported all around the world for over twenty centuries, it is only recently that the techniques for experiencing them have been systematically taught. The non-profit Monroe Institute has taught tens of thousands of people, both in residence and through distance learning, to undertake out-of-body journeys. So useful was his program that it was adopted by the American military as part of the standard training for remote viewers.

An out-of-body experience (OBE) happens when a person's duplicate invisible body, sometimes called the astral or etheric body, is able to move out of the physical body with full consciousness. For this reason it is sometimes called "astral projection." For most people there is no control at all over the OBE - it just happens spontaneously. A person who experiences an OBE does not have to be ill or near death.

Dr. Dean Sheils analyzed over a thousand studies of OBE's in seventy non-Western cultures. His conclusive results showed that whereas it was expected that there would be significant variation in the experience, there was absolute consistency. Dr. Sheils claimed that the results were so universal that the phenomenon had to be genuine.

Many of the literary giants of the twentieth century publicly stated that they had had an OBE, and others included: Ernest Hemingway, Tolstoy, Dostoevsky, Tennyson, Edgar Alan Poe, D.H. Lawrence and Virginia Woolf.

(Lazarus 1993: 167).

Conviction about Life after Death
A most highly credible scientist, Dr. Robert Crookall, analyzed over seven hundred reports of OBE's. He found that 81% of those who had experienced them had a firm conviction of life after death owing to their personal experience. What astounded Crookall, a meticulous

scientist, was the consistency of the reports of OBE's coming from all over the world with near-death experiences and with the communications coming from high-level mediums (Crookall 1970).

The Society for Psychical Research has a great number of cases of OBE's on record. One of the most interesting involved the person experiencing the out-of-body state being actually perceived, as if in the flesh, by another person:

Mr Landau reports that in 1955 his wife-to-be told him of her OBE's. One night he gave her his diary and asked her to move it to his room during her next OBE. Early the following morning he saw her apparition, which backed out of his room across a landing to her room. He watched while the apparition vanished into her body sleeping on the bed. When he returned to his room he found her rubber toy dog, which he had last seen on a chest of drawers beside her bed, lying beside his. When questioned about it, she stated that she had felt uncomfortable moving the diary as she had been taught as a child never to handle other people's letters and diaries

(Landau1963: 126-128).

In the United States, Karlis Osis and Boneita Perskari spent several years doing scientific research with an excellent OBE subject, Alex Tanous, and were able to achieve significant results. One particular test involved Tanous traveling astrally to a different place miles away to visit a particular office to see what was on the table and then report back. Tanous did not know that at this office a psychic, Christine Whiting, was waiting to see if she could see anyone coming to visit. With her clairvoyant sight, she was able to see Tanous come into the office and, as well, she described in detail his position and the shirt with rolled-up sleeves and the corduroy pants he was wearing

(Williams 1989: 35-36).

Because of the cooperation of some gifted OBE experiencers, the phenomenon has come within the ambit of science.

● Dutch scientists succeeded in weighing the physical body before, during and after exteriorization (OBE). They found a weight loss of 2¼ ounces during exteriorization.

(Carrington, 1973).

● French researchers, including Professor Richet, spent many years having the exteriorized body move material objects, produce raps at a distance and affect photographic plates and calcium screens, thus photographing exteriorization.

● Other experimenters, including Robert Morris at the Psychical Foundation of North Carolina, who spent two years investigating OBES. A volunteer subject, Keith "Blue" Harary, claimed to have been having out-of-body experiences since childhood. He was able to lie down in a sealed laboratory room and project himself to another house twenty yards away. While there he was able to read letters and report accurately to the experimenters.

In 1965 Dr. Charles Tart, a psychologist at the University of California, conducted controlled experiments with Robert Monroe, a highly gifted out-of-body experiencer who died in 1995. A former vice-president of Mutual Broadcasting Corporation, Robert Monroe was president of two corporations active in cablevision and electronics and produced over 600 television programs.

Monroe developed a system called Hemi-Sync which he claimed could trigger altered states of consciousness and OBE's by sending different sounds (tones) to each ear through stereo headphones. The two hemispheres of the brain then act in unison to "hear" a third signal- the difference between the two tones. His work is being carried on by the Monroe Institute, in Charlottesville Virginia (USA) which offers six day residential Gateway Programs for people wishing to experience for themselves "development and exploration of human consciousness; deeper levels of self-discovery; expansion of one's awareness; wilful control of that awareness; communication with and visits to other energy systems and realities."

Like Swedenborg, Monroe too talked about traveling to the "astral" worlds of heaven and hell complete with spirits and thought-forms. One of the graduates of his program, Bruce Moen, has written a number of books claiming that anyone can learn how to use Monroe's techniques to explore the afterlife for themselves.

The Out of Body Research Foundation (OBERF), founded by Jeffrey Long, M.D. and Jody A. Long, J.D., focuses on scientifically researching the phenomena and its relationship with the afterlife.

Travelling Clairvoyance
They made the interesting discovery that the psychometer could look at a map, then close his eyes and experience a sensation of flying through the air until he came to the place he had seen. This faculty is known as 'travelling clairvoyance', and has been the subject of a great deal of modern research (for example, at Stanford University in the mid-1970s where, under laboratory conditions, the psychic Ingo Swann was able to demonstrate his ability to travel mentally to other places and describe accurately what was happening there). They chose at random the island of Socatra in the Gulf of Aden, and Mrs Denton was first asked to describe it. She stated that it was a rocky island, 'almost a rock in the sea', with one coast high and mountainous and the other- the inhabited coast - low. There seemed to be two types of people. Those inland, the natives, were poor, and 'there seems to be a wandering disposition about them'. Near the coast the people were 'yellowish' and engaged more in business. All this proved (from an encyclopaedia article on Socatra) to be remarkably accurate. The geographical description is

precise. The population consisted of two types - the original inhabitants, Bedouins, who lived inland and who were nomadic, and Arab traders and agriculturalists who lived near the coast.

By comparison, Sherman Denton's description sounds vague and inaccurate; he described it as a green island without mountains (in fact, the mountains are five thousand feet high), and continued with descriptions of natives who lived a hand-to-mouth existence. But the fact that Denton includes this relative failure is a testimony to his honesty. (176)

A young man lies on a simple cot in a soundproof room. He closes his eyes and takes several deep breaths, then subsides into a pattern of shallow regular breathing. Instruments attached to his body show a slight increase in pulse beat as his heart accelerates to compensate for reduced blood pressure. The electrical potential of his skin decreases. His brain-waves slow to a steady alpha rhythm and from time to time his eyes flick rapidly from side to side, but there are no signs of sleep as such. He is in a normal relaxed waking state. (177)

Stuart Blue Harary calls this his "cool down" procedure. He regards it as an essential part of preparing to do something which he and a few others can do on demand under such controlled conditions. When Harary feels that everything is right, he says, "Now. I'm going." The twelve channel polygraph registers an increase in both heart and respiration rates, implying a greater degree of arousal, but his skin potential slides even further into a state of deep relaxation. Two minutes later, all these signs reverse themselves and Harary says out loud "That's it. I'm back." And then he "cools down" and goes through the whole performance again.

His Kitten Senses his Astral Presence

There's not a lot of excitement in it for the scientist monitoring Harary's behaviour, but half a mile away on the other side of Duke University in North Carolina, there is considerable interest. A kitten called "Spirit" is confined to a large wooden box whose floor is marked off into twenty-four numbered squares. He is a very active and unhappy kitten, wandering all over the board meowing frequently. But twice during the 40-minute observation period he stops moving and sits quietly in one square for two minutes at a time - precisely those times when Harary at the other end of the campus claims to be "out'

Stuart Blue Harary, who seems now to be called Keith, believes that he can leave his body and travel. He describes it as feeling like floating in space, sometimes in body form, sometimes as a ball of light, occasionally as a pin-point of concentrated awareness. Always he sees and feels and hears things and sometimes others are aware of him being there. In these tests at Duke, his instructions are to go to where his kitten is confined, to comfort it and play with it. A battery of instruments, including thermistors, photo multi-pliers and devices for measuring electrical conductivity and magnetic permeability, are scattered strategically about the target room. None of them registers anything at any time in the test, but during those four minutes out of forty when Harary claimed to be out of his body, the kitten's behaviour changed dramatically. "Spirit" meowed 37 times during the control period, but not once when it seems that it was getting a ghostly grooming. (178)

Ghosts & Apparitions

The literature on ghosts and apparitions is filled with cats whose hair stands on end and, dogs that growl or cower in a corner for no apparent reason. Robert Morris, recently appointed to the Koestler Chair in Parapsychology at Edinburgh University, once took a whole menagerie with him into an allegedly haunted house in Kentucky to test their effectiveness as ghost detectors. He chose a dog, a cat, a rat and a rattlesnake and sent each of these occult equivalents of the miner's canary with their owners into a room in which a murder had occurred. The dog refused to go beyond the threshold. It snarled and "no amount of cajoling could prevent it from struggling to get out". The cat leaped up on to its owner's shoulder and "spent several minutes hissing and spitting at an unoccupied chair in the corner of the room". The rat remained unmoved, but the rattlesnake "immediately assumed an attack posture facing the same chair". None of the animals responded to any other room in the house. (179)

I have dealt with the problem of survival elsewhere, and mention hauntings here only as a reminder of the relative acuteness of the sense systems of other species. (180)

It is probably no accident that witches are so often associated with cats and owls - two animals whose choice as "familiars" suggests that they may be very useful for picking up subtle signals. It could be productive to join forces with other species far more often in this kind of investigation, but sometimes it is not necessary to have any intermediary at all. As previously reported, Robert Monroe lives in the Blue Ridge mountains of Virginia. He used to work in the communications business, but now runs an Institute at which he trains others in a technique he discovered twenty-five years ago, which seems to make it possible to travel out of the body at will. His results have been impressive, but perhaps his most interesting achievement to date was to make a disembodied call on a friend holidaying in a country cottage. He found her talking to a neighbour and, unable to attract her attention and despite his insubstantial condition, decided to give her a playful pinch. She jumped and rubbed herself and looked puzzled. When asked later if she remembered anything untoward happening, she replied by displaying a small bruise on the precise spot. (181)

In 1863 the *City of Limerick* ran into a fierce storm in mid-Atlantic. Aboard her was a man called Wilmot, a manufacturer on his way home to Connecticut, who dreamed one night that his wife appeared in his cabin in her nightdress, kissed him and vanished again. He said nothing about the dream, but the following morning his cabin-mate remarked, "You are a lucky fellow, to have a lady come to visit you like that!" On arrival in Bridgeport, the first thing Mrs Wilmot asked her husband was whether he had received her visit that night. She explained that there had been news of shipwrecks and that she had been worried and tried to make contact with him. She had visualized herself flying, finding the ship, and going to his stateroom. "There was a man in the upper berth who looked straight at me, and for a moment I was afraid to come in, but at last I came up to you, bent over you, kissed you, pressed you in my arms, and then I went away." She was able to describe the ship and the cabin and his cabin-mate in accurate detail. (182)

A little after 2.00 a.m. on the morning of January 27th, 1957, Martha Johnson saw herself travelling from Plains, Illinois, to visit her home 926 miles away in northern Minnesota. She found her mother in the kitchen and after I entered, I leaned up against the dish cupboard with folded arms. I looked at my mother who was bending over something white and doing something with her hands. She did not appear to see me at first, but she finally looked up. I had a sort of pleased feeling, and left. Martha's mother wrote to her daughter the following day to say: It would have been about ten after two, your time. I was pressing a blouse here in the kitchen. I looked up and there you were at the cupboard just standing smiling at me. I started to speak to you and you were gone. I forgot for a moment where I was. I think the dogs saw you too. They got so excited. (183)

In 1886, Edmund Gurney collected 350 case histories of "spontaneous apparitions. (184)

In 1951, Sylvan Muldoon and Hereward Carrington concentrated on experience induced by drugs, illness or accident and collected together another hundred cases in which separation of a "spirit" seemed to have occurred. There were 255 In 1954. Hornell Hart analyzed 288 cases of what he called "ESP projection. (185)

Between 1961 and 1978, Robert Crookall published nine books with painstaking records of several hundred further cases of "astral travelling". In 1968, Celia Green made a press appeal that resulted in 326 reports of "ecsomatic experiences. (186)

In 1975, John Poynton made a survey of 122 "separative experiences. (187)

In 1978, Dean Sheils looked at comparable beliefs and experiences in over 60 other cultures. (188)

And finally in 1982, Susan Blackmore of the University of Bristol gathered all these surveys and some of her own research into a detailed analysis of the whole out of body experience. (189)

The results are hard to dispute. It seems that about one in every ten people everywhere claims to have left their body at some time. Most do so only once in their lives, often at a time of crisis, but about 40 per cent go on to have further such experiences. Some, perhaps as many as 18 per cent, learn to separate more or less at will, particularly if the first experience took place when they were very young. Women seem to do it slightly more often than men. Apart from accidents and illness, detachment usually takes place in states of relaxation on the verge of sleep, though it can occur during intense activity. There are reports of motorcycle riders and airline pilots suddenly finding themselves floating high above a speeding bike or perched in terror on the outside of a jet aircraft. Most people have less traumatic experiences, describing floating gently above the ground, from where it is possible to look down at leisure and see details, including very often their own bodies. Many find that their senses in this situation are more than usually acute, but sensations are usually confined to sight and sound. Roughly 20 per cent claim to "travel" away from the vicinity of their bodies, and less than 10 per cent seem to succeed in making their presence felt there. Around 14 per cent come back with information that can be checked and when it is, there are many convincing details, but there are also many mistakes and a blurring and blending of experience of the sort that takes place in dreams or distant memory.

There have been several determined attempts to tame these talents in the laboratory, but apart from Harary's success with his kitten, the results - as far as "travel" is concerned - have been disappointing. Charles Tart of the University of California managed on one occasion to get a young girl to "read" the five-digit display on a random number generator placed out of her sight. (190)

And Karlis Osis in New York has had some success with a psychic from Maine, who was asked to take a look at a complex piece of apparatus that only makes sense when examined through a peephole that was beyond his reach. (191)

In the foregoing paragraphs we have been considering out-of-body awareness only in relation to the experiences of persons who have come close to dying but recovered sufficiently to be able to describe their short out-of-body sojourns. Even better evidence of the ability of the mind, personality and soul to leave its physical cloak or overcoat has been given in recent years by persons who develop the ability to leave their bodies whenever they so desire.

Again as previously reported, one of the most accomplished out-of-body "travellers" is Robert Monroe, a former radio and television broadcasting executive and electronic engineer. In his book journeys *Out of the Body*, he tells how he developed the ability, and of his actual experiences with out-of-body travel over a 20-year period.

Monroe is now teaching this ability to small groups of people throughout the United States. Several years ago, I spent ten days at a lovely ranch in Montana where Monroe conducted training sessions, during which he acquainted fifty people with the basics of the technique. In the year following this indoctrination workshop, approximately twenty percent of the people learned to leave their bodies at will. To show the reality of this activity, consider this example from Monroe's personal experiences:

One Saturday in 1963 when Bob Monroe was 55 years old, he decided to see if he could contact a woman friend of the family who had gone someplace on vacation, but he did not know where. He lay down, relaxed, and left his body. He travelled until he found himself in the kitchen of a beach cottage where his friend was sitting, talking with two teenage girls. He tried to 'communicate' with her but had no success. He decided to give her a pinch on her right leg. She suddenly jumped up in surprise. A week later when they met, he asked her if she had felt anything at the time the incident took place. She exclaimed in surprise, pulled her dress just above the knee and showed a discoloured spot and said, "Don't you ever try that trick again without giving me warning!" The description of the kitchen, the teenage girls and many other details which he had written down upon returning to his body agreed precisely with what the woman was able to report.

Remote Viewing by the Russian Military

The parapsychology literature is now full of reports of scientific research dealing with this new awareness of the mind's ability to leave temporarily its physical habitat. No distance limitation on such travel has yet been observed. Subjects at Stanford Research Institute report back from their travels around the state of California. The Russians are reported to have developed these remote viewing abilities for purposes of military surveillance. Experimenters have even "travelled" to the back side of the moon and recorded their observations, which were later confirmed by American and Russian astronauts who made investigations.

Consciousness remains when the Body Dies

It should be obvious that if the mind, personality and soul can take leave of the physical body and function in space adjacent to or far away from the body without losing consciousness, then it can remain outside of the body when the body decays in death, since it is obviously independent of the body. (192)

Although the OBE's experienced by such patients are spontaneous, some people have mastered the ability well enough to leave their body at will. One of the most famous of these individuals is a former radio and television executive named Robert Monroe. When Monroe had his first OBE in the late 1950s he thought he was going crazy and immediately sought medical treatment. The doctors he consulted found nothing wrong, but he continued to have his strange experiences and continued to be greatly disturbed by them. Finally, after learning from a psychologist friend that Indian yogis reported leaving their bodies all the time, he began to accept his uninvited talent. "I had two options he recalls. One was sedation for the rest of my life; the other was to learn something about this state so I could control it. (193)

From that day forward Monroe began keeping a written journal of his experiences, carefully documenting everything he learned about the out-of-body state. He discovered he could pass through solid objects and travel great distances in the twinkling of an eye simply by "thinking" himself there. He found that other people were seldom aware of his presence, although the friends whom he travelled to see while in this "second state" quickly became believers when he accurately described their dress and activity at the time of his out-of-body visit. He also discovered that he was not alone in his pursuit and bumped into other disembodied travellers. Thus far he has put his experiences into two fascinating books, *Journeys Out of the Body* and *Far Journeys.*

OBE's have also been documented in the lab. In one experiment, parapsychologist Charles Tart was able to get a skilled OBEer he identifies only as Miss Z to identify correctly a five-digit number written on a piece of paper that could only be reached if she were floating in the "out-of-body state." In a series of experiments conducted at the American Society for Psychical Research in New York, Karlis Osis and psychologist Janet Lee Mitchell found several gifted subjects who were able to "fly in" from various locations around the country and correctly describe a wide range of target images, including objects placed on a table, coloured geometric patterns placed on a free-floating shelf near the ceiling, and optical illusions that could only be seen when an observer peered through a small window in a special device. (194)

Dr. Robert Morris, the director of research at the Psychical Research Foundation in Durham, North Carolina, has even used animals to detect out-of-body visitations. In one experiment, for instance, Morris found that a kitten belonging to a talented out-of-body subject named Keith Harary consistently stopped meowing and started purring whenever Harary was invisibly present. (195)

Journeys into the Future

Harary has also made occasional OB journeys into the future and agrees that the experiences are qualitatively different from other precognitive experiences. "OBE's visit to future time and space differ from regular precognitive dreams in that "I am definitely 'out' and moving through a black, dark area that ends at some lighted future scene," he states. When he makes an OB visit to the future he has sometimes even seen a silhouette of his future self in the scene, and this is not all. When the events he has witnessed eventually come to pass, *he can also sense his time-traveling OB self in the actual scene with him.* He describes this eerie sensation as "meeting myself 'behind' myself as if I were two beings," an experience that surely must put normal deja vu to shame!! (196)

There are also cases on record of OB journeys into the past. The Swedish playwright August Strindberg, himself a frequent OB traveller, describes one in his book *Legends*. The occurrence took place while Strindberg was sitting in a wine shop, trying to persuade a young friend not to give up his military career.

To bolster his argument Strindberg brought up a past incident involving both of them that had taken place one evening in a tavern. As the playwright proceeded to describe the event he suddenly "lost consciousness" only to find himself sitting in the tavern in question and reliving the occurrence. The experience lasted only for a few moments, and then he abruptly found himself back in his body and in the present.

The argument can also be made that the retrocognitive visions we examined in which clairvoyants had the experience that they were actually present during, and even "floating" over, the historical scenes they were describing are also a form of OB projection into the past.

Poltergeist Activity

In 1968, following an outbreak of poltergeist activity in his family home, Matthew Manning realized that he was somehow responsible and began to exploit and direct the phenomenon. He produced "automatic writing" in a variety of scripts, including Arabic, and even more impressively - a portfolio of "automatic drawings" in the style of Durer, Picasso, da Vinci, Beardsley and Klee. Although Manning has no appreciable artistic talent in his own right, the drawings are highly accomplished, done very quickly, always in the distinctive style of a particular well-known artist, but are not always reproductions of any known work. "It's not me," says Manning. "I simply switch on the energy. (197)

The sudden acquisition of linguistic, musical and artistic skills presents a real problem for any explanation of the paranormal. They seem to rule out any possibility of telepathy or extrasensory perception - even of the more naturalistic saman kind I have been suggesting. Which would appear to leave us with just two other possibilities: true possession - the actual invasion of an alien entity; or reincarnation - which in the final analysis amounts to the same thing, except that the entity involved is dead.

Physicists Russell Targ and Harold Puthoff joined forces at the Stanford Research Institute in California in 1972. They built themselves a visually opaque, acoustically sealed, electrically shielded, double-walled steel isolation chamber deep in the heart of their laboratory. Into it they placed a man, the "receiver", wired up to an electro-encephalograph. In another room they put a second man, the designated "sender", facing a photo stimulator, an instrument designed to produce patterns of bright light which flashed into his eyes in trains ten seconds long. He was also attached to an EEG machine and the pattern of his brain-waves soon began to flicker in synchrony with the lights. The "receiver" was never conscious of any change, but soon after the "sender" established the photo rhythm, there was an equivalent shift, a sympathetic response, in his EEG, matching the rhythm of his brain-waves precisely to a visual display that his eyes could not see. The experimenters concluded that "a person can perceive a remote state of affairs, even though his perception might be below the level of awareness." (198)

The importance of this experiment is not only that it succeeds in demonstrating that people can share events to which they have no direct anatomical access; but that a capacity for such perception could be latent in all of us. It gives things like telepathy and extra sensory experience a firm biological base. And it makes it seem somehow less absurd to assume that individuals, even those widely separated in space, can be linked at a saman level and, in effect, share the same sense system.

Targ and Puthoff went on to explore distant connections in a more naturalistic way. They developed a procedure which involved pairs of researchers, one of whom would act as a "beacon" - going out to a target site chosen at random from a list of sixty, and staying there for fifteen minutes, while the "viewer" back at base concentrated on trying to pick up information of the partner's experience. The "viewer" gave a verbal description, and some-times a sketch, to an interviewer, and an independent judge was then taken to all the listed sites to see if any matched the drawings or descriptions. They did so surprisingly often - on average 66 percent of the time. (199)

This technique for "remote viewing" has now been replicated in forty-six separate studies at places such as Princeton University, Mundelein College in Chicago and the Institute for Parapsychology in North Carolina. (200)

Communication with a Submarine under Water
Distances involved varied from half a mile to several thousand, including on one occasion a "viewer" who worked

several hundred feet underwater on a submarine, and the overall success rate - that is the number of descriptions by "viewers" which were judged to be appropriate to sites visited at random by their partners - was around 50 per cent. (201)

I find this astonishing. The tests are designed only to deal with pictorial information coming from a person who is anxious perhaps that the experiment should succeed, but under no environmental pressure. There is no biological need to speed a message on its way. And yet, despite the emotional and mental noise which must be present at both ends of this tenuous connection, between people who do not necessarily know or mean anything to each other, information still gets through half the time and in sufficient detail for it to be meaningful to a third party. Something amazing is going on.

Those doing the studies say that the best results seem to come from viewers who are "relaxed, attentive and meditative", excited by the task, which they see as an adventure rather than as a test of their worth. Viewers are told not to try to analyze their impressions, but simply to say what they are feeling or experiencing at the test time. There is no doubt that something is lost in translation of such feelings to words - in transfer from the right to the left brain. Viewer drawings tend to be more accurate than their verbal descriptions. Successful viewing seems to involve an intuitive perception of general form rather than precise detail – viewers often provide astonishingly good diagrams of the shape of buildings, but get the number of columns or windows wrong. And experienced viewers, those who have had enough feedback from successful experiments to see a pattern in them, say that the best impressions are clearly recognizable as such at the time. They have a gentle and fleeting form, starting with vague impressions that gradually evolve into an integrated image which always comes as a surprise, because it is so clear and so clearly elsewhere. (202)

So far, so good. As a biologist, I *(Watson)* have no great difficulty with the concept that individuals of the same species could share at least part of their experience, even at a distance. But now we move into a problem area.

In 1978, the Stanford Research Institute team began tests of a different kind with a freelance photographer called Hella Hammid, who had been found to be a particularly successful viewer. A large pool of objects ranging from a steam iron to a banana were handed over to an independent person who, at random, placed one of the objects in each of sixteen numbered boxes in a locked room. At the Institute, an interviewer simply gave Hella the number of one of the boxes, again chosen at random, and asked her to describe what was in it. Her descriptions were given to a neutral judge to compare with the original objects. In six such tests, she scored what were judged to be four direct hits: describing a trumpet as "a gold, bell-shaped object, brass"; and a rag doll as something "velvety, pliable and floppy, with knots of material and midcalf boots with striped socks".

To avoid the possibility that Hella was getting her information, normally or paranormally, from the person who put the objects into the boxes before the test, a second series of experiments was done with smaller objects sealed in metal film containers. These were shuffled, kept in a safe, and selected by a random number generator, so that nobody anywhere knew what was in a specific can. And yet Hella still succeeded in scoring four out of five direct hits, describing a map pin as "silver coloured, thin and long, with a nail head at the end"; and a leather belt as precisely that, "the image I get is of a belt." And to push her talent to the limit, Hella was asked to try and "see" a series of posters reduced to micro dots and double-sealed in opaque envelopes, one of which was chosen at random for her to focus on. She again hit four out of six: describing a Swiss alpine scene as "a snow covered mountain encircled with highways"; and a photograph of an open human hand as "a round thing with five points. (203)

This is not telepathy of any kind any more. There seems to be no other mind involved. This is clairvoyance - an ability to acquire information from a distant, inanimate, source - and you can see why that could be problematic for a biologist. There are no brains, no sense systems, no theoretical sama to lean on.

Precognition
Some parapsychologists go even further and suggest that precognition may be involved. That Hella, or anyone showing such talents, could be getting her information from the future, looking at the actual object when the can or envelope is eventually opened to confirm impressions of it. Logically, they are right; but biologically, I find this even more difficult to accept. It may well be true, as Einstein suggested, that "the distinction between past, present and future is only an illusion", but until we can travel through time at will, that explanation remains one more relevant to theoretical physics than it is to practical biology."

It is also wasteful, because we already have some evidence to suggest that it is possible for a subject, without physical movement, to succeed in travelling through space.

If we are aside from and greater than the body, then you'd think we could learn some things about the world without using the body. In other words, if someone could prove that we can see without using our eyes, then that would mean the eyes, retina, optic nerve, and optical cortex in our brains aren't necessary for us to be able to see; they're just options the mind uses in the physical realm.

But seeing without using the eyes is very common today. Thousands of people are able to see without using their eyes through a very common ability called "remote viewing." The remote viewer sits quietly with his or her eyes closed and focuses on something hundreds or thousands of miles away. The remote viewer is able to see it. Not only that, but the person is often able to hear it, smell it, feel the texture, sense movement, and sense emotions involved with it. In other words, the person is doing things outside of the body while the body is sitting quietly with its eyes closed.

The CIA & Remote Viewing

For several decades at the end of the twentieth century, the CIA had a remote viewing program named Operation Stargate that attempted to use remote viewers to spy on the Russians. The program had remarkable results. In 1974, a remote viewer named Pat Price was to view a mysterious, unidentified research centre at Semipalatinsk, USSR, to see what was there. He sat with his eyes closed and focused on the area. His sketch of what he saw in his mind, had all the distinguishing marks of a gantry crane. (204)

Later, the CIA obtained satellite photos of the site. A CIA artist created a sketch of part of the site based on photos of the actual Semipalatinsk site. It was a gantry crane.

The government wanted to be sure that their investment in remote viewing was going into a valid enterprise, so to find out whether people can really view things from a distance using remote viewing, the government agencies commissioned the Stanford Research Institute (SRI) to perform 154 experiments with 26,000 separate trials over 16 years. At the end of that testing period, Edwin May, Ph.D., a researcher in low energy experimental nuclear physics, headed a team of researchers that analyzed the experiments and reported to the government.

They concluded that the odds against someone merely guessing what remote viewers had described when focusing on a target at a distant location were more than a billion billion to one. His only explanation was that they genuinely were seeing without using their eyes and without regard for how many miles away the target was. (205)

Now satisfied that remote viewing existed, the government sponsors of the remote viewing activity requested a second evaluation to find out how it worked. Congress and the CIA commissioned a study by the Science Applications International Corporation (SAIC). The result of the study was that Jessica Utts, professor in the Division of Statistics at the University of California at Davis, prepared a report assessing the statistical evidence for remote viewing in the U.S. government-sponsored research. She uses the term "anomalous cognition" to refer to remote viewing. This is her conclusion:

"It is clear to this author that anomalous cognition is possible and has been demonstrated. This conclusion is not based on belief, but rather on commonly accepted scientific criteria. The phenomenon has been replicated in a number of forms across laboratories and cultures. The various experiments in which it has been observed have been different enough that if some subtle methodological problems can explain the results, then there would have to be a different explanation for each type of experiment, yet the impact would have to be similar across experiments and laboratories. If fraud were responsible, similarly, it would require an equivalent amount of fraud on the part of a large number of experimenters or an even larger number of subjects."

"I believe that it would be wasteful of valuable resources to continue to look for proof. No one who has examined all of the data across laboratories, taken as a collective whole, has been able to suggest methodological or statistical problems to explain the ever-increasing and consistent results to date. Resources should be directed to the pertinent questions about how this ability works. I am confident that the questions are no more elusive than any other questions in science dealing with small to medium sized effects, and that if appropriate resources are targeted to appropriate questions, we can have answers within the next decade." (206)

Former President Jimmy Carter

"She went into a trance. And while she was in the trance, she gave us some latitude and longitude figures. We focused our satellite cameras on that point, and the lost plane was there."

Former President Jimmy Carter (207)

The psychic researcher Ingo Swann coined the term "remote viewing" as a neutral scientific term to describe a process by which a viewer perceives information about a distant location using something other than the known five senses. Initially it referred only to situations in which a very disciplined research protocol was used by the U.S. Military, but gradually the term has come into general use as the ability to perceive hidden or remote information by psychic means.

Although not direct evidence of the afterlife, it is included here because its validation by extensive testing is evidence of "the sixth sense," the same ability which psychic detectives and mediums call upon to go forward or back in time and to solve crimes.

Puthoff and Targ wrote in their classic paper "*A Perceptual Channel for Information over Kilometre Distances*" (1976) that for these mechanisms, they were choosing the term "remote viewing" as a neutral term, free from prior associations and bias such as in terms such as autoscopy (medical literature), exteriorization or dissociation (psychological literature), clairvoyance or out-of-body experience (parapsychology), or astral projection (occult literature). Other investigators prefer the neutral term "anomalous cognition."

Researchers who intentionally practice both remote viewing and out-of-body experience claim that there is a difference between the two kinds of experience. They say that in an out-of-body experience the viewer perceives things as if physically present, whereas in remote viewing the viewer is able to clairvoyantly tune into all sorts of information about the target that would not be physically observable.

As Joseph McMoneagle puts it in his book *Remote Viewing Secrets* (2000), the remote viewer sits in a room and describes perceptions of a target in another location. While he / she may accurately describe that other location there is never any doubt that he / she is in the room where his or her body is located. On the other hand, in out-of-body experiences people actually perceive that they have travelled to that location and are present there in all ways except the presence of their physical bodies. (208)

For more than 20 years, the United States military had a multi-million dollar a year budget for the purpose of psychic research with special emphasis on "remote viewing."

The United States, Russia & China
Stunning as it may sound to those who are unfamiliar with psychic phenomena, these and greater things have been done and are being done today in the United States, Russia, and China.

In his most interesting book, *Remote Viewers - The Secret History Of America's Psychic Spies* (1997), Jim Schnabel cites a number of highly credible sources, including an

American President (see above), about the reality of remote viewing as applied for military objectives. Here are some of them making some stunning statements that by now have found their place in the history of psychic phenomena: "I never liked to get into debates with the sceptics, because if you didn't believe that remote viewing was real, you hadn't done your homework." (209)

"You can't be involved in this for any length of time and not be convinced there's something here." Norm J., former senior CIA official who tasked remote viewers (Cover of Schnabel 1997).

'There were times when they wanted to push buttons and drop bombs on the basis of our information." Dr. Hal Puthoff, a former manager of the remote viewing program (Cover of Schnabel 1997).

"She went into a trance. And while she was in the trance, she gave us some latitude and longitude figures. We focused our satellite cameras on that point, and the lost plane was there." Former President Jimmy Carter, recalling a 1978 remote viewing operation (Cover of Schnabel1997).

The Stanford Research Institute in the United States was the venue where many of the original experiments were conducted. Physicist Hal he was the chief of the Remote Viewing Program there. Some of the personnel involved in this military astral projection / remote viewing program (Schnabel 1997) included:

• Admiral Stanfield Turner, Director of the CIA, 1977-1991

• Major General Ed Thompson, Assistant Chief of Staff for Army Intelligence. He had special knowledge that the Russians had advanced techniques in psychic phenomena which were used for military espionage in remote viewing and long-distance telepathic hypnosis

• Sergeant Mel Riley (1978-90)

• Sergeant Lyn Buchanan, Major Ed Dames and Colonel John Alexander, from U.S. Army Intelligence & Security Command

• Gifted remote viewer Ingo Swann, who was Puthoff's first test OBE subject

• CIA scientist Richard Kennet, who worked with Pat Price and Hal Puthoff

• Keith Harary, a gifted remote viewer

• John MeMahon, chief of the CIA's Office of Technical Service during 1974-76 and later the CIA's Deputy Director; he was a major supporter of remote viewing and became a remote viewer himself – he was convinced when he himself experienced stunning psychic phenomena

• Patrick Price, a highly gifted psychic and highly consistent with the remote viewing of Ingo Swann. Price through remote viewing accurately described "details of a secret Pentagon facility in the hills of West Virginia village of Sugar Grove..." Among its secret functions were the interception of intercontinental telephone communications and the control of U.S. spy satellites. Price was also deadly accurate in his remote viewing in penetrating the Russian installation at Mount Narodnaya in the remote northern Ural Mountains. The CIA confirmed the accuracy of Price's remote viewing.

Another Strange Story
A youth of about sixteen, the son of an old friend of Mr. Erskine's, came to see him one day, and Mr. Erskine, in the course of conversation, chanced to ask him where his father was. The boy replied that he did not know. It then occurred to the hypnotist to wonder what his answer

would have been if he had put him into hypnotic sleep. Accordingly he asked the boy if he was willing to be hypnotized. The boy readily consented, and was soon off. Mr. Erskine proceeded to put to him the identical question that he had asked him before, and he thereupon answered him at once, giving him the minutest details of what his father was doing. Mr. Erskine took down what he said then and there. For three hours the boy in his trance condition followed his father through the streets of London and described him as making various calls on his way. Neither the father nor the boy knew before-hand of Mr. Erskine's experiment, which was entirely unpremeditated, and the boy, when awakened, knew nothing of the answers which he had given.

At this point Mr. Erskine got into touch with the father and asked him to come round to see him. This is the story of the interview as he tells it:

"I saw him privately" (he tells us) "and he had rather a shock when at my first question I asked him if he had felt the invisible eye of his son following him. He had not. I showed him what I had written down. He was staggered. For a few moments he did not speak. Then he asked for an explanation. I gave it to him. He could not believe it. Then he admitted that his son's accounts of his movements, of the people he had spoken to, and of the scenes described were accurate. Every note I had made was correct in the minutest detail. (210)

That remarkable mystic, Emanuel Swedenborg, devoted the first fifty-six years of his life to science and engineering; then he began having strange dreams, hallucinations and trances. In these visionary states, he believed he had visited heaven and hell, and his books contain detailed accounts of the 'afterworld', all of which his disciples - who were soon numbered in thousands - accepted as literal truth. A century before the rise of spiritualism, Swedenborg claimed to be able to converse with spirits of the dead. When the queen of

Sweden asked him to give her greetings to her dead brother, the prince royal of Denmark, Swedenborg said he would. Soon after, he told her that her brother sent his greetings, and apologized for not answering her last letter. He would now do so through Swedenborg. As Swedenborg delivered the detailed message, the queen turned pale, and said, 'No one but God knows this secret.' On another occasion, in 1761, the widow of the Dutch ambassador told Swedenborg that she was having trouble with a silversmith who was demanding payment for a silver tea service; a few days later, Swedenborg told her he had spoken to her husband, and that he had paid for the tea service; the receipt would be found in a secret compartment in his bureau drawer. Swedenborg also mentioned some secret correspondence that would be found in the same drawer. Both the receipt and the correspondence were found where Swedenborg had said.

In July 1759, Swedenborg was able to tell guests at a party in Gothenburg that a great fire had broken out in Stockholm, three hundred miles away. Two hours later he told one of the guests that the fire had been extinguished only three doors from his home. Two days later, a messenger arrived confirming these details. (211)

The Shoe on the Ledge
Maria told Clark that she had experienced something very strange. After her heart had stopped she suddenly found herself looking down from the ceiling and watching the doctors and the nurses working on her. Then something over the emergency room driveway distracted her and as soon as she "thought herself" there, she was there. Next Maria "thought her way" up to the third floor of the building and found herself "eyeball to shoelace" with a tennis shoe. It was an old shoe and she noticed that the little toe had worn a hole through the fabric. She also noticed several other details, such as the fact that the lace was stuck under the heel. After Maria finished her account she begged Clark to

please go to the ledge and see if there was a shoe there so that she could confirm whether her experience was real or not.

Sceptical but intrigued, Clark went outside and looked up at the ledge, but saw nothing. She went up to the third floor and began going in and out of patients' rooms looking through windows so narrow she had to press her face against the glass just to see the ledge at all. Finally, she found a room where she pressed her face against the glass and looked down and saw the tennis shoe. Still, from her vantage point she could not tell if the little toe had worn a hole in the shoe or if any of the other details Maria had described were correct. It wasn't until she retrieved the shoe that she confirmed Maria's various observations. "The only way she would have had such a perspective was if she had been floating right outside and at very close range to the tennis shoe," states Clark, who has since become a believer in OBE's. "It was very concrete evidence for me." (212)

--o--

CHAPTER TWELVE

CLAIRVOYANCE & PRECOGNITION

There is a lot of similarity between precognition, clairvoyance, psychometry and maybe even dowsing. It also goes into the subject of "time", none the less I believe that precognition is an important subject which should stand on its own (213)

One topic which many people find difficult to accept, and get their head around, is that of precognition. It raises questions such as "is everything pre-determined?" and, "do I have a free will?" I will try to answer these questions in this book. But for starters, let's have a look at some experiments done by Puthoff and Targ, and others.

Stanislov Grof
Grof says that he has repeatedly observed, in psychedelic sessions and in holotropic therapy, verified instances of precognition, clairvoyance of past and future events, and psychometry. I have also had the privilege to witness repeatedly reliable performances in these areas by such accomplished psychics as Anne Armstrong and Jack Schwartz. Of particular interest in this context are controlled experiments of future remote viewing conducted at the Stanford Research Institute by Russel Targ, Harold Puthoff, and Keith Harary not only with famous psychics, but with many ordinary people not known for having special psychic ability. (214)

In their two recent successful remote viewing experiments, Russel Targ and Keith Harary used a Soviet subject who was able to describe not only a randomly chosen target location in the United States visited by the "beacon" person (the person who visits the target area at the time the psychic is trying to describe it) but also one that would be visited in the future. (215)

Einstein
Einstein suggested that "the distinction between, past, present, and future is only an illusion", but until we are able to travel through time at will, that explanation remains one more relevant to theoretical physics than it is to practical biology. (216)

In the long series of card-guessing tests at Duke University most of the subjects were trying to guess the card being looked at by another person; these were genuine telepathy tests. But in a few, the subjects were aiming at a target nobody knew, such as the sequence in a shuffled deck. When these tests returned results better than chance, Rhine was forced to recognize a new phenomenon-clairvoyance. (217)

One of the most exhaustively tested subjects in the history of parapsychological research is a young Czechoslovakian student, Pavel Stepanek. He has produced phenomenal scores in all the classic card tests, but he has also introduced a variation of his own that has come to be known as the 'focusing effect' (218).

He scores particularly well with certain favourite cards and can find them when they are enclosed in envelopes and shuffled so that even the experimenter does not know which is which. After a while his focus comes to include the envelope too, and this has then to be placed in another wrapping. In his latest tests he is being offered a card in an envelope enclosed in a cover that is placed in another jacket, but still he gets them right. (219)

Most of these clairvoyance experiments provide evidence that becomes apparent only on statistical analysis, but two Dutch psychics offer much more dramatic demonstrations. In 1964 Gerard Croiset of Utrecht was consulted by the police in the murder case of three civil-rights workers in Mississippi, and reports indicate that he was able to give accurate information and descriptions of the area in which the bodies were eventually found and to correctly implicate certain local policemen in the killings.

In 1943 Peter Hurkos fell from a ladder, fractured his skull, and found that he had lost the power of concentration, but had gained a new faculty instead. When asked recently to assist the police of The Hague, he had only to hold the coat of a dead man to be able to describe the man's murderer in detail that included glasses, moustache, and wooden leg. When the police admitted that they already had such a man under arrest, Hurkos told them where to find the murder weapon. (220)

Nellie Titus
A case in point was drawn to James's attention shortly after it took place. At six o'clock on a frosty October morning in 1898, a girl named Bertha Huse left her house in Enfield, New Hampshire, and walked down to the Shaker Bridge that ran across the surface of Mascoma Lake. Her family became alarmed when she failed to return and the search began. By the end of the day a hundred and fifty men had joined in the search, and a local mill owner sent along a man in a diving suit, who investigated the water on either side of the Shaker Bridge.

Two days later, while the search was still going on, Mrs Nellie Titus, who lived in the nearby village of Lebanon, fell asleep in a rocking chair after dinner. She began to twitch and groan, and when her husband shook her awake, said: 'Why did you .disturb me? In a moment I would have found the body.

That night, Nellie Titus screamed in her sleep and tossed restlessly; but her husband did not repeat his mistake. Instead he lit the lamp. Then, in a kind of trance, his wife began to speak. She described how Bertha Huse had walked on to the Shaker Bridge - which was an eighth of a mile long and floated on the lake - and had climbed out on to a jutting beam covered with hoar frost. Her foot slipped, and she went in backwards. Her body was now jammed head downward, caught in the timberwork of the bridge.

The next morning, George Titus told his story to his employer and asked leave of absence. Then he and his wife went to Enfield in a buggy. On the bridge, Mrs Titus pointed out the beam from which the girl had slipped, and said that the body was in the water below it. They drove to the house of the mill owner who had sent the diver; he was sceptical, but agreed to send for the diver again. The man said that he had already been down below the beam, but Mrs Titus told him he was mistaken. (Later the diver said: 'I was more afraid of the woman on the bridge than of the one down below.') The diver climbed down a ladder, groped around on the bottom, and suddenly found himself a foot. The body was jammed head downward in a hole, just as Nellie Titus had said. (221)

My own dream records convince me that in dreams we do receive information concerning future events - information we could not have received in any other manner. This data may come from the personal subconscious. It may come from deeper areas of the human personality. Regardless of its source, the information may be useful, and can sometimes be used in quite a practical manner. Your own dream records should allow you to perceive the ways in which you personally foresee the future events. Most likely you have always had clairvoyant dreams, though you were not consciously aware of them. You were not in the habit of recalling any of your dreams except the most unusual ones. It is, therefore, not strange that you did not recognize the foreseen events when they occurred in physical reality. (222)

Extra Sensory Perception
Parapsychology is a branch of psychology concerned with the investigation of evidence for telepathy, clairvoyance and the like, and also with experimentation in the field of extrasensory perceptions. Parapsychologists insist that ESP is a proven fact. Men like J.B. Rhine in this country and Willem Tenhaeff of Holland, among others, have spent their entire adult lives studying ESP under strict laboratory conditions. With some notable exceptions, psychologists will often state emphatically that ESP has not been scientifically demonstrated. Those of you who have read *Croiset the Clairvoyant* by Jack Harrison Pollack will find it difficult to believe that the evidence for ESP can be doubted.

Indeed, telepathy and clairvoyance have been demonstrated under scientific conditions by Croiset countless times, and the Rhine experiments with Zenar cards also present their own evidence. Various out-of-body experiences have been documented by investigators of whose integrity there can be no doubt. Apparitions do appear, regardless of our dismay. Countless cases of such events are in the records of the various psychic societies.

ESP is a proven fact. We know that it exists and is part of the framework within which we operate as human beings. We do not know how it works, why it works, or when it works, though we do have some partial answers to these questions. Often the very attempt to test an individual's abilities makes these abilities inoperable, at least temporarily. Success at home under familiar conditions is one thing. Success in a laboratory with the resulting tension is something else again. ESP happens spontaneously often enough. Until we know more about its characteristics we shall probably continue to have difficulties under test conditions. Luckily some psychics are gifted enough to put their abilities to practical use and allow their talents to be investigated. Professor Tenhaeff, working with Croiset, has added to our knowledge concerning ESP and its connection to the associative processes of the mind.

There is no doubt that ESP abilities are more closely connected with the intuitions and the subjective self than with the logical part of the self. One theory suggests that these abilities were much more prominent in prehistoric uncivilized man, and that they have tended to recede with the advance of evolution. It is also possible, however, that we have simply ignored them in our headlong plunge into materialism and technology.

The more pragmatic and "objective" we are, the less we use our ESP abilities. This, of course, leads us into one of our difficulties. Those who investigate ESP with a strictly pragmatic attitude are often prejudiced against it. Those who are not pragmatic are accused of lacking scientific objectivity. The ideal investigator would be an individual who was both intuitive and trained in scientific methods. Since these abilities are subconscious rather than conscious, they show the characteristics displayed by the personality in subjective states. Often subconscious symbolism is involved. Here again Pollack's Croiset gives excellent examples of the importance of association (one idea leading into the next) and how it can operate to build up a clairvoyant image. Distortions occur at times, however. The language of the subconscious must be investigated. We must learn to decipher it with some precision. (223)

The Dream Laboratory
Another researcher who believes Bohm's implicate order has applications in psychology is psychiatrist Montague Ullman, the founder of the Dream Laboratory at the

Maimonides Medical Center in Brooklyn, New York, and a professor emeritus of clinical psychiatry at the Albert Einstein College of Medicine, also in New York. Ullman's initial interest in the holographic concept stemmed also from its suggestion that all people are interconnected in the holographic order. He has good reason for his interest. Throughout the 1960s and 1970s he was responsible for many of the ESP dream experiments conducted. Even today the ESP dream studies conducted at Maimonides stand as some of the best empirical evidence that, in our dreams at least, we are able to communicate with one another in ways that cannot be explained.

In a typical experiment, a paid volunteer who claimed to possess no psychic ability, was asked to sleep in a room in the lab while a person in another room concentrated on a randomly selected painting and tried to get the volunteer to dream of the image it contained. Sometimes the results were inconclusive. But other times the volunteers had dreams that were clearly influenced by the paintings. For example 'when the target painting was Tamayo's *Animals*, a picture depicting two dogs flashing their teeth and howling over a pile of bones, the test subject dreamed she was at a banquet where there was not enough meat and everyone was warily eyeing one another as they greedily ate their allotted portions.

In another experiment the target picture was Chagall's *Paris from a Window,* a brightly colored painting depicting a man looking out a window at the Paris skyline. The painting also contained several other unusual features, including a cat with a human face, several small figures of men flying through the air, and a chair covered with flowers. Over the course of several nights the test subject dreamed repeatedly about things French, French architecture, a French policeman's hat, and a man in French attire gazing at various "layers" of a French village. Some of the images in these dreams also appeared to be specific references to the painting's vibrant colors and unusual features, such as the image of a group of bees flying around flowers, and a brightly colored Mardi Gras-type celebration in which the people were wearing costumes and masks. (224)

Although Ullman believes such findings are evidence of the underlying state of interconnectedness Bohm is talking about, he feels that an even more profound example of holographic wholeness can be found in another aspect of dreaming. That is the ability of our dreaming selves often to be far wiser than we ourselves are in our waking state. For instance, Ullman says that in his psychoanalytic practice he could have a patient who seemed completely unenlightened when he was awake, mean, selfish, arrogant, exploitative, and manipulative; a person who had fragmented and dehumanized all of his interpersonal relationships. But no matter how spiritually blind a person may be or unwilling to recognize his or her own shortcomings, dreams invariably depict their failings honestly and contain metaphors that seem designed tp prod him or her gently into a state of greater self-awareness.

Moreover, such dreams were not one-time occurrences. During the course of his practice Ullman noticed that when one of his patients failed to recognize or accept some truth about himself, that truth would surface again and again in his dreams, in different metaphorical guises and linked with different related experiences from his past, but always in an apparent attempt to offer him new opportunities to come to terms with the truth.

Because a man can ignore the counsel of his dreams and still live to be a hundred, Ullman believes this self-monitoring process is striving for more than just the welfare of the individual. He believes that nature is concerned with the survival of the species. He also agrees with Bohm on the importance of wholeness and feels that dreams are nature's way of trying to counteract our seemingly unending compulsion to fragment the world. "An individual can disconnect from all that's cooperative, meaningful, and loving and still survive, but nations don't have that luxury. Unless we learn how to overcome all the ways we've fragmented the human race, nationally, religiously, economically, or whatever, we are going to continue to find ourselves in a position where we can accidentally destroy the whole picture," says Ullman. "The only way we can do that is to look at how we fragment our existence as individuals. Dreams reflect our individual experience, but I think that's because there's a greater underlying need to preserve the species, to maintain species-connectedness. (225)

What is the source of the unending flow of wisdom that bubbles up in our dreams? Ullman admits that he didn't know, but he offers a suggestion. Given that the implicate order represents in a sense an infinite information source, perhaps it is the origin of this greater fund of knowledge. Perhaps dreams are a bridge between the perceptual and non manifest orders and represent a "natural transformation of the implicate into the explicate." (226) If Ullman is correct in this supposition it stands the traditional psychoanalytic view of dreams on its ear, for instead of dream content being something that ascends into consciousness from a primitive substratum of the personality, quite the opposite would he true.

Bohm's assertion that every human consciousness has its source in the implicate implies that we all possess the ability to access the future and this is also supported by the evidence. Jahn and Dunne's discovery that even normal individuals do well in precognitive remote-viewing tests is one indication of the widespread nature of the ability. Numerous other findings, both experimental and anecdotal, provide additional evidence. In a 1934 BBC broadcast Dame Edith Lyttelton, a member of the politically and socially prominent Balfour family in England and the president of the

British Society for Psychical Research, invited listeners to send in accounts of their own precognitive experiences. She was inundated with mail, and even after eliminating the experiences that did not have corroborative evidence, she still had enough to fill a volume on the subject. (227) Similarly, surveys conducted by Louisa Rhine revealed that precognitions occur more frequently than any other kind of psychic experience. (228)

Precognition of Tragedies
Studies also show that precognitive visions tend to be of tragedies with premonitions of unhappy events outnumbering happy ones by a ratio of four to one. Presentiments of death predominate, with accidents coming in second, and illnesses third. (229) The reason for this seems obvious. We are so thoroughly conditioned to believe that perceiving the future is not possible, that our natural precognitive abilities have gone dormant. Like the superhuman strengths individuals display during life-threatening emergencies, they only spill over into our conscious minds during times of crisis, when someone near to us is about to die; when our children or some other loved one is in danger, and so on. That our "sophisticated" understanding of reality is responsible for our inability to both grasp and utilize the true nature of our relationship with time is evident in the fact that primitive cultures nearly always score better on ESP tests than so-called civilized cultures. (230)

Further evidence that we have relegated our innate precognitive abilities to the hinterlands of the unconscious can be found in the close association between premonitions and dreams. Studies show that from 60 to 68 percent of all precognitions occur during dreaming. (231) We May have banished our ability to see the future from our conscious minds, but it is still very active in the deeper strata of our psyches.

Tribal cultures are well aware of this fact, and shamanic traditions almost universally stress how important dreaming is in divining the future. Even our most ancient writings pay homage to the premonitory power of dreams, as is evidenced in the biblical account of Pharaoh's dream of seven fat and seven lean cows. The antiquity of such traditions indicates that the tendency of premonitions to occur in dreams is due to more than just our current sceptical attitude toward precognition. The proximity the unconscious mind has to the atemporal realm of the implicate may also play a role. Because our dreaming self is deeper in the psyche than our conscious self-and thus closer to the primeval ocean in which past, present, and future become one, it may be easier for it to access information about the future.

Whatever the reason, it should come as no surprise that other methods for accessing the unconscious can also produce precognitive information. For example, in the 1960s Karlis Osis and hypnotist J. Fahler found that hypnotized subjects scored significantly higher on precognition tests than non hypnotized subjects. (232) Other studies have also confirmed the ESP-enhancing effects of hypnosis. (233) However, no amount of dry statistical data has the impact of an example from real life. In his book *The Future Is Now (The Significance of Precognition)*, Arthur Osborn records the results of a hypnosis-precognition experiment involving the French actress Irene Muza. After being hypnotized and asked if she could see her future, Muza replied, "My career will he short: I dare not say what my end will be: it will be terrible."

Muza Predicted a Terrible Death for herself
Startled, the experimenters decided not to tell Muza what she had reported and gave her a posthypnotic suggestion to forget everything she had said. When she awakened from her trance she had no memory of what she had predicted for herself. A few months later her hairdresser

accidentally spilled some mineral spirits on a lighted stove, causing Muza's hair and clothing to be set on fire. Within seconds she was engulfed in flames and died in a hospital a few hours later. (234).

The American Society for Psychical Research was formed in 1884 to "explore the borderland of human experience". It adopted somewhat wider grounds of interest than the British Society and succeeded immediately in recruiting biologists, physicists, and astronomers; but ran foul of psychologists, who had just established their first laboratory at Johns Hopkins and were intent on keeping their young science strictly experimental. Psychotherapists, however, were less concerned with methodological purity, and more sympathetic; so psychic research in the United States became associated with studies of abnormal psychology.

Neither Society was part of a strictly scientific movement, but as a result of early scientific antipathy, both developed a bad case of "physics envy" and tried to bury scientific incredulity under a heap of facts. They are still trying to do so.

I have glossed over the first half-century of active psychic research with unseemly speed, in order to arrive at the landmark year of 1934 in which a young psychologist published a slim volume called *Extra-sensory Perception*, which threw the subject open to a new and enthusiastic audience. (235)

Naturalizing the Supernatural
J. B. Rhine set out to add scientific plausibility to the discoveries of psychical research. He wanted to naturalize the supernatural. And so, instead of working with recognized psychics or spirit mediums, Rhine developed simple techniques that he used on unselected subjects, mostly students, showing that telepathic and clairvoyant talents could be found even in ordinary people. And the people loved it. Polls continue to show that seven or eight

out of every ten adults in our culture believe in "ESP", most of them on the basis of some personal experience.

Rhine also succeeded in establishing psychical research as an experimental science in an academic setting. He took the subject out of the séance, gave it the new and less emotional name of "parapsychology" and began awarding graduate degrees for work done under his direction in the new laboratory at Duke University. All of which became possible because of the enormous public interest which his books inspired. As a result of private donations at one point in the late 1930s, Rhine personally controlled over 10 percent of the entire research budget of his university. Which naturally led to jealousy and hostility and to a pattern of criticism, much of it in the popular arena that lowered the quality of dialogue about the paranormal in a way which persists to this day. (236).

Australian Aborigines

The Australian anthropologist A. P. Elkin found that Aborigines frequently seemed to be aware of events taking place at their homes, even when they were hundreds of miles distant and they had been away from them for months. He was particularly impressed by their absolute assurance. "A man will suddenly announce one day that his father is dead, that his wife has given birth to a child, or that there is some trouble in his country. He is so sure of his facts that he would return at once if he could (237) Elkin checked on several such examples and, finding them too often correct in substantial detail to be dismissed as chance or coincidence, decided that contact of some sort was being established. He studied Aboriginal shamans or "clever men" and concluded that deliberate communication might be possible. The vision of a shaman, he said, "is no mere hallucination. It is a mental formation visualized and externalized, which may even exist for a time independent of its creator (238). These entities are described by Aborigines as "power animals", which can sometimes be seen by others, and are capable themselves of working or "seeing" at a distance.

One of the best examples in my own files concerns a Cajun from New Orleans, a tough thirty-two-year-old Creole called Shep, who joined the crew of a fishing boat working deep waters at the north-west end of the Hawaiian archipelago. On the evening in question, they had been trawling and, in a quiet moment, Shep decided to go to the crew quarters. He grabbed the hatch rail and swung himself, as he always did, down into the forecastle. This time, however, his hands were slippery with fish scales and he fell flat on his back on the deck below. Nobody saw the accident and Shep lay there, paralyzed and in intense pain. He was convinced that he was about to die, wondered what would become of his young American friend Milly, noticed that the time was 9.12 and passed out.

On the main island 600 miles away, Milly was visiting the home of the boat's captain, passing the evening in a little social embroidery. The wife of the skipper was a full-blooded Samoan, who was intent on her needlework, chatting away cheerfully, until she felt what she later described as "a blow at the back of the head". She slipped semi-conscious to the floor and when she could speak, said "Something very bad has happened on the boat." And then added, "It isn't Bill" – (her husband). When Milly looked at the clock on the wall, the time was 9.14. It was not until the early hours of the following morning that the Coast Guard called to tell her that Shep had been landed on Kauai with a broken back and was being flown home (239).

Professor Dick J. Bierman of the University of Amsterdam and Utrecht University has been active in the field of parapsychology for over two decades, though he had been sceptical about the reality of psychic phenomena for much of that time. After receiving his Ph.D. in experimental physics, he became involved in research in artificial intelligence, specifically intelligent tutoring systems. This resulted in a focus on individual learning and later on learning during altered states of consciousness, especially learning during sleep.

His decades of research into how people know, led him to change his viewpoint about psychic phenomena. This is his description of the conclusion he came to about people's ability to sense the future:

People Sense the Future
We're satisfied that people can sense the future before it happens. We'd now like to move on and see what kind of person is particularly good at it.

Professor Brian Josephson, a Nobel Prize winning physicist from Cambridge University, similarly concluded: "So far the evidence seems compelling. What seems to be happening is that information is coming from the future (240).

A meta-analysis of all precognition experiments conducted at Stanford Research Institute from 1973 to 1988 was conducted by Edwin May, Ph.D., a researcher in low-energy, experimental nuclear physics, and his colleagues. The analysis was based on 154 experiments with more than 26,000 separate trials conducted over 16 years. They concluded that the studies showed that people were able to predict the future. The statistical results of this analysis showing odds against chance that were more than a billion billion to one (241).

Sensory experience confines a person to knowing about what is happening currently, in the immediate environment of the body. These studies and the conclusions by the researchers who have reviewed them indicate that the mind must be obtaining information from some source outside of the body and brain that it knows and remembers. That suggests that the mind is not in the brain (242)

--o--

CHAPTER THIRTEEN

NEAR DEATH EXPERIENCES

With the advancements in resuscitation techniques there has been a tremendous increase in the number of people who have near-death-experiences and they bring back convincing stories from the Afterlife.

Sceptics say that there is no such thing as the etheric body but, as we have seen in an earlier chapter, there is lots of convincing evidence. Also about the human double and about the Afterlife.

What is more, those having an OBE, find that it has been a 'life changing' experience.

"There seems little doubt that NDEs occur in all cultures and have occurred at all times through recorded history ... the NDE happens to young and old, to people from all walks of life, to those whose life has a spiritual dimension and to those who profess no faith at all ... there are many examples of people who have an NDE at a time when they did not even know that such a phenomenon existed." (243)

Dr. Peter Fenwick

Near Death Experiences
Blind people, including those blind from birth, can actually see during near-death experiences (NDE'S) and out-of-the-body experiences (OBE's), suggesting that their

minds must be independent of their bodies, which are unable to see.

Kenneth Ring, Ph.D., professor emeritus of psychology at the University of Connecticut, and Sharon Cooper interviewed 31 blind and sight-impaired persons who had NDE's and OBE'S, and found that 80 percent of them reported correctly "visual" experiences, some in detail. For example, they reported correctly actual colours and their surroundings. One patient who had become totally blind after having been sightless for at least 40 years "saw" the pattern in colours on a new tie during an out of body experience, even though everyone denied having ever described it to him. The results of the two-year research study were published in the book *Mindsight*. (244)

Dr. Larry Dossey, former chief of staff of Medical City Dallas Hospital, describes this case of a woman's being able to see clearly during her near-death experience:

The surgery had gone smoothly until the late stages of the operation. Then something happened. As her physician was closing the incision, Sarah's heart stopped beating. When she awoke, Sarah had a clear, detailed memory of the frantic conversation of the surgeons and nurses during her cardiac arrest; the operating room layout; the scribbles on the surgery schedule board in the hall outside; the colour of the sheets covering the operating table; the hairstyle of the head scrub nurse; the names of the surgeons in the doctors lounge down the corridor who were waiting for her case to be concluded; and even the trivial fact that her anaesthesiologist that day was wearing unmatched socks. All this she knew even though she had been fully anesthetized and unconscious during the surgery and the cardiac arrest.

But what made Sarah's vision even more momentous was the fact that, since birth, she had been blind. (245)

It appears that Sarah's mind was seeing when her body was unable to see because she was both unconscious and blind since birth.

The Near-Death Experience (NDE) is a powerful argument for the existence of the afterlife that, because of recent advances in medical science, is becoming widely reported. As medical resuscitation techniques are being improved, more and more people are being brought back from the border of clinical death. A number of them recount an intense, profoundly meaningful experience in which they seem to be alive and functioning outside their body. For many, a near-death experience is an extremely powerful emotional and spiritual experience.

The evidence for the NDE is consistent, overwhelming, and experienced by many. It is also consistent with evidence for other psychic phenomena such as OBE'S, and with the information obtained from mental and physical mediums.

The more informed closed-minded sceptics now acknowledge that there is no dispute at all about the existence of the NDE. The dispute is about what it means and its interpretation.

Psychics say that in a crisis situation, where death is almost inevitable or is perceived to be inevitable, the duplicate physical body, the astral or etheric body, sometimes leaves the physical body and experiences the first stages of the afterlife. When death does not occur, the duplicate body resumes its place in the physical body. Studies have shown that NDE's occurred following illness, surgery, childbirth, accident, heart attack and attempted suicide.

Sceptics say that there is no such thing as a duplicate body and whatever one experiences has to do with the problems of the physical body itself - "it's all in the mind."

One pioneer in this area was Dr. Raymond Moody, Jr., who began his work as a sceptic. His first book *Life After Life* in 1975, considered the classic work that opened this area to modern research, was followed by two others in 1983 and 1988.

Since 1975 there have been many studies in many countries, so much so that there are now several international associations and journals for the investigation of near-death studies. Cherie Sutherland's excellent Australian book (1992) contains a selected bibliography of over 150 scholarly research reports.

Millions around the World have had NDE's
There are now literally millions of people from all over the world who have undergone a near-death experience. In 1983 a major American survey by George Gallup, Jr. reported that eight million Americans, approximately five percent of the adult population, had experienced one (Gallup 1982). A 1989 Australian survey by Allan Kellehear and Patrick Heaven found that ten percent of 179 people claimed to have experienced at least five typical elements of an NDE.

Studies in widely differing geographic locations have produced remarkably similar findings, such as Margot Grey's study of NDE's in England (Grey 1985), Paola Giovetti's study in Italy (Giovetti 1982), 'Dorothy Counts' study in Melanesia (Counts 1983) and Satwant Pasricha and Ian Stevenson's (1986) study in India. More studies are coming out from different countries on a regular basis, and historical examples show that the experience has been remarkably consistent over time (see Plato's example of Er's NDE in The Republic).

Yet while these experiences have been happening throughout human history, in Western culture it is only in the last twenty or so years that people have felt free to talk about them and the effect that they have had on their lives.

There are many accounts of people having near-death experiences returning with factual information of which they had no prior knowledge. These include being 'able to identify ancestors from pictures, learning about siblings who had died before their own birth, learning about family secrets, etc. Others were able to document information they had learned about future events (see for example Eadie 1992, Brinkley 1994 and Atwater 2000).

Lives are changed Forever
According to the International Association for Near-Death Studies, around eighty percent of the people who experience near-death states claim that their lives are changed forever. They experience specific psychological and physiological differences on a massive scale which may cause major adjustment difficulties for, on average, seven years, but especially during the first three years. This is true with child experiencers as well as with teenagers and adults.

These after-effects are shared by people, including children, who had intense experiences in a particularly vivid dream, while meditating or who have narrowly escaped death.

Cherie Sutherland, an Australian. researcher, interviewed 50 NDE survivors in depth and found that the effects on the lives of survivors had been remarkably consistent and quite different from the effects of drug or chemical-induced hallucinations. She identified many effects which have been substantiated by other studies, e.g. Ring (1980 and 1984) Atwater (1988).

These included:
- a universal belief in life after death
- a high proportion (80%) now believed in reincarnation
- a large shift from organized religion to personal spiritual practice
- a statistically significant increase in psychic sensitivity.
- a more positive view of self and of others,
- an increased desire for solitude and an increased sense of purpose.
- a lack of interest in material success coupled with a marked increase of interest in spiritual development.
- fifty percent experienced major difficulties in close relationships as a result of their changed priorities
- an increase in health consciousness
- most drank less or gave up alcohol and almost all gave up smoking, most gave up prescription drugs
- most watched less television and read fewer newspapers.
- an increased interest in alternative healing
- an increased interest in learning and self-development
- seventy-five percent experienced a major career change in which they moved towards areas of helping others. (246)

Other researches have shown that the NDEers are almost always profoundly changed by the journey to the beyond. They become happier, more optimistic, more easy going, and less concerned with material possessions. Most striking of all, their capacity to love expands enormously. Aloof husbands suddenly become warm and affectionate, workaholics start relaxing and devoting time to their families, and introverts become extroverts. These changes are often so dramatic that people who know the NDEer frequently remark that he or she has become an entirely different person. There are even cases on record of criminals completely reforming their ways, and fire-and-brimstone preachers replacing their message of damnation with one of unconditional love and compassion.

NDE'ers return to say that the Universe is Compassionate
NDEers also become much more spiritually oriented. They return not only firmly convinced of the immortality of the human soul, but also with a deep and abiding sense that the universe is compassionate and intelligent, and this loving presence is always with them. However, this awareness does not necessarily result in their becoming more religious. Like Sri Aurobindo, many NDEers stress the importance of the distinction between religion and spirituality, and assert that it is the latter that has blossomed into greater fullness in their lives, not the former. Indeed, studies show that following their experience, NDEers display an increased openness to ideas outside their own religious background, such as reincarnation and Eastern religions. (247)

Truck Driver becomes a Physicist after an NDE
This widening of interests frequently extends to other areas as well. For instance, NDEers often develop a marked fascination for the types of subjects discussed in this book, in particular psychic phenomena and the new physics. One NDEer investigated by Ring, for example, was a driver of heavy equipment who displayed no interest in books or academic pursuits prior to his experience. However, during his NDE he had a vision of total knowledge, and although he was unable to recall the content of the vision after he recovered, various physics' terms started popping into his head. One morning not long after his experience he blurted out the word quantum. Later he announced cryptically, "Max Planck. you'll be hearing about him in the near future," and as time continued to pass, fragments of equations and mathematical symbols began to surface in his thoughts. Neither he nor his wife knew what the word quantum meant, or who Max Planck (widely viewed as the founding father of quantum physics) was until the man went to a library and looked the words up. But after discovering that he was not talking gibberish, he started to read

voraciously, not only books on physics, but also on parapsychology, metaphysics, and higher consciousness; and he even enrolled in college as a physics major. The man's wife wrote a letter to Ring trying to describe her husband's transformation.

Many times he says a word he has never heard before in our reality. It might he a foreign word of a different language but learns it in relationship to the "light" theory.... He talks about things faster than the speed of light and it's hard for me to understand.... When he picks up a book on physics he already knows the answer and seems to feel more. (248)

The man also started developing various psychic abilities after his experience, which is not uncommon among NDEers. In 1982 Bruce Greyson, a psychiatrist at the University of Michigan and IANDS's director of research, gave sixty-nine NDEers a questionnaire designed to study this issue, and he found that there was an increase in virtually all of the psychic and psi-related phenomena he assessed. (249)

Phyllis Atwater, an Idaho housewife who became an NDE researcher following her own transformative NDE, has interviewed dozens of NDEers and has obtained similar findings. "Telepathy and healing gifts are common," she states. "So is 'remembering' the future. Time and space stop, and you live in a future sequence in detail. Then, when the event occurs, you recognize it. (250)

Near Death Experiences are Universal
Like OBES, NDEs appear to be a universal phenomenon. They are described at length in both the eighth-century 'Tibetan Book of the Dead and the 2,500-year-old Egyptian Book of the Dead. In Book X, *The Republic,* Plato gives a detailed account of a Greek soldier named Er, who came alive just seconds before his funeral pyre was to be lit and said that he had left his body and went through a "passageway" to the land of the dead. The

Venerable Bede gives a similar account in his eighteenth century work *A History of the English Church and People,* and, in fact, in her recent book *Otherworld Journeys* Carol Zaleski, a lecturer on the study of religion at Harvard, points out that medieval literature is filled with accounts of NDES.

NDEers also have no unique demographic characteristics. Various studies have shown that there is no relationship between NDEs and a person's age, sex, marital status, race, religion and / or spiritual beliefs, social class, educational level, income, frequency of church attendance, size of home community, or area of residence. NDES, like lightning, can strike anyone at any time. The devoutly religious are no more likely to have an NDE than nonbelievers.

One of the most interesting aspects of the ND phenomenon is the consistency one finds from experience to experience. A summary of a typical NDE is as follows:

A man is dying and suddenly finds himself floating above his body and watching what is going on. Within moments he travels at great speed through a darkness or a tunnel. He enters a realm of dazzling light and is warmly met by recently deceased friends and relatives. Frequently he hears indescribably beautiful music and sees rolling meadows, flower-filled valleys, and sparkling streams-more lovely than anything he has seen on earth. In this light-filled world he feels no pain or fear and is pervaded with an overwhelming feeling of joy, love, and peace. He meets a "being (or beings) of light" who emanate a feeling of enormous compassion, and is prompted by the being(s) to experience a "life review," a panoramic replay of his life. He becomes so enraptured by his experience of this greater reality that he desires nothing more than to stay. However, the being tells him that it is not his time yet and persuades him to return to his earthly life and re-enter his physical body. (251)

Much of the search for evidence that one's mind, personality and soul survive death of the physical body is to be found in death-bed, near-death and out-of-body experiences.

The past few years have seen books on these subjects become over-night bestsellers. *On Death and Dying*, by Elisabeth Kubler-Ross, M.D., and *Life After Life*, by Raymond Moody, M.D., have each sold more than 3,000,000 copies and have each been translated into more than 25 languages, while subsequent books by these and other authors have also received acceptance throughout the world. Their popularity testifies to a thirst for knowledge that reassures there is a life after death.

One might think that the above activities represent a completely new area for research, but this is not the case. The references at the end of this book show that writing on these subjects started more than 100 years ago. During this past century, many persons laboured to add to the great body of knowledge which now fully supports and substantiates the work set forth in the above mentioned bestsellers. In fact, it is most significant that Dr. Moody and Dr. Kubler-Ross had very little knowledge of the work of prior researchers. The fact that their work dovetails so precisely with the findings of Cobb, Crookall, Savage, Hyslop, Richet and others serves to add great significance to this area of survival research.

Because of the ready availability of books on deathbed and near-death experiences, I will not make an in-depth report on them. I will, however, briefly review the subject. Then I will do something that has been widely overlooked. I will relate these experiences, particularly near-death ones, to the rapidly increasing findings of researchers working with out-of-body experiences.

First, let's define our terms:

Deathbed Cases: Observations by medical people and psychical researchers of what a dying person reports in the moments before death of the physical body. Often these reports include visions of deceased loved ones, religious figures and afterlife scenes.

Out-of-Body Experiences are experiences in which the consciousness of a person seems to get outside that person's physical body. This consciousness then reports what it sees, hears, and does, and where it travels during the time when it is seemingly displaced from its physical body.

One of the most extensive pieces of research yet done on *deathbed experience* is the death-bed *"visions"* published in 1961 by Dr. Karlis Osis, a lengthy monograph, *Deathbed Observations by Physicians and Nurses.* Dr. Osis sought the experiences of 10,000 American physicians and nurses. An analysis was made of the detailed reports of 640 respondents. A high proportion of these had witnessed their patients' reactions to and reports of unseen deathbed visitors. Dr. Osis drew these major conclusions:

1. The dying often go into inexplicable exaltation before death.
2. They see visions of apparitions to a much greater extent than persons who are not approaching death.
3. Usually, these apparitions are of persons who have died. However, visions of living or religious personages are occasionally seen.
4. Drugs or other aspects of illness seemingly do not account for these visions.
5. Many of the dying persons intuitively realize that these apparitions are coming to take them into death and a continued existence.

In 1977, Dr. Osis and a colleague, Dr. Erlendur Haraldsson, published *At the Hour of Death.* This book extended the above studies and included reports of experiences of more than 1,000 additional doctors and nurses. Significantly, this work was based on the experiences of persons dying in India as well as in the United States. The deathbed visions were very similar in spite of racial, cultural and religious differences.

These scholarly and scientific studies in turn have been found to correlate very well with the pioneering work done over a period of 30 years and reported in the several works of Dr. Robert Crookall of England.

The Silver Cord
In Near-Death Experiences the nonphysical part of a person is outside of the physical body but attached with a tenuous connection known since early Biblical days as the silver cord.

This ability of the mind, personality and soul to detach itself from the physical body should be kept in mind in reading through this short selection of excerpts of near-death cases reported by Dr. Moody in *Life After Life:*

A woman recalls, "About a year ago, I was admitted to the hospital with heart trouble, and the next morning, lying in the hospital bed, I began to have a very severe pain in my chest. I pushed the button beside the bed to call for the nurses, and they came in and started working on me. I was quite uncomfortable lying on my back so I turned over, and as I did I quit breathing and my heart stopped beating. Just then, I heard the nurses shout, 'Code pink! Code pink!" As they were saying this, I could feel myself moving out of my body and sliding down between the mattress and the rail on the side of the bed. Actually it seemed as if I went through the rail on down to the floor. Then, I started rising upward, slowly. On my way up, I saw more nurses come running into the room. There must have been a dozen of them. My doctor happened to be making his rounds in the hospital so they called him and I saw him come in, too. I thought, "I wonder what he's doing here." I drifted on up past the light fixture. I saw it from the side and very distinctly and then I stopped floating right below the ceiling and looked down. I felt almost as though I were a piece of paper that someone had blown up to the ceiling.

"I watched them reviving me from up there! My body was lying down there stretched out on the bed, in plain view, and they were all standing around it. I heard one nurse say, "Oh, my God! She's gone," while another one leaned down to give me mouth-to-mouth resuscitation. I was looking at the back of her head while she did this. I'll never forget the way her hair looked; it was cut kind of short. Just then, I saw them roll this machine in there, and they put the shocks on my chest. When they did, I saw my whole body just jump right up off the bed, and I heard every bone in my body crack and pop. It was the most awful thing!

Why are they going to so much trouble to keep me Alive? As I saw them below beating on my chest and rubbing my arms and legs, I thought, "Why are they going to so much trouble? I'm just fine now."

Everything we know about the afterlife tells us that the Higher Power has set up life so the transition into the next plane of eternal life is as easy as possible; the universe is filled with love and compassion. Pre-death visions are an example of that preparation for a gentle transition.

Pre-death visions are visions of deceased loved ones patients commonly have in the weeks before they die. Deathbed visions are the visions dying patients have in the days or hours immediately preceding death. Both help the person prepare for the transition. They are God's counsellors, bringing reassurance to those about to cross over.

Dr. James L. Hallenbeck, director of palliative care services with the Veterans Administration Palo Alto Health Care System, estimates that these pre-death visions or deathbed visions of deceased loved ones occur for at least 25 percent of deaths. (252)

Stephen Wagner estimates the number of people who experience deathbed visions as even more because only about 10 percent of dying people are conscious shortly before their deaths. Looking just at those who are conscious, between 50 and 60 percent experience deathbed visions. (253)

Children Tell the True Story
Children are truth-tellers because of their youthful naiveté, so when they experience such visions, they describe them matter-of-factly. In Closer to the Light, Dr. Melvin Morse describes children's deathbed visions, explaining that they are astonishing scientific proof of the validity of the near-death experiences. (254)

Dr. Diane Komp, a Yale paediatric oncologist, described a 7-year-old girl who sat up in bed just before her death from leukaemia and said, "The angels, they are so beautiful, can't you hear them singing Mommy?" A boy dying of leukaemia said that God spoke to him and that he asked God to live another year so he could explain his death to his 3-year-old brother. Amazingly, against medical odds, the boy lived one more year. (255)

Elisabeth Kubler-Ross described a healthy 4 year old girl who had a vivid dream she described to her mother. She said she saw a beautiful golden heaven and that it was "really, really, real," with gold angels, diamonds, and jewels. It was a fun place. There, she met Jesus. She told her mother not to worry because Jesus would take care of her. She then went out to play and sadly was murdered only hours later. (256)

AFTERLIFE – THE PROOF

In 1959, Karlis Osis, Ph.D., psychology professor at the University of Freiburg, and Erlendur Haraldsson, Ph.D., psychology professor at the University of Munich, studied deathbed visions in the U.S. and India by interviewing doctors and nurses who had been present when people died. They mailed out questionnaires to 5,000 physicians and 5,000 nurses, providing information on over 35,000 observations of dying patients. Over 1,300 dying patients saw apparitions and almost 900 reported visions of an afterlife. (257)

--o--

CHAPTER FOURTEEN

GHOSTS & APPARITIONS

Ghosts are nothing new; maybe **you** *have seen one. Many people have.*

They have been seen by many credible witnesses from all professions, including Judges and Lawyers. Ghosts have been seen by sceptics and unbelievers; they have even been observed scientifically.

Don't be afraid of ghosts. Usually they are simply people who have moved over to the Afterlife but, for some reason or other, have remained attached to this life.

Mind you – if someone said 'Boo' behind me in a dark graveyard at night I'd probably run like hell!!

Apparitions are a recurring theme in the literature and folklore of all countries and throughout all of recorded history. They have been scientifically studied since at least 1882 and the results have consistently showed them to be very widely experienced (Currie 1978:17 and Bayliss 1973:17).

Thirty-two thousand sightings reported in 1894
The first systematic inquiry into apparitions was instituted by the English Society for Psychical Research in 1882. The result was embodied in *Phantasms of the Living* by Myers, Podmore and Gurney. A further, far more detailed

international study was commenced in 1889. Thirty-two thousand cases of sightings of apparitions were received, 17,000 were in England. The 1894 report fills almost the whole of Volume X of the Proceedings of the Society for Psychical Research.

Further studies by the American Society for Psychical Research and by the French researcher Camille Flammarion, who compiled thousands of cases in his books *The Unknown* (1900) and *Death and Its Mystery* (1925), also found that after-death communications occurred very widely.

In 1973 a University of Chicago sociologist asked a sample of 1,467 Americans if they had ever felt they had contact with someone who had died. Twenty-seven percent answered that they had (Greenicy 1975). A similar survey in Iceland (Haraldsson et al. 1976) found that thirty-one percent said yes.

Dr. W.D. Rees, a British physician, found that of a sample of widows in Wales, forty seven percent had experiences - often repeatedly over a number of years - that convinced them that their dead spouses had been in contact with them (Rees 1971:37-41). An earlier British experiment by Dr. P. Marris (1958) had found a figure of fifty percent.

This study was repeated in Canada by Dr. Earl Dunn (1977:121-122), also found that fifty percent of widows and widowers had contact experiences. Many of these people had thought that they were "going crazy" and had not previously told anyone of their experiences as they expected to be ridiculed. (258)

Judges & Lawyers witnessed Ghosts
"Furthermore, let me say that over twenty years in the active practice of law, largely in trial cases, coming in contact with many great minds, has qualified me to do certain things: i.e.

to estimate the weight and value of evidence fairly; to detect fraud in any guise; to know when a fact is proved." (259)
Edward C. Randall,
Attorney and afterlife researcher
(Heagerty 1995:39)

Space does not permit us to delve deeply into the writings of the number of lawyers who have investigated and accepted the paranormal and the afterlife. Accordingly, I have chosen three very exceptional lawyers who would be representative.

More than the members of any other profession, lawyers and judges are trained to evaluate the credibility of witnesses, and the strength of evidence. So I was impressed when I found a number of lawyers and judges, at the top of their profession, who investigated the evidence for the afterlife and were prepared to make a public stand to support it, with absolutely nothing to gain, and often at great personal cost.

These were men of the highest intellectual calibre who all approached the subject in a rational and objective manner applying the legal test of 'beyond reasonable doubt'. All had been open-minded sceptics to begin with and all maintained their conviction until their deaths.

Judge Edmonds was at the height of his career in early 1851 when he decided to investigate the mediumship of the Fox sisters. He had been a member of both branches of the New York State Parliament, and, for some time, President of the Senate and a Judge of the New York State Supreme Court.

He detailed his investigation of the afterlife and his conclusions with the same precision as he would write a judgment on a matter before the court, in a letter addressed "To the Public," published in the New York Courier and dated New York, August 1, 1853.

It is worth quoting this judge, using his own words. It shows his depth, his intellect, his emotions, his empirical perception, his feelings and his rationale. It also shows the long process which all informed open-minded sceptical enquirers go though, as they try to balance the evidence of their own eye-witness experiences with their "intellect" and materialist conditioning:

Sceptics & Unbelievers witnessed Ghosts
It was January 1851 that my attention was first called to the subject of "spiritual contact." I was at the time withdrawn from general society; I was labouring under great depression of spirit. I was occupying all my leisure in reading on the subject of death and man's existence afterwards. I had, in the course of my life, read and heard from the pulpit so many contradictory and conflicting doctrines on the subject, that I hardly knew what to believe.

I could not believe what I did not understand, and was anxiously seeking to know, if, after death, we should again meet with those whom we had loved here, and under what circumstances. I was invited by a friend to witness the "Rochester Knockings." I complied more to oblige her, and to while away a tedious hour. I thought a good deal on what I witnessed, and I determined to investigate the matter and find out what it was. If it was a deception, or a delusion, I thought that I could detect it.

For about four months I devoted at least two evenings in a week and sometimes more to witnessing the phenomena in all its phases. I kept careful records of all I witnessed, and from time to time compared them with each other, to detect inconsistencies and contradictions. I read all I could lay my hands on, on the subject, and especially all the "professed" exposures of the humbug.

I went from place to place, seeing different mediums, meeting with different parties or persons, often with persons whom I had never seen before, and sometimes where I was myself entirely unknown, sometimes in the dark and sometimes in the light, often with inveterate unbelievers, and more frequently with zealous believers.

I availed myself of every opportunity that was afforded, to thoroughly sift the matter to the bottom. I was all this time an unbeliever, and tried the patience of believers sorely by my scepticism, my fault finding, and my obdurate refusal to yield my belief.

I saw around me some who yielded a ready faith on one or two sittings only; others again, under the same circumstances, avowing a determined unbelief; and some who refused to witness it at all, and yet others were confirmed unbelievers. I could not imitate any of these parties, and refused to yield unless upon the most certain testimony. At length the evidence came, and in such force that no sane man could withhold his faith.

After depending upon my senses, as to these various phases of the phenomenon, I invoked the aid of science, and, with the assistance of an accomplished electrician and his machinery, and eight or ten intelligent, educated, shrewd persons, examined the matter. We pursued our inquiries many days, and established to our satisfaction two things: first, that the sounds were not produced by the agency of any person present or near us; and, second, that they were not forthcoming at our will and pleasure.

The Press described it as Humbug

While these things were going on, there appeared in the newspapers various explanations and "exposures of the humbug," as they were termed. I read them with care, in the expectation of being assisted in my researches, and I could not but smile at once at the rashness and the futility of the explanations. For instance, while certain learned professors in Buffalo were congratulating themselves on having detected it in the toe and knee joints, the manifestations in this city changed to ringing a bell placed under the table. (cited by Doyle, 1926, i, 126)

The judge went on to explain how his own secret thoughts had been revealed (much as was reported in the Scole experiments) and that plans he had kept in his own mind and spoken of to no-one were known to the spirit communicators (Doyle, 1926, i, 129).

He notes also that he had heard the mediums use Greek, Latin, Spanish, and French when they were ignorant of these languages. He records that facts were revealed which were unknown to any of the people present but afterwards found to be true. (Doyle, 1926, i, 129)

Judge Edmonds maintained his convictions in spite of attempts to ridicule and attack him and preferred to resign his position as a Supreme Court Judge rather than keep quiet about his life-changing discoveries.

He went on to become a medium himself and also detailed the trance mediumship of his daughter, Laura, who in trance spoke in nine languages unknown to her in waking life.

Above all, he retained until his death his excitement about what he had learned through communication with higher spirits.

Judge John Worth Edmonds' decision to make his discoveries public would have influenced many American people.

As a senior judge, he would have had in-depth understanding of assessing credibility of anything presented to him for consideration and an expert in the admissibility of evidence. He had the opportunity of examining the evidence at first hand and then building on it with personal experience.

Edward C. Randall practiced law in Dunkirk, New York, and in the city of Buffalo, where he has attained distinction both as a lawyer and businessman. He acquired not only high professional honour, but organized and financed various industrial enterprises. He was one of the leading men in the industrial world, and was the executive head of various companies in addition to being president of a number of corporations.

Medium Emily French
Initially an open-minded sceptic, he came to accept the evidence for the afterlife through hearing the incredible voices that came in the presence of direct voice and materialization medium, Emily French.

He and his wife spent twenty two years in recording sittings with her and he became a major writer on the afterlife. (See Randall *The Dead Have Never Died*).

For five years they were joined by a prominent judge, Dean Stuart of Rochester, "a learned jurist and man of such impeccable character that he had been repeatedly elected to the responsible office of Surrogate Judge."

Randall writes that every person who attended the circle was initially sceptical and sure that the voices were fraudulent. And that each person was allowed to conduct however many exacting experiments there needed to be. I strongly recommend the reader to obtain a copy of Edward C Randall's *The French Revelation.*

Dr. Aubrey Rose OBE, CBE, a leading British Human Rights lawyer, has stated in his recent book *The Rainbow Never Ends* that he totally accepts the evidence for the existence of the afterlife.

After empirically investigating transmissions made by one of his colleagues through direct voice medium, Leslie Flint, he stated that without doubt the voice came from the afterlife, and was that of Judge Lord Birkett, who had crossed over some time before.

From the afterlife, he says, he heard Lord Birkett state: When I was on your side, I supported the death penalty, but now I am here, I can see that it was wrong. We have no right to take life.

These highly intelligent, logical, successful lawyers and judges were fortunate to have had the opportunity of sitting with brilliant direct voice / materialization mediums who provided them with evidence of the afterlife that they simply could not deny.

All were initially sceptical, but, to their credit, once they had the opportunity of carefully examining the evidence for themselves, they accepted the evidence and had the courage to become open campaigners for the existence of the afterlife.

I would suggest that there are many cases of haunting where there is as little consciousness in the so-called "ghosts" as there is in the clothes that he appears to be wearing. But assuredly there are hauntings and hauntings, and to place all such phenomena under one category would be a grave error even though for many it might appear a tenable hypothesis. (260)

At the University of Colorado, Nicholas Seeds has taken mouse brains and teased them apart into their component cells. (261)

These he put into a culture solution in a test tube and shook gently for several days. At the end of this time the separate cells reaggregated and formed pieces of brain in which cells were connected by normal synapses, they showed the usual biochemical reactions, and grew a natural myelin protective sheath. Somehow cells are capable of recreating past patterns; they have a molecular memory, which is passed on from one cell to another so that a new one can reproduce the behaviour of its parents. If a change, or mutation, occurs, this, too, is faithfully duplicated by the descendants. The dead live again in defiance of time.

Living Matter doesn't die, it just recycles again
The cyclical patterns of life mean that matter is never destroyed but goes back into the system to re-emerge sometime later. Living organic matter rises again in the same form with the same behaviour patterns in a process of reincarnation. Each new generation is a reincarnation of the species, but this does not mean that individuals reappear. The Greeks believed in metempsychosis-the transmigration of the soul into a new body, and similar ideas are so widespread among all cultures that they can be considered almost universal. But despite some sensational stories, there is little real evidence that anything of the sort occurs. It is difficult enough to prove that we have souls in the first place. While apparent knowledge of other times and places can be attributed to telepathic contact with someone still alive, it seems unnecessary to assume that the phenomena are produced by an eternal spirit

Souls or spirits that occur without benefit of body are a separate kind of phenomenon, but can be considered in much the same way. For the sake of argument, it is worth considering the possibility that man can produce an 'astral projection," or part of himself that can exist without his normal physical body and perhaps even survive his death. These spirits are said to wander at will and there are countless records of their having been seen, in whole or in part, in a great variety of situations. In England, one person in six believes in ghosts and one person in fourteen thinks that he has actually seen one. (262)

After publishing her careful report on 307 cases of 'phantasms Mrs Eleanor Sidgwick may well have felt that she had established her case once and for all. After her investigation, no cultured person could ever again dismiss ghosts as old wives' tale or delusions of credulous or over-excitable people. As another eminent investigator, Andrew Lang, pointed out, most people who have seen ghosts are not hysterics, but 'steady, unexcitable people with just one odd experience. Had Mrs Sidgwick's 180-page report appeared as a book with a title like *Ghosts and Apparitions* - perhaps it might have achieved its intended effect of placing ghosts on the same scientific footing as radio or photography. But buried away in the pages of the *Proceedings* of the SPR, it never reached the general public. (263)

Since the beginning of recorded history, people in all parts of the world have reported apparitions, hauntings and ghosts. To what extent, if any, does this throw light on the survival question?

There is considerable overlapping of these terms in many people's minds, so I will clarify them here. Webster's Third New International Dictionary defines apparition as "the unexpected or supernormal appearance of someone living or dead." It is obviously unnecessary to consider living apparitions; those of the dead will be included in my references to ghosts.

The term haunting is defined as "an act of frequenting, especially by a disembodied spirit." Here we come a bit closer to the survival question. Centuries of reports of hauntings establish two essential elements in the phenomenon: an old house or dwelling place of some kind, and the restlessness of a human spirit. The first represents an unbroken link with the past life of a former occupant. The second is believed to be caused by various factors. These include the person's remorse over an evil life, his shock at a violent death, important unfinished business in the physical world, excessive attachment to material life, or the failure to realize that he has "died" and is now living in another realm.

<u>Hauntings show themselves in many ways</u>
Such hauntings provide many types of activity. Strange noises are heard, objects are displaced, lights are seen where none exist, existing lights are turned on and off, and objects are moved about. An actual temperature drop may be felt in the atmosphere. Sometimes an unbearable stench is detected, and often people on the premises experience a feeling of discomfort or even horror. They sometimes report seeing insubstantial shapes, phantoms, apparitions or ghosts.

What are ghosts? Webster's dictionary tells us that a ghost is "a disembodied soul; the soul of a dead person believed to be the inhabitant of the unseen world, or to appear to be living in bodily likeness." A disembodied soul, inhabiting an unseen world. Yes, these certainly relate to the question of survival. At least this gives us indication that perhaps there is a soul and perhaps it can leave the physical body at death. So that brings us face to face with ghosts. Are ghosts real? There is ample – and increasing – evidence that they are. (264)

The notion that some events leave stronger imprints in the holographic record than others is also supported by the tendency of hauntings to occur at locations where some terrible act of violence or other unusually powerful emotional occurrence has taken place. The literature is filled with apparitions appearing at the sites of murders, military battles, and other kinds of mayhem. This suggests that in addition to images and sounds, the emotions being felt during an event are also recorded in the cosmic hologram. Again it appears that it is the emotional intensity of such events that makes them more prominent in the holographic record, and that allows normal individuals to unwittingly tap into them.

Fairies and Supernatural Beings

And again, many of these hauntings appear to be less the product of unhappy earthbound spirits, and more just accidental glimpses into the holographic record of the past. This, too, is supported by the literature on the subject. For example, in 1907, and at the prompting of the poet William Butler Yeats, a UCLA anthropologist and religious scholar named W. Y. Evans-Wentz embarked on a two-year journey through Ireland, Scotland, Wales, Cornwall, and Brittany to interview people who had allegedly encountered fairies and other supernatural beings. Evans-Wentz undertook the project because Yeats told him that, as twentieth-century values replaced the old beliefs, encounters with fairies were becoming less frequent and needed to be documented before the tradition was lost completely.

As Evans-Wentz went from village to village interviewing the usually elderly stalwarts of the faith, he discovered that not all of the fairies people encountered in the glens and the moon-dappled meadows were small. Some were tall and looked like normal human beings except that they were luminous and translucent and had the curious habit of wearing the clothing of earlier historical periods.

Moreover, these "fairies" often appeared in or around archaeological ruins, burial mounds, standing stones, crumbling sixth-century fortresses, and so on, and participated in activities associated with bygone times. Evans-Wentz interviewed witnesses who had seen fairies that looked like men in Elizabethan dress engaging in hunts, fairies that walked in ghostly processions to and from the remains of old forts, and fairies that rang bells while standing in the ruins of ancient churches. One activity of which the fairies seemed inordinately fond was waging war. In his book *The Fairy-Faith in Celtic Countries* Evans-Wentz presents the testimony of dozens of individuals who claimed to see these spectral conflicts, moonlit meadows thronged with men battling in medieval armour, or desolate fens covered with soldiers in coloured uniforms. Sometimes these frays were eerily silent. Some-times they were full-fledged dins; and, perhaps most haunting of all, sometimes they could only be heard but not seen.

From this, Evans-Wentz concluded that at least some of the phenomena his witnesses were interpreting as fairies were actually some kind of afterimage of events that had taken place in the past. "Nature herself has a memory," he theorized. "There is some indefinable psychic element in the earth's atmosphere upon which all human and physical actions or phenomena are photographed or impressed. Under certain inexplicable conditions, normal persons who are not seers may observe Nature's mental records like pictures cast upon a screen, often like moving pictures. (265)

As for why encounters with fairies were becoming less frequent, a remark made by one of Evidence convi's respondents provides a clue. The respondent was an elderly gentleman named John Davies living on the Isle of Man, and after describing numerous sightings of the good people, he stated, "Before education came into the island more people could see the fairies; now very few people can see them." (266)

Since "education" no doubt included an anathema against believing in fairies, Davies's remark suggests that it was a change in attitude that caused the widespread retrocognitive abilities of the Manx people to atrophy. Once again this underscores the enormous power our beliefs have in determining which of our extraordinary potentials we manifest and which we do not.

Ghosts are described by those in the afterlife as being impressions on the memory of the "ether," the unseen spiritual atmosphere surrounding Earth. When emotional events occur, the ether may retain a memory of the event. Later, sensitive people may be able to see the memory act out. The memories are described as ghosts, and generally appear in relationship to traumatic events. These ethereal memories have no spirit attached to them, can move only in the ways the living person moved when the memory was created, cannot communicate, and are completely harmless. That is why hauntings often involve the same spirit seeming to perform the same actions repeatedly, with no communication between the apparitions and the witnesses. When the conditions between the Earth's atmosphere and the ether are just right, the memories may play out like a movie so more than one living person witnesses them. That is what happens when people witness a battle scene being played out by what people call "ghosts." In any event, there is no living spirit there when the memory comes from the ether.

Poltergeists, on the other hand, can be earthbound people who are not able or willing to change their mental condition to allow themselves to leave the Earth plane. They are almost always simply trying to attract attention and are frustrated that no one can see them or respond to their communication. As a result, they may bang on things, move things about if they can, and otherwise disrupt the Earth plane.

Some are immature spiritually, and may have been mischievous on Earth. They continue their mischievous activities by staying on the Earth plane and influencing people on this side of life who are susceptible because of their natural inclinations toward the same sort of mischief. Drugs or alcohol make a person on the Earth plane even more susceptible. In addition, some people still alive on Earth open themselves to influence because they have latent medium abilities, but they are not spiritually mature enough to keep the lower-level people in the afterlife from intruding. (267)

During the last days of March 1848, the Fox family of Arcadia, New York, was kept awake for several nights running by loud rapping noises. John Fox and his wife Margaret had been in the house for less than six months, and the previous tenant – so they later discovered - had left it because he had been disturbed by noises. It was a windy March, and at first they were not unduly bothered. But on the night of Friday 31 March, the bangings and rattlings were so loud that John Fox made a thorough search of the house, watched by his two daughters, Margaret, fifteen, and Kate, twelve. He tried shaking the window sashes, to see if they could be responsible, and Kate observed that as her father rattled the windows, the sounds seemed to reply, like an echo. Mrs Fox was convinced that she had heard footsteps walking downstairs on the previous night. Now, worn out by lack of sleep, they decided to go to bed at about eight o'clock and try to get a good night's rest.

All four slept in the same room, and the noises soon began again. Kate tried snapping her fingers in imitation of the raps; then she said perkily: 'Mr. Splitfoot, do as I do,' and clapped her hands. The raps promptly imitated her. Margaret, just as unconcerned, said: 'No, do as I do', and began to count as she slowly clapped. The raps imitated her. The children suddenly remembered that tomorrow would be April Fools' Day, and concluded that someone was playing a joke. Mrs Fox thought of a test; she asked the unknown knocker to rap her children's' ages; it did so correctly, convincing her that this was not some mischievous neighbour's child. She asked: 'Is it a human being who makes these raps?' There was no sound. 'Is it a spirit?' There were two raps. 'If it is an injured spirit, make two raps.' The two raps were so loud that the house shook.

By questions, Mrs Fox obtained the information that the knocker was thirty-one - or had been at the time of his death - and that he had been murdered in the house and buried in the cellar. She asked if the 'ghost' had any objection to her calling in the neighbour's. It said no. Within an hour, the house was crowded with neighbours who listened breathlessly to the noises. Most of them did not dare to venture into the bedroom. One of the braver participants, a Mr. William Duesler, not only went into the bedroom, but continued to question the knocker. He was told, by a code of knocks, that the man had been murdered in the east room of the house, by having his throat cut; this had happened five years earlier, and the murderer was the man who then lived in the house, a Mr. Bell. The murder had been committed for the $500 carried by the man, who was a pedlar. It also rapped out Duesler's own age correctly, that of his wife, and of various other people in the neighbourhood.

By means of an alphabetical code, the 'spirit' later identified itself as Charles B. Rosma. A maid named Lucretia Pulver, who had worked for the Bells, could recall the pedlar's arrival, and how she was sent off to her parents' home for the night. When she came back the next day, she was told the pedlar had left.

Mr. and Mrs Bell had moved to Lyon, New York, and he indignantly denied the accusation, producing a testimonial to his good character signed by his neighbours. The spirit had already prophesied that he would never be brought to justice.

The Foxes tried digging in the cellar, but at a depth of a few feet the hole began to flood with water. At a later date, when the water had subsided, they tried again. Five feet down they encountered a plank, and underneath this, in quicklime and charcoal, human hair and a few bones. But there were not enough of these to justify a charge of murder against Mr.

Bell. It was to be another fifty-six years before, in November 1904, the collapse of a wall in the cellar revealed another wall a few feet behind it. This time, digging between the two walls revealed most of a human skeleton, and a pedlar's tin box. It looked as if someone had dug up the body from its original burial place, buried it close to the wall, then built another wall to confuse searchers. (268)

--o--

CHAPTER FIFTEEN

POLTERGEISTS

Poltergeists are often caused by people moving to the Afterlife – but with unfinished business. Children, particularly adolescent teenagers, can often be the cause.

Poltergeists often throw things around, cause fires, and cause electrical appliances to blow up.

There is a great case of a disused hotel lift in Southport which continued to operate on its own and without any electrical supply. It continued to do until it was battered to pieces with sledge-hammers!!!

The word "poltergeist" is German for "noisy spirit." Research into this area from the United States, Brazil, England, Scotland, Ireland, Canada, Finland, Germany, France, Italy, India, Russia and other countries is quite objective and conclusive. The behaviour of poltergeists ranges from the very gentle to the very destructive.

Poltergeists
In 1968, following an outbreak of poltergeist activity in his family home, Matthew Manning realized that he was somehow responsible and began to exploit and direct the phenomenon. He produced "automatic writing" in a variety of scripts, including Arabic, and even more impressively - a portfolio of "automatic drawings" in the style of Durer, Picasso, da Vinci, Beardsley and Klee. Although Manning

has no appreciable artistic talent in his own right, the drawings are highly accomplished, done very quickly, always in the distinctive style of a particular well-known artist, but are not always reproductions of any known work. "It's not me," says Manning, "I simply switch on the energy. (269)

> In some cases poltergeist activity is consistent with the information transmitted from the afterlife from hundreds of different sources, that there are people who physically die and who, upon finding themselves conscious in an apparently solid body in a new dimension, refuse to believe they are physically dead - some become confused and cause a lot of mischief for a time.

Information transmitted from the afterlife tells that just because we enter into a different dimension at the point of death, it does not mean that our personality changes.

Personality Doesn't Change when we enter the Afterlife
The state of mind at the point of death is crucially important. The mind, character and personality immediately after death do not change, not one iota. And if a person is extremely disturbed at the time of death, there is a likelihood that the person will continue to be disturbed in the next world - for an indefinite period of time.

We are told that sometimes people do get caught between the physical world and the afterlife. They think that they are still alive and continue to live in the same house.

In his book The Strangers, Matthew Manning writes of his poltergeist experiences when he was a teenager. He claims they were triggered by a deceased previous occupant of his family home, a Robert Webbe, who, unaware that it was a different century, was complaining of other people living in his house.

Matthew Manning has since gone on to become an internationally-known psychic and healer. At the time he was experiencing the poltergeist phenomena, he was thoroughly investigated by Professor George Owen of Cambridge, a world expert on poltergeists. Later he was investigated by a number of other scientists including Charles Tart and Nobel Prize-winning physicist Brian Josephson. These scientists with the highest credibility and with international reputations confirmed that Matthew Manning's psychic experiences were genuine (Manning 1974)

Unfinished Business
In many instances, the motivation for poltergeist's activity is directly related to some serious unfinished business. Sometimes serious crimes such as murder, rape, torture and some other form of injustice motivates the afterlife intelligence to seek justice or revenge.

While each case needs to be investigated thoroughly to rule out fraud and other natural explanations, there is no doubt that some of the objective evidence available about poltergeist activity can only be explained by the existence of the afterlife. (270)

There have been tens of thousands of poltergeist incidents recorded around the world, with solid objects flying in the air, huge kitchen cabinets levitating, plates and glasses, and clothing set on fire, human voices being heard from unknown sources, vases being smashed on floor and stones being thrown and other material things being moved, at times eliciting terror in those who happen to be present.

Michael Gross, a British writer, has written a very scholarly annotated bibliography of 1,111 sources of poltergeist cases from different countries (Gross 1979). Colin Wilson has produced a very easy-to-read and comprehensive 382-page book packed with cases (Wilson 1981). Guy Playfair's "This

House is Haunted" is an excellent account of the Enfield poltergeist case.

Sometimes hardened police officers have witnessed and testified to this poltergeist phenomenon that cannot be explained other than by a disturbed intelligence from the afterlife. Many times professional mediums were able to contact the poltergeist, who was able to explain why it was disturbed.

One of Britain's most amazing poltergeist activities was at the Harper home in Enfield and lasted for more than sixteen months from. August 1977 to October 1978. Mrs. Harper, a divorcee, lived there with her four children - two boys and two girls aged seven to thirteen.

Events witnessed by a range of Professional People
The disturbances, which did not come from physical or human origin, were witnessed by a number of different people with different backgrounds and different religious beliefs, including sceptics, police, politicians, psychologists, psychiatrists, journalists and social workers all reported the poltergeist activities.

Two consistent investigators were writer Guy Lyon Playfair, a highly experienced observer of poltergeist activities in Brazil, and Maurice Grosse, a highly motivated member of the Society for Psychical Research (SPR). Playfair and Grosse estimated that over 2,000 inexplicable incidents were observed by at least 30 witnesses. Some of the activities of this particular poltergeist included:

● throwing household items around; chairs were smashed and children's toys were seen flying in the air, thrown from an invisible source.
● lighting fires which extinguished themselves

- draining the power out of the journalists' camera and other electronic batteries immediately after the batteries had been charged
- throwing an iron grille from the bottom of the fireplace across the room, narrowly missing Jimmy, one of the Harper boys.
- ripping a heavy gas fire out of the wall.

Answering an investigator, one of the poltergeists stated he was "Joe Watson." Asked the reason for the activity the poltergeist answered: "I was sleeping here," - implying everybody else was a trespasser!

An indentation appeared on one of the pillows - as if an invisible head was resting there; this was witnessed by the investigator Guy Playfair.

A voice saying "F--- off you," "I was sleeping here," and "I like annoying you" were heard directed towards investigator Playfair.

Thousands of poltergeist cases have been reported in the United States. In one well-attested case, the police arrived on 19 December 1976 at the home of Mrs. Beulah Wilson of Pearisburg, Virginia, after she complained of regular poltergeist activities. Previously sceptical, the police had ignored the complaint, but it is reported that when they went into the house, they witnessed the destructive behavior of some invisible intruder, who was smashing dishes, wooden chairs, and other household items. In this particular incident the police witnessed the amazing sight of a 200-pound kitchen cabinet floating in the air without any means of support.

Annemarie Schneider
A most powerful poltergeist activity occurred in a lawyer's office in the Bavarian town of Rosenheim, in Germany, in 1967.

The poltergeist activity centered around an eighteen year old secretary, Annmarie Schneider. One morning when she first got the job at the office, she walked down the entrance hall.

Witnesses stated that:
- the hanging lamp started to swing,
- the lamp in the cloakroom started to swing too,
- a bulb directly above her exploded, and
- the fluorescent lighting went out in the next room.

At other times:
- loud bangs were heard
- all the lights in the office went out at the same time. Electrical fuses would blow without any cause
- cartridges fuses ejected themselves from the sockets
- all four telephones would ring simultaneously with no one on the line.
- calls were frequently cut or interrupted for short periods
- telephone bills suddenly soared to very high levels
- developing fluid in the photostatic copiers would often spill out without any disturbance
- investigating technicians captured swinging lamps and games on cameras
- physicists F. Karger and G. Zicha could not find anything wrong with the electrical and other material things in the office.
- drawers were witnessed opening by themselves
- twice a 400-pound cabinet was seem to move by itself.

Professors, journalists, police and other witnesses testified to the poltergeist phenomenon. Professor Bender, a parapsychologist who also investigated this special poltergeist, stated that the poltergeist phenomenon was centered around Annmarie. When Annmarie had to leave to work somewhere else, the poltergeist phenomenon stopped abruptly. No investigator raised any issue of cheating by Annmarie or by anybody else.

Elsewhere, in 1969 in Nicklheim, Germany, it was reported that parascientists investigated apportations - the moving of solid objects by themselves" from one place to a different place. Parascientists communicated with this particular poltergeist and instructed it to remove perfume bottles from one room to be taken outside. Soon afterwards, in the presence of many witnesses, these bottles were seen falling from the sky. (271)

Occasionally, one of the living people occupying the same house may be mediumistic, a developing psychic sensitive. In the presence of this person the entity is able to make its presence felt. (272)

While each case needs to be investigated thoroughly to rule out fraud and other natural explanations, there is no doubt that some of the objective evidence available about poltergeist activity can only be explained by the existence of the afterlife.

Modem parapsychologists have described many important observations involving various psychokinetic activities and have conducted systematic laboratory research of this phenomenon with some remarkable results. Their methodology evolved from simple dice-throwing experiments to sophisticated designs using randomization based on the emission of electrons in radioactive decay, electronic devices, and modern computers. They have studied Psychokinesis on targets in motion (PK-MT), such as dice thrown by special machines, electric clocks, the flow of liquids, and the emanation of electrons. Significant advances have been made in the area of studying, Psychokinesis on the more difficult static targets (PK-ST). Para-psychological experiments with living targets (PK-LT) involved controlled studies of healing in animals, growth in plants, and activity of enzymes.

Some other studies conducted in the United States, in the Soviet Union, and elsewhere focused on systematic observation of individuals capable of moving objects without touching them, projecting mental pictures onto photographic film, influencing others by hypnosis at a distance, and psychokinetic bending of metals. I am mentioning these here without making any conclusions; this has to be left to researchers and experts in this field. (273).

There is no shortage of good evidence for poltergeist activity, much of it provided by sceptical scientists, professional police officers, and hard-nosed reporters. The phenomenon is the, same all over the world. Things fall off tables, light bulbs drop from their fixtures, liquids are upset, meaningless knocking occurs, stones fly through windows, and taps are left running. These apparently childish tricks often seem to be associated with an adolescent, usually a girl at the stage of puberty or a teen-ager in a stage of emotional adjustment. (274) In one well-known case, a twenty-year-old girl with delicate feelings was just getting involved in married life.

The association of poltergeist activities with a person, rather than a place, is crucial. It suggests that unusual geophysical phenomena, such as a local aberration in gravity, play a less important part than forces of psychological origin. There is an area at the head of the Songe Fjord in Norway and another in the volcanic crater of Kintamani on Bali, where pebbles are not as firmly anchored to the ground as they should be. But investigation, such as George Owens's meticulous study of the Sauchie poltergeist, show that when the central figure in one of these cases moves, the phenomena follow close behind. (275).

Little Sister

The household was small, a man and his wife, their two small boys and the husband's young unmarried half-sister - and it was clear to me from the moment I arrived where the source of trouble lay. The mother and father were typical Tetum, dark-skinned people with curly hair, more Papuan in their appearance than Malay. The children resembled them, but the girl was very different, lighter-skinned with almost Chinese features, which in that community would have made it difficult for her to find a husband. They called her Alin - "little sister" - and treated her with courtesy, but it was plain that she was the odd one out and ended up with most of the dirty work.

I ate with the family that evening, or started to, before things began to happen. We sat on the ground around a rough wooden table in the centre of a large grass-roofed room. There was a fire in an open hearth on one wall and a kerosene lantern on the low table. A dish of grilled fish and maize meal had been placed in front of the father and each of us had a clay cup of sweet tea. Alin was busy at the fire opposite when the eldest boy, about eight years old, screamed and dropped his cup, which broke in two on the table beside me. The back of his right hand began to bleed from fresh punctures that suddenly appeared there in a semi-circle, like the mark of a human bite, but with a diameter larger than his own.

As I was examining the wounds, the lamp flame turned blue and flared up, and in the suddenly brighter light I watched a cascade of salt pour down over the food until the entire dish was covered in the coarse grains and completely inedible. It wasn't a sudden deluge, but a slow and deliberate action which lasted long enough for me to look up and see that it seemed to begin in mid air, just above eye level, perhaps four feet over the table. I stood up immediately and walked round to stand near the fire, from which I could see the whole room. Nobody else moved. But the table did.

There was a slow cracking sound, as though the thick wood was tearing itself apart; silence, then a series of sharp raps, the sound of urgent knocking at a door; then it began to wobble. The family got up in a hurry and we all watched in horror as the heavy table heaved and bucked like the lid on a box containing some wild animal, and finally flipped over on its side and burst into flame as the lamp on it shattered on the floor. And, I am ashamed to say, I joined the others and ran.

We stood outside the door for a while and when nothing further seemed to be happening, the father and I went back in and put out the fire. I had by now recovered some presence of mind and enough scientific curiosity to look very carefully at the table, walls and ceiling for any signs of strings, pulleys and other devices. I found none, nor did I really expect to. Everything I had seen could have been arranged for my benefit, but I was certain by then that 1was watching a typical, if more than usually violent, poltergeist in action. (276).

"Poltergeist" is an old German' world', meaning "noisy spirit", the sort of thing that went bump during medieval nights, but it has never been confined to Germany. Such disturbances seem to have happened during the times of the Emperor Vespasian and Saint Caesarius of Arles; they were recorded in tenth-century China and twelfth-century Wales; and they appear to be perfectly ecumenical, making life equally difficult for Martin Luther and the Bishop of Zanzibar. (277)

In 1948, Nandor Fodor - an Hungarian American psychoanalyst- noticed that several of his patients with unresolved emotional tensions were associated with, or lived in, houses where poltergeist activity had been reported. He saw some of the phenomena, was satisfied that they were genuine, and took to analyzing the poltergeist itself as though it were a disturbed person.'" His diagnosis was one of fear or guilt that had been concealed, and he suggested that deeply repressed drives or conflicts in individuals with hysteric tendencies, could produce "conversion" symptoms and be externalized in some way - perhaps as classical poltergeist phenomena. This diagnosis was particularly convincing in the case of an adolescent boy who was a potentially creative writer oppressed by lack of recognition even from his family, who soon became the victims of inexplicable disturbances and breakages in their home. (278).

--o--

CHAPTER SIXTEEN

TELEPATHY

The Oxford Dictionary defines Telepathy as: 'communication between minds otherwise than by the known senses. It is possible that all of us can communicate in this way although most of us seem to have lost the ability. Even animals and plants can communicate in this way (see elsewhere in this book).

Telepathy has been well demonstrated and it is well known that identical twins communicate in this way particularly in times of distress.

The Russians and Americans are experimenting with telepathic contact with space vehicles (important here because the communication is instantaneous), and with submarines under the sea.

Despite the immense amount of evidence there are still many sceptics who say that it is absolutely whacky.

We would expect that the minds of people who are close to one another and love one another would be even more closely linked. We've all experienced a sense of knowing what's going on with a person we love or knowing what they're thinking or even finishing their sentences.

To learn whether the minds of people close to one another actually are linked, studies have been done with children in the same family. (279)

Tests Performed on TV
One test performed under the intense scrutiny of television cameras was performed in 1997 on a program titled *Carlton TV's Paranormal World of Paul McKenna*. The subjects on this occasion were Elaine and Evelyn Dove.

Elaine sat in the studio in front of a large pyramid. Evelyn was in a separate room sealed off from all communication from outside the room, with electrodes attached to her fingers to measure her stress level. She went through some relaxation exercises and her polygraph showed that she was nicely relaxed.

Meanwhile, in the other room, sealed away from Evelyn, Elaine continued watching the pyramid. Suddenly, without warning, the pyramid exploded in a burst of sparks, flashes and coloured smoke, startling Elaine and giving her a considerable shock. At exactly that moment, Evelyn's polygraph pen recorded a huge swing, with one pen running off the top of the paper. Without trying to communicate with her sister, Evelyn automatically picked up her distress. When asked whether she felt or sensed anything, Evelyn said she experienced nothing out of the ordinary. Her mind outside of the body had communicated to the body and bypassed the brain entirely. (280)

It is widely known that twins communicate telepathically, and when something happens to a twin, the other very often feels the same emotions or pain in exactly the same way even though they can be separated by thousands of miles. A well-known, extensive review of the studies was written by Guy Lyon Playfair. The conclusion of the review of the studies was that here is powerful evidence that twins are joined telepathically through shared emotions, thoughts, tactile sensations, and even physical manifestations such as bruising or burning.

The journal Science published a study by two physiologists who reported finding significant correlations in brain waves between isolated identical twins. These sorts of studies came to be known as Distant Mental Intention on Living Systems (DMILS). (281)

A demonstration of this link between twins was shown before a vast audience on January 10, 2003. Richard. Powles and Damien Powles, identical twins, were invited to a television studio to participate in a telepathy experiment to be shown later that day on a chat show named Channel 4's Richard and Judy Show.

Richard Powles was taken to a soundproof room in the television studio and was asked to sit before a bucket of ice-cold water. In another studio well out of sight and earshot, his identical twin brother Damien was sitting quietly connected to a polygraph machine. Sitting beside Damien was polygrapher Jeremy Barrett, who was monitoring his respiration, abdominal muscles, pulse, and skin conductance. Barrett and Damien had no idea what Richard, in the other room was about to do.

When told to do so, Richard plunged his arm into the bucket of near-freezing water, giving a gasp as he did so.

At the exact moment of Richard's sharp gasp caused by the freezing water, there was a sudden blip on the line monitoring Damien's respiration rate. It was as though he too had gasped, but he actually hadn't. The effect was so obvious that Barrett pointed to it with his thumb to indicate that he knew something had happened to Richard.

They continued the experiment with the twins on the same show. Richard was asked to open a cardboard box placed before him. He did, excitedly, expecting to find something nice (preferably edible) in it. Instead, a huge rubber snake shot out of it at him, giving him a fright. His twin Damien's pulse rate, indicated by the pen on the polygraph shot up at the same moment. (282)

It is Proof that Minds cannot be in the Brain
The ability of twins to link telepathically is a commonly known phenomenon. What is important is that they couldn't link if their minds were confined to the brain. They feel the emotions and pain their twin feels without using any part of the body to receive the feelings. That is further evidence that our minds outside of the body are one.

Contact a distant relative or friend without writing a letter or using a telephone? This may sound improbable, yet it is very possible that all of us can do this on a sub-conscious level a good deal of the time. In fact, such telepathic messages may be received so easily and smoothly that we act on them automatically, without giving them any conscious attention at all. (283)

The Russians have been experimenting with telepathy as a method of communication between Earth and space vehicles. The U.S. government is experimenting in the transmission of telepathic command to volunteers aboard Polaris submarines. Telepathy could conceivably end up as a weapon in some future war.

But what about telepathy (thought transference) in ordinary everyday life? Here are some experiences told to me by a neighbour, a teacher in his thirties. Coincidence is a possible explanation for anyone instance, yet when we consider groups of such happenings, certain patterns seem to present themselves which make coincidence less likely as an explanation.

One weekend morning this neighbour felt a sudden strong impulse to visit his sister. He felt particularly impelled to go to her house for dinner that evening, though she lived forty miles away, and he was not in the habit of making such a trip unless he planned to stay for a longer period of time.

That afternoon he finally decided to make the drive. As he left his apartment, the phone rang and he returned to answer it. His sister was calling him. She asked him to drive down for dinner, saying that she had thought about calling him all morning, but hesitated. She did not think that he would want to make such a long trip for such a short visit. Finally she had decided to call. Apparently in this case, the actual phone call was quite unnecessary. My neighbour had already received the message, and was acting upon it.

A recent definition of telepathy describes it in these terms. "If one individual has access to information not available to another, then under certain circumstances and with known sensory channels rigidly controlled, the second individual can demonstrate knowledge of this information at a higher level than that compatible with the alternative explanation of chance guessing. (284)

Emotional Bonds
There are thousands of records of what seems to be communication of this kind between two people who already have strong emotional bonds. The evidence is largely anecdotal and deals usually with knowledge of crises affecting one member of a pair-husband / wife, parent / child, brother / sister, that is communicated at the time of the occurrence to the other member, somewhere else. Rapport is said to be most effective between identical twins, who suffer the same diseases at the same time and seem to lead very similar lives even when separated at birth. These accounts are interesting but almost impossible to assess in retrospect and offer no real clues as to the nature and origin of telepathy.

The most painstaking attempt to deliberately keep knowledge of a given fact from an individual to see if he could guess the target correctly is the work done by Rhine and his associates at Duke University. They took the public feeling that there was an area of human experience in which people seem to know, by "hunch" or 'intuition," about things that are out of direct reach of eye or ear, and examined it under laboratory conditions, in which the odds against knowing by pure coincidence could be computed. This work began in the early 1930s, when Rhine first used the term extrasensory perception, or ESP, to describe the process and began a lengthy series of tests on card guessing.

Rhine used the Zener pack, which consists of twenty-five cards carrying five symbols: square, circle, cross, star, and wavy lines. In any test the chance score is five out of twenty-five, but in a variety of test situations with a number of subjects, Rhine found that many times scores were so high that they had odds of more than a million to one against chance. On one occasion a nine-year-old girl from an unhappy home scored twenty-three when tested at her school, and when brought into the Duke laboratory by an experimenter to whom she had become emotionally attached, succeeded in guessing all twenty-five cards correctly. A Duke student, Hubert Pearce, became very involved with the research and, when specifically challenged by Rhine to do well in an important test, identified every single card in the pack. These were exceptional results clearly influenced by the personalities involved, and in longer series of the basically monotonous tests both subjects continued to do better than chance, but at the level of only seven or eight out of twenty-five. So most of his research, which has now been going on for almost forty years, is providing telepathic evidence that shows up only in statistics. But even if the margin of success is small, it is so persistent, over tens of millions of tests, that it shows that something is taking place to produce this bias.

The statistical methods used at Duke have been criticized, but the president of the American Institute of Mathematical Statistics says, "If the Rhine investigation is to be fairly attacked it must be on other than mathematical grounds." (285) Spencer-Brown of Cambridge suggests that the deviation from chance may be real, but that it is caused not so much by telepathy as by an as yet unrecognized factor that affects randomness itself. To many other researchers the surprising thing about the statistics is that there should have been any success at all in experiments of this kind. Gaither Pratt describes the card tests as 'a grossly inefficient instrument,' which is "choking off the very function which it was designed to measure." (286) And the Soviet worker Lutsia Pavlova regards the Rhine tests, which involve transmitting a great many bits of information in a short time, as the most difficult way imaginable of trying to generate telepathy. She says, "We find it best not to send signals too quickly. If different bits come too rapidly, the changes in the brain associated with telepathy begin to blur and finally disappear." (287)

Telepathy now widely Accepted

By 1949, telepathy was so widely accepted, even by scientists that Sir Alister Hardy could say, in his presidential address to the zoological section of the British Association: "I believe that no one who examines the evidence with an unbiased mind can reject it" - a statement that would have brought catcalls a century earlier. (288)

The evidence for direct extrasensory contact between human brains is extensive, even if most of it remains anecdotal. Experimental work under controlled conditions has been going on now for over fifty years. Procedures range from the painstaking efforts of J. B. Rhine at Duke

University to make coincidence measurable by restricting response to limited targets such as the five Zener cards; to more refined, and certainly more natural, assessments made on sleeping receivers at the Maimonides "dream laboratory" in Brooklyn. Most such protocols produce statistics that tend to support a telepathic interpretation, but their results come from what psychiatrist Jan Ehrenwald calls "flaw-determined" incidents - those that take place for no very good reason, when there is a temporary or local breakdown of the barrier that normally keeps us from being overwhelmed by stray information. As a biologist, I find these card-guessing tests some-what meaningless. They seem to me to lack significance and survival value.

I am far happier with the incidents which Ehrenwald classifies as "need-determined" - those which occur when communication is vital and ordinary sensory channels are blocked. It is difficult, perhaps impossible, to reproduce such life-threatening situations in a laboratory, but I find the quantity and variety of spontaneous experience from all over the world very persuasive. (289)

Consider just two examples.

In 1930, an English pilot called Hinchcliffe tried to make the first flight across the Atlantic from east to west. It was a distinctive attempt - he had just one eye and his co-pilot was a woman. In mid-Atlantic, two old friends of his were on their way to New York in an ocean liner, unaware that he was making the attempt or that he planned to take anyone with him. Squadron Leader Rivers Oldmeadow was in bed when Colonel Henderson, in his pyjamas, burst in and said:

God, Rivers, something ghastly has happened. Hinch has just been in my cabin. Eye-patch and all. It was ghastly. He kept repeating over and over again, "Hendy, what am I going to do? What am I going to do? I've got the woman with me and I'm lost. I'm lost." Then he disappeared in front of my eyes. Just disappeared. (290)

It was during that night that Hinchliffe and his co-pilot died in a crash. This experience is typical of many in which the need is clear. The information is important and meaningful, and seems to be aimed at someone in particular - even if there is little that the recipient can do to help.

The second account is similar and though less dramatic, is even more convincing because it suggests the existence of a biological connection at an unconscious level.

James Wilson was a student at Cambridge at the time and in the best of health. Except that one evening he suddenly felt extremely ill and started to tremble. He tried to ignore the feeling, but it became so severe that he became convinced that he was dying. He went down to the rooms of a friend, who was alarmed at his appearance and produced a bottle of whisky. After three hours, the feeling passed and Wilson felt well enough to go off to bed. He didn't hear until the next day that his brother had died that that evening 75 miles away in Lincolnshire. (291).

The pioneer primatologist Wolfgang Kohler once said that "a solitary chimpanzee is no chimpanzee." (292) The same is clearly true of human beings, who go to pieces rather rapidly in solitary confinement. But it seems that, in a very real sense, we are never completely alone. There are strange tendrils that reach out, apparently quite independent of time and space, to touch us all, giving us a common experience of reality.

Bad News Travels Quickly
Again, the evidence shows that the most effective telepathic messages involve trauma and crisis and that no news travels so well or so quickly as bad news. Biologically this makes sense. There is no urgency attached to pleasure and well-

being; these are states that can be communicated in the usual leisurely way by normal channels, such as greeting cards, but if alarm signals are going to serve any useful function, they must travel by the fastest possible telegraphic or telepathic route. (293)

Telepathic Communication with Subarines

In 1960 a French magazine splashed the news that the United States Navy was using telepathy to solve the old problem of communication between a submarine under water and its base on the shore. They reported that the atomic submarine Nautilus was in telepathic contact with trained receivers on the shore and that ESP had become a new secret weapon. The American authorities were quick to deny the reports, but the Russians were equally quick to point out that they had been using the system for years. The Soviet method involved rabbits instead of radio. They took newly born rabbits down in a submarine and kept the mother ashore in a laboratory with electrodes implanted deep in her brain. At intervals, the underwater rabbits were killed one by one, and at the precise time that each of her offspring died there were sharp electrical responses in the brain waves of the mother. There is no known physical way in which a submerged submarine can communicate with anyone on land, and yet even rabbits seem to be able to make contact of a kind in a moment of crisis.

The possibility of actually using telepathy as a means of communication to submarines and spaceships has been entertained by both the United States and the U.S.S.R., and in both countries scientists have used the ideas as an instrument to pry more money for research out of their governments. As far as we know, nothing really practical has emerged. The difficulty is that in deep-sea or outer-space exploration, reliability is essential, and nobody has yet managed to produce telepathic contact that works every time and on demand. Perhaps the closest so far is the Kamensky

/ Nikolaiev combination, in which EEC records show when contact is taking place and how long it lasts. Using a Morse signal in which a contact of forty-five seconds is read as a dash and a contact of less than ten seconds as a dot, they have succeeded in getting seven consecutive signals across space to spell out the Russian word MIG, which means "instant." (294)

It seems to me that telepathy, defined as 'access to information held by another without use of the normal sensory channels,' is proved beyond reasonable doubt. It is too much a part both of common experience and of controlled investigation to be dismissed any longer. We now have a great many records of communication taking place outside the normal channels, but still very little idea of how it might operate. (295)

We know a fair amount about how it does not work. Leonid Vasiliev, physiologist at the University of Leningrad, has done a long and painstaking series of experiments in an attempt to track down the telepathic wavelength. He started with two hypnotic subjects that could be put into a trance from a distance by what can only be telepathic means. This provided him with a repeatable phenomenon that could be switched on and off at will and probed and pulled apart to reveal what he hoped would be the physical basis of transmission. He eliminated most of the normal electromagnetic possibilities by putting the subjects into a, Faraday cage, but still they fell asleep on telepathic cue. He built a lead capsule with a lid that sealed itself in a groove filled with mercury, but still the message got through. Finally, when he found that it worked regardless of the distances involved, Vasiliev admitted defeat. (296)

--o--

CHAPTER SEVENTEEN

PSYCHOMETRY

We have already talked about ghosts. Some ghosts you can actually communicate with but there are some ghosts which do not communicate and are more like memories of the past. Psychometry is like that.
It is also a supernormal thing with which I have had some contact myself, as I shall describe later.

Psychometry is the astonishing and recurrent phenomenon of those who can simply touch a garment or some other item to trigger their extraordinary psychic powers to delve into history, locate a missing person, solve a crime, locate a corpse, and even predict where a killer will strike again.

The phenomenon of psychometry and psychic detection has its roots in the extraordinary powers – recorded through history – of those who can 'see' things totally unknown to them as a response to handling an inanimate object. (297)

I was recently talking to a man who is not only a gifted Medium but is also adept at Psychometry. It is not unusual for him to hold an object in his hand and know immediately who owned the object, and to go even further back in time and explain where it had been and who had had it before.

Some artefacts have taken him back thousands of years. He sees the tribe and their surroundings; he even recognizes ancient languages and hieroglyphs. His abilities have been used by museums where, sometimes, what he says contradicts what they had previously thought to be the case. They have slowly learned that when there are such differences he inevitably turns out to be correct.

I am amazed at what is stored on a memory stick but it is even more amazing to think what can be stored in the everyday objects around us.

When my wife and I were living in Saudi Arabia, we travelled once to a place called Al Kharj. It was a small town, but a town with a lot of history.

Our look around Al Kharj took us to an old, broken down, palace. I found the place very interesting and, before we even got inside the building, we unearthed a lot of old leather bullet pouches.

Eventually we moved inside the building. It had a high, long, central gallery which ran right down the length of the building. It was cluttered with rubble and bits and pieces of military equipment.

I moved eagerly forward anxious to explore what there was there until I realized that Margaret was no longer walking behind me. I turned back. She was twenty-five yards behind me and she looked terrified. I hurried back to her side and put my arm around her.

"What is it?" I asked.

"It's all these soldiers milling around carrying weapons."
I looked around. The place was quiet and I could see no one. We hurried out of the place and, once outside, she relaxed.

"There were lots and lots of them," she said, when we got outside.

I never knew Margaret to have any psychic experience before or after that, but she certainly did on that day.

As the man gazed off into space, the room he was in became ghostly and transparent, and in its place materialized a scene from the distant past. Suddenly he was in the courtyard of a palace, and before him was a young woman, olive-skinned and very pretty. He could see her gold jewelry around her neck, wrists, and ankles, her white translucent dress, and her black braided hair gathered regally under a high square-shaped tiara. As he looked at her, information about her life flooded his mind. He knew she was Egyptian, the daughter of a prince, but not a pharaoh. She was married. Her husband was slender and wore his hair in a multitude of small braids that fell down on both sides of his face.

He Fast- Forwards the memories like a Movie
The man could also fast-forward the scene, rushing through the events of the woman's life as if they were no more than a movie. He saw that she died in childbirth. He watched the lengthy and intricate steps of her embalming, her funeral procession, the rituals that accompanied her being placed in her sarcophagus, and when he finished, the images faded and the room once again came back into view.

The man's name was Stefan Ossowiecki, a Russian-born Pole and one of the century's most gifted clairvoyants, and the date was February 14, 1935. His vision of the past had been evoked when he handled a fragment of a petrified human foot.

Ossowiecki proved so adept at psychometrizing artifacts that he eventually came to the attention of Stanislaw

Poniatowski, a professor at the University of Warsaw and the most eminent ethnologist in Poland at the time. Poniatowski tested Ossowiecki with a variety of flints and other stone tools obtained from archaeological sites around the world. Most of these *lithics*, as they are called, were so nondescript that only a trained eye could tell they had been shaped by human hands. They were also pre certified by experts so that Poniatowski knew their ages and historical origins, information he kept carefully concealed from Ossowiecki.

It did not matter. Again and again Ossowiecki identified the objects correctly, describing their age, the culture that had produced them, and the geographical locations where they had been found. On several occasions the locations Ossowiecki cited disagreed with the information Poniatowski had written in his notes, but Poniatowski discovered that it was always his notes that were in error, not Ossowiecki's information.

Ossowiecki always worked the same. He would take the object in his hands and concentrate until the room before him, and even his own body, became shadowy and almost nonexistent. After this transition occurred, he would find himself looking at a three-dimensional movie of the past. He could then go anywhere he wanted in the scene and see anything he chose. While he was gazing into the past, Ossowiecki even moved his eyes back and forth as if the things he was describing possessed an actual physical presence before him.

He could see the vegetation, the people, and the dwellings in which they lived. On one occasion, after handling a stone implement from the Magdalenian culture, a Stone Age people who flourished in France about 15,000 to 10,000 B.C., Ossowiecki told Poniatowski that Magdalenian women had very complex hair styles. At the time this seemed absurd, but subsequent discoveries of statues of

Magdalenian women with ornate coiffures proved Ossowiecki right.

Over the course of the experiments Ossowiecki offered over one hundred such pieces of information, details about the past that at first seemed inaccurate, but later proved correct. He said that in the Stone Ages they used oil lamps. That was vindicated when excavations in Dordogne, France, uncovered oils lamps of the exact size and style he'd described. He made detailed drawings of the animals various peoples, the style of the huts in which they lived, and their burials, assertions that were all later confirmed by archaeological discoveries. (298).

His sister, Anne Cridge, seemed a suitable subject for experiment, since she was 'highly impressible'. Denton began by trying Buchanan's experiments with letters. Mrs. Cridge revealed herself to be an excellent psychometrist; 'She saw and described the writers of letters she was examining, and their surroundings, telling at times even the colour of hair and eyes correctly.'

The next step was to try her with a geological specimen. Denton selected a piece of limestone which he had picked up near Quindaro, Kansas, on the Missouri River; it was full of tiny fossil shells. His sister was not told anything about the specimen, and it was wrapped in paper so she could not tell what it was. Her response was:

"It seems to me there is a deep hole here. Oh, what shells! Small shells; so many. I see water; it looks like a river running along. What a high hill! almost perpendicular; it seems as if the water had cut it in two; it is not so high on the other side. The hill is covered with sand and graves."

This was an excellent beginning. Denton admitted that, as far as his memory served him, it was a very accurate description. This piece of rock had taken in the pictures of the turbid Missouri that swept past it, the hill that hung over it, and the country in general around it, and, to the eye of the psychometer, they became apparently as plainly visible as to a spectator on the spot.

His wife, Elizabeth Denton, also proved to be a good psychometer. When he handed her a piece of quartz from Panama, she received an impression of a huge insect, with antennae' nearly a foot long, resting its head against a quartz rock, and could see a snake coiled in the wiry grass. She remarked that the country seemed much warmer than North America, with tropical vegetation.

She sees Boiling Lava Pouring into the Sea

These experiments were encouraging. But the result of the next was spectacular. He handed his sister a fragment of volcanic lava from Kilauea, on Hawaii, wrapped in paper. Mrs Cridge had an impression of an ocean, with ships sailing on it, and could tell that it was an island. Then she saw 'an ocean of fire pouring over a precipice and boiling as it poured. I see it flow into the Ocean, and the water boils intensely.' The vision was so real that it shattered her nerves, and the feeling of fear remained for the next hour. Denton knew that the piece of lava had, in fact, been ejected in the eruption of 1840, so the vision of ships was probably accurate.

At this point, Denton took a precaution which reveals that he was a genuine scientist, determined to rule out all possibility of auto-suggestion. He tried wrapping several specimens in separate sheets of paper, then mixing them up, so he had no idea which was which. Then he handed his wife one of them. She had a vision of a volcano, with molten lava flowing down its side. 'The specimen must be lava," said Mrs Denton, and she was right.

Denton was understandably elated, 'from the first dawn of light upon the infant globe, when round its cradle the steamy curtains hung, to this moment, Nature had been busy photographing every moment.' It was – and is – a perfectly reasonable hypothesis. We now know that matter and energy are the same frozen energy. Energy from space - light, heat, cosmic rays - fall upon us in a continuous cosmic hail, knocking electrons from the surface of everything it strikes. Light failing on a sheet of metal 'evaporates' electrons as sunlight evaporates a sheet of water, producing the 'photoelectric effect', an electric current. So there can be no doubt that everything that happens in daylight is 'photographed' by the surrounding objects. (299).

Lodge suggested that strong emotions could be unconsciously recorded in matter, so that on a psychometric hypothesis the original tragedy had been literally photographed on its material surroundings and thenceforth in certain persons an hallucinatory effect is experienced corresponding to such an impression. That comment: 'in certain persons', is important. Mrs Sidgwick records a number of cases in which one or more people have seen a 'ghost' while others who were there at the same time saw nothing. (300).

Some days later, Denton decided to try her again. This time she immediately saw a distinctly Roman scene, with a large building with pillars and steps leading up to it. In a room with uncomfortable furniture ('if furniture it can be called') the walls were hung with crimson velvet. She saw lines of helmeted soldiers, then a 'fleshy man with a broad face and blue eyes'. He wore a 'dress like a gown' (presumably a toga). 'He is majestic yet has a good deal of geniality about him too. He regards himself as superior, and withdraws from others. It seems to me that he has something to do with those troops'. (301)

The Porcelain Tower in China
When Denton handed his wife a fragment of the Porcelain Tower, near Peking, he knew nothing whatever about it,

except that it came from a place called the Porcelain Tower in China. His wife described a place like a temple, with massive walls and large urns; she saw a bell-shaped roof and a spire. After writing down her description, Denton checked in the Iconographic Encyclopedia to find out what the Porcelain Tower was used for (for all he knew, it was simply a monument like the leaning tower of Pisa). He discovered that it was a temple, with walls twelve feet thick.

If we can make the assumption that Denton's own knowledge of the objects had no telepathic influence on the psychometrist, then the experiments he describes in the first volume of *The Soul of Things* are stunningly impressive. Again and again they were able to pin down the place from which the object came. A piece of a limestone slab from Nineveh brought an impression of a vast temple; a Greek coin (kept unseen) brought a detailed description of the mint; a piece of curtain from the House of Representatives brought a large council chamber, and an impression of some members talking glibly and superficially; a piece of sandstone from Melrose Abbey in Scotland brought a description of an abbey with arched doorways, Gothic windows and an aisle. Three months later, Mrs Denton was handed the fragment a second time, with no knowledge that she had handled it before. Again she saw arches and a 'place of worship', but this time with some conference going on there. 'These people are ignorant and bigoted.' A check with an encyclopedia revealed that Melrose Abbey was 'usually involved in the rancorous events of border feud and international war'. ('Ignorant and bigoted' is an admirable description of the Scottish religious temperament of earlier centuries.) A piece of mosaic from a Roman bath brought a detailed description of a Roman bath, with an atmosphere of gaiety and voluptuousness'.

A Description of Pompeii
A piece of mosaic from Pompeii brought an interesting description of an ancient town with narrow streets, and a

populace in the grip of war fever; Denton had hoped for some mention of the destruction of Pompeii. But a piece of volcanic rock from Pompeii brought far more satisfying results. It was the size of a small bean, and the psychometer was not allowed to see it. (Denton does not explain how he did this, but presumably it was wrapped in paper or cloth.) Mrs Denton saw coloured figures on a wall - frescoes - and observed that the building overlooked the sea. Out of the window, she could look towards the mountaintop, and see smoke and cinders rising up in a column. The black cloud of dust was spreading across the countryside. From a situation higher up the mountain she was able to observe the eruption. 'I feel the influence of human terror that I cannot describe.' The land below finally became a desert of cinders. Watching crowds fleeing from Pompeii (in fact, most of the population escaped before the final catastrophe) she is surprised that it resembles a modern town more than she had expected.

One interesting observation was that the volcano had also vomited water. In fact, Pompeii was engulfed by a kind of mud, not by molten lava. Bodies found encased in the hardened material were unscorched. A description of the eruption by Pliny the Younger describes a tree-like column of smoke rising from the volcano, then spreading out like branches ~ or a mushroom-cloud ~ which then descended and covered the town. Elizabeth Denton's description was startlingly close.

Almost a decade later, Denton returned to the subject of Pompeii. By now, his son Sherman was in his mid-teens; he had been practicing psychometry since he was a child, and was in some ways more sensitive than his mother. The tests Denton conducted occupy more than fifty pages of his second volume, and they provide a remarkably rich and complex picture of life in Pompeii.

Sherman's first session - with a piece of plaster from the 'House of Sallust' - immediately brought one remarkable 'hit'. Over a doorway, Sherman 'saw' a painting of two winged children drawing a cart with another winged child riding in it. Denton later discovered an engraving of the painting in a book on Pompeii (which, he insists, neither he nor Sherman saw before the test), and he reproduces it in his text.

When Sherman spoke of wide streets, Denton was dubious; most streets in Pompeii were hardly six feet across. But he later discovered that the House of Sallust was not in the residential section, but on a square, in an area with wide streets. Sherman described a Pompeiian boat with a prow like a swan's head and neck. Denton found engravings from nearby Herculaneum (also engulfed in the eruption) of the *cheniscus*, a birdlike head and neck attached to the prow of Roman vessels.

Sherman also comments: 'The labouring people seem to hate the rich. Where there are a number of them together, the rich pass them quickly, and seem to regard them as a man would a snake.' Denton makes no attempt to verify this statement. But from a modern book, *Pompeii and Herculaneum* (1960) by Marcel Brion, we learn that the walls of Pompeii contained such graffiti as 'This city is too rich' and 'I propose a share-out of the public wealth among the inhabitants'. The attitude of the rich must have added fuel to this feeling of social injustice; in the hall of the House of Vedius Siricus there was an inscription, *Salve Lucrum* - 'Hail, Profit!' It also, comments Brion, meant 'Welcome to, money', addressed as a welcome to other moneyed people who came to the house. 'The Pompeiians, it becomes clear, took money-making very seriously indeed. In her earlier examination of a fragment from Pompeii, Mrs Denton had commented on the difference she sensed between the Pompeiians and the ancient Egyptians: that for the Egyptians, religion was inherent in their way of life, while for the Pompeiians, it was largely a matter of forms and observances. But the wealthy had statues of Mercury in their houses to bring luck to their business and ward off evil spirits that might harm it. 'Hail, profit!'

Another of Sherman's comments was that women seemed to play a prominent part in the life of Pompeii; Brion remarks that in Pompeii the women took a hand in business; even a rich woman advertised that she had shops to let.

Sherman's description of a theatrical performance makes it sound more like a circus with clowns and acrobats, and makes no mention of the kind of things a modem reader would expect- comedies by Plautus, Statius and Terence, Greek tragedies and so on. Denton remarks that his son's description of acrobats and comics sounds very modern. But Marcel Brion comments that the favourite form of dramatic entertainment at this time was the *atellanae*, popular farces that took their name from their town of origin, Atella; originally intended to relax the audience after performance of tragedies, they became so popular that they were performed on their own. Brion says of these performances: (they might be compared to music hall numbers of a rather low level), interspersed with dancing, clowning, obscenities, feats of skill and athletic exhibitions, the whole ending with a procession of nude girls'. Apart from the nude girls (which Denton would no doubt have censored out), this is a fairly accurate summary of Sherman Denton's lengthy description of a theatrical performance in Pompeii. (302).

A bloodhound can detect the traces of a particular person in a room long after he has left it, perhaps even after he has died elsewhere. The psychometrist claims to do the same, but not by smell. If a healer changes the structure of water just by holding it in his hand for half an hour, what effect does he have on a wristwatch he wears for half a lifetime? If a barley seed can tell the difference between ordinary and handled water, is it unreasonable to assume that a man can distinguish a brand-new object, untouched by human hand, from one that has been fondled for twenty years? I believe that there are differences and that they are discernible, but proving this is another matter. There have been casual tests made by presenting objects for psychometry in sealed containers, but no good, controlled investigation has yet been made. I predict that when one is, it will provide evidence of our ability to detect traces of human contact with things, but that there will be a limit to the amount of information we can get in this way. A fox can tell from traces on a tree not only that there is a male in the territory but who he is and what he last had to eat. Our territorial displays are now predominantly visual: the initials carved on the tree include a date and perhaps even an address, but there must have been a time when early man, with a comparatively poor sense of smell, could have made good use of a talent such as psychometry. (303). There are people today who claim to be able to tell the sex of the person who last used a particular Stone Age hand axe. This might once have been a very useful piece of information.

Robert Pavlita Discovers Strange Properties

The nearest we can get to some sort of understanding of psychometry is an extraordinary series of experiments still going on in Czechoslovakia. They began with Robert Pavlita, design director of a textile plant near Prague. He invented a new weaving process that was so successful he could afford to retire and devote all his attention to his hobby of metallurgy. This continued until he discovered that an alloy of a particular shape had strange properties. If handled often, it seemed to accumulate energy and to attract even non-magnetic objects. This sounds like electrostatic energy, which can be built up by friction in amber until it is strong enough to pick up paper, but static electricity does not work underwater-and Pavlita's 'generator' does.

He took it to the physics department at Hradec Kralove University. There they sealed it on his instructions into a metal box alongside a small fan driven by an electric motor. Pavlita stood six feet away and did no more than stare hard at his generator. After a while the blade on the fan began to slow down, as though the current had been cut off; then it stopped altogether and began to rotate in the opposite direction (304). For two years the department worked with him to try to unravel the mystery, but got nowhere. It has nothing to do with static electricity, air currents, temperature changes, or magnetism, but it works, and they now have a whole collection of generators in a variety of shapes that look like miniature metal sculptures by Brancusi. All of them have the same inexplicable ability to store energy from a particular person that can be released later to do a particular job, such as driving an electric motor.

At this point the government stepped in and appointed the physiologist Zdenek Rejdak to investigate the claims. He could find no indications of fraud and continued to work with Pavlita. Together they produced a generator shaped like a doughnut that killed flies placed inside the ring; then they went on to build a square one that accelerated the growth of bean seeds when placed in a pan of soil. And finally they turned out a small one that could be dropped into water polluted by factory effluent and would leave it crystal clear in a short while. An official chemical analysis of the water concluded that it could not have been purified with a chemical agent and added the splendid comment that the molecular structure of the water was slightly altered. Again this fact crops up, and we find reactions working first on the instability of the universal trigger substance-water.

So far the only theory put out about the generators is that their secret lies in the form, which is critical and that only one configuration can produce a particular effect. These developments are very difficult to follow from a distance since, as yet, no details of any of the generators have been published, but Pavlita has said that he got his original description and inspiration from an ancient manuscript, and we know that the libraries of Prague abound in untranslated and unexplored texts of the alchemists.

In 1941, Stanislaw Poniatowski, Professor of Ethnology at the University of Warsaw, handed a small stone to an elderly Pole. For twenty minutes, Stefan Ossowiecki felt the object, rolling it over and clasping it in his hand, and then he spoke:

"I see very well, it is part of a spear. I see round houses, wooden, covered with grey clay, over walls of animal hide ...People with black hair, enormous feet, large hands, low fore-heads, eyes deeply set."

He went on for an hour, giving a detailed view of the daily life, dress, appearance and behaviour of a Palaeolithic people; including an account of their ritual use of red ochre and lime as cosmetics, and a description of a cremation ceremony. All of which was totally appropriate for a projectile point identified by the Warsaw Museum as belonging to the fifteen-thousand-year-old Magdalenian culture (305).

Ossowiecki was murdered by the Gestapo in 1944, but he was tested further during the war years with another thirty-two assorted objects from the Museum - including stone tools, bone fishhooks and ceramic figurines. And in each case he provided vivid panoramic descriptions that read like eye-witness accounts of communities and technologies ranging from half-a-million-year-old Acheulian times, through Mousterian, Aurignacian and Neanderthal cultures, to the present day. These accounts were stimulated by objects that only experts could be sure to recognize, and were supported by further complementary detail when the same object was given to him again at a later date. Despite the fact that Ossowiecki was a chemical engineer with no conscious interest in prehistoric archaeology, his descriptions are not only consistent with what was then known about the cultures in question, but sometimes included information that has only come to light as a result of discoveries made since he died. (306)

Maria Zierold
He was not the only one with such a talent. In the early 1920s, a German physician in Mexico discovered that one of his patients, Maria Zierold, was able to do something similar under hypnosis. She was particularly good at describing the recent history of fragments of pumice stone that seemed to soak up impressions like sponges and release them to her later." She was officially tested by Walter Prince, President of the American Society for Psychical Research, with a number of objects sealed in envelopes and shuffled so that even he did not know which one she would receive. Zierold never opened any of the envelopes, but nevertheless described one as a farewell message from a man on a sinking ship, and she described the man. The object was in fact a piece of paper with a message found in a bottle washed up on the Azores – and when the man's widow was later contacted, she confirmed that the description of her husband was accurate, right down to the scar over his right eyebrow. And in the most impressive demonstration of all, Zierold held a sealed envelope containing a letter sent to Prince from a clergyman friend and, once again without opening it, she gave him thirty-eight pieces of information about the sender. This was information neither contained in the letter nor known to Prince, but which he was later able to verify (307).

More recently, the Dutch clairvoyant Gerard Croiset has demonstrated a comparable talent. In 1953, working with nothing more than a tiny fragment of bone, he described a cave, its inhabitants, its surroundings and a religious ceremony connected with it - astonishing the Dean of the University of the Witwatersrand who, having brought the relic from a cave in Lesotho, could vouch for the accuracy of the "reading".

This odd ability to "read" an object's world line like a book, has in it a suspicion of telepathy and clairvoyance but it is better and more precisely described as "psychometry" - which literally means "measurements made by the mind". The term was coined in 1893 and has since fallen into disrepute with parapsychologists who, fearing that it might be confused with "psychometrics" – which describes the general application of mathematics to psychology -prefer to talk instead of "token-object reading".

I don't think that does it justice. It is a talent that is virtually ignored by most modern researchers, which is a pity, because there is far more to it than a clinical test with a token. I find that psychometry is one of those bridging phenomena that helps to knit together a number of other loose ends in experience of the paranormal.

For a start, it provides easy experimental access to a faculty which seems to operate in the same strange void as mind and memory. We know from studies of learning that memory seizes most readily on items that are recent, frequent or vivid. Psychometry seems to do the same, most often picking up traces of events which have just happened, or have happened very often, or which have a strong emotional connection. When psychic Eileen Garrett was once asked to "read" a box containing a cuneiform tablet, she gave a vivid and unmistakable description of the secretary who was the last person to handle it before the test (308) But with most antique objects, it is more usual to get accounts of things like richly emotive ceremonies. And if the object is a room or a house, the dominant impression will not be of any of the everyday conversations which must have taken place there, but will concentrate on the one murder or rape with which it might be associated.

Unlikely as it may sound, it begins to look as though information about past events can indeed be stored in physical objects. And if this is true, then it is not impossible that memory, in its intricate dance with the environment, leaves similar traces on, or interacts with the physical world in ways which are perceptible to all of us, even if it is only a few active psychometrists who can bring these cues to conscious attention.

Do We All Have the Ability?
I suspect that we all do enjoy something of the sort. It has never been put to the test, but I would be willing to bet that a majority of subjects, chosen at random and blindfold, could just by holding a ring or wristwatch in their hands, distinguish one worn constantly for years, from another identical but unworn object.

It is part of common experience too that some objects have a good "feel". They carry what amounts to a patina laid down by events with which they have become associated. Dealers in antiques, of course, exercise their own special discernment in these things, but when it comes to discriminating between superb fakes and the real things, all rely in the end on a very personal assessment of whether or not an object "feels right".

--o--

CHAPTER EIGHTEEN

CHILDREN

Jesus said, "I tell you the truth, anyone who will not receive the kingdom of God like a little child will never enter it."
*There is no doubt that children are special in so many different ways. Lyall Watson once watched a 3 year old girl bend a shanked key after watching Yuri Geller on TV. She didn't realize that it was against the laws of nature. No doubt she would lose that ability later when she discovered that it **was** against the laws of physics.*
Many young, children see and hear invisible playmates. Again, that is something which they lose later when they discover adults consider it negative.

Perception is Artificial

Children as a whole are usually more open to the true natures of things. Their experience, according to pioneer psychologist 'William James' is "a blooming , buzzing, confusion", which only settles into formal patterns as we mature and learn to construct a personal view which is more socially acceptable. But we should never lose sight of the fact that this perception is essentially artificial. As psychologist Robert Ornstein points out, "Nothing sacred occurs in nature between the electromagnetic wavelengths of 380 and 370 billionths of a metre, yet we can perceive one and not the other. (309)

What is still more exciting is that through meditation techniques it is possible to sit down in a quiet and secure spot, relax, and then attune to the higher planes and let the astral body travel. Remember, the levels of mind and soul are contained in the astral body so that they, too, are out of the body. This allows direct mental contact with intelligences on the astral plane. Not only can such contact vastly increase the knowledge available to the meditator, but it can also bring to him the increased wisdom that can be gleaned from much older and wiser souls.

Often small children insist that they see and hear other children or playmates which are invisible to adults. When they get older they seem to grow out of this. Are their 'playmates' a figment of their imagination?

Most certainly not! We have recently learned that up until the age of six or seven, the eyes of many children can see light at wavelengths considerably shorter than those detected by the eyes of adults. But they also have a high sensitivity to energies outside our known electromagnetic spectrum. Sensitivity to this latter type of energy in adults is possessed only by those relatively rare individuals who are known as clairaudients and clairvoyants (310).

This is also the conclusion reached by many NDE researchers. One such researcher is Dr. Melvin Morse, a pediatrician in Seattle, Washington. Morse first became interested in NDEs after treating a seven-year-old drowning victim. By the time the little girl was resuscitated she was profoundly comatose, had fixed and dilated pupils, no muscle reflexes, and no corneal response. In medical terms this gave her a Glasgow Coma Score of three, indicating that she was in a coma so deep she had almost no chance of ever recovering. Despite these odds, she made a full recovery and when Morse looked in on her for the first time after she regained consciousness she recognized him and said that she had watched him working on her comatose body. When Morse questioned her further she explained that she had left her body and passed through a tunnel into heaven where she had met "the Heavenly Father." The Heavenly Father told her she was not really meant to be there yet and asked if she wanted to stay or go back. At first she said she wanted to stay, but when the Heavenly Father pointed out that that decision meant she would not be seeing her mother again, she changed her mind and returned to her body.

Morse was sceptical but fascinated and from that point on set out to learn everything he could about NDES. At the time, he worked for an air transport service in Idaho that carried patients to the hospital, and this afforded him the opportunity to talk with scores of resuscitated children. Over a ten-year period he interviewed every child survivor of cardiac arrest at the hospital, and over and over they told him the same thing. After going unconscious they found themselves outside their bodies, watched the doctors working on them, passed through a tunnel and were comforted by luminous beings

Morse continued to be sceptical, and in his increasingly desperate search for some logical explanation he read everything he could find on the side effects of the drugs his patients were taking, and explored various psychological explanations, but nothing seemed to fit. "Then one day I read a long article in a medical journal that tried to explain NDEs as being various tricks of the brain," says Morse. "By then I had studied NDEs extensively and none of the explanations that this researcher listed made sense. It was finally clear to me that he had missed the most obvious explanation of all- NDEs are real. He had missed the possibility that the soul really does travel" (311).

Children commonly see things with enormous clarity. It is possible that what we call hallucinations are a normal part of every child's psychic experience (their paintings seem to show this), but as we grow older our visions are dimmed and eventually suppressed altogether, because they come to have a negative social value. Each society lays down certain guide-lines of what constitutes sanity, and by a combination of these cultural pressures and our own needs for acceptance and conformity, most of us end up inside these prescribed limits. A few break out and are classified insane and deprived of their freedom on the grounds that they need to be taken care of, but in fact their confinement is designed far more to protect society than to save these individuals from themselves. The Soviet Union makes no bones about this and regularly certifies troublesome dissenters on the grounds that they must be mad if they don't agree with the State. A few individuals manage to shake off the restrictions of sanity and get away with it, because they do so within the sphere of a religion in which such revolutionary activities are permissible because they have been labeled "divinely inspired." Far from being confined, many of the people who have had this kind of transcendental experience return to society with a new view of things and proceed to change their way of life and ours; not always for the best (312).

I reserve judgment on Geller, because I have never examined him personally under controlled conditions. But there is no doubt in my mind about our joint ability as a species to do in private the things he appears to do on stage. I have watched a three-year-old child, while sitting on my lap, bend a long-shanked key that I wasn't strong enough to restore to its original shape. She did this after watching a video of Geller doing it - and because no one had yet explained to her that by doing so she might be violating the laws of nature, destroying our view of the world, or condemning scientists everywhere to the whims of a hostile and in-comprehensible universe. I sincerely doubt that she will be able to go on doing so when she is older and wiser in the ways of our world (313)

A Child has no concept of Death

A child under the age of two has no concept of death, and from two to five years, the child has a limited understanding that death is when the body stops moving. However, NDEs are described as occurring to infants and young children who have a different concept of death and have not yet experienced ego differentiation. Pediatric nephrologists from Massachusetts General describe a childhood NDE in which the child suffered a cardiac arrest from renal failure at 8 months of age and began to articulate her NDE at age 3. She described going into a tunnel and seeing a bright light (314).

Melvin Morse, Associate Professor of Pediatrics, University of Washington School of Medicine, Seattle Children's Hospital, presents another report of an NDE involving a child described by Gabbard and Twemlow (315).

Todd was age 2 years 5 months old when he bit into an electric cord from a vacuum cleaner. Medical records stated that he was in ventricular asystole with no spontaneous respirations for approximately 25 minutes. After his resuscitation, he slowly recovered cortical and neurologic functions over the next 4 to 6 months. At age 33 months, he was playing in the living room when his mother asked him about biting into the cord. He stated: "I went into a room with a very nice man and sat with him. (The room) had a big bright light in the ceiling. The man asked if I wanted to stay or come back with you." He then looked up at his mother and stated: "I wanted to be back with you and come home." He then smiled and went back to playing with his toys. This occurred in 1972, before the publication of Raymond Moody's book [naming and describing near-death experiences. (316)

Mature Spiritually by becoming more like a Child
The first requirement for maturing spiritually is that you become humble and naively open, like a child. You must have a child's willingness to grow into spiritual adulthood without expectations and plans, just as a child grows inexorably into physical and emotional adulthood not knowing what an adult mind and life will be like.

You must be willing to clean out the closet of your mind and throw out all the old assumptions and perspectives that no longer fit you, transforming your mind with new assumptions and perspectives you likely don't even know about right now, but that will fit who you are becoming spiritually.

In other words, you must be willing to release your grip on assumptions that were called "right" and "commonsense" and "righteous" and "godly" and all the other words our parents, teachers, and clergy used to enforce the assumptions you learned from society in the physical realm. When you let go, you will find materializing in your open hands what the Higher Power has brought to you to replace what you released. But you won't know what that is until you receive it.

You are becoming a new person. You don't know what that person will be like, just as when you were 10 years old you didn't know the adult you would become. You couldn't know. For this person to come into your life, you have to be willing to allow yourself to be different, but you don't know what that difference will be.

If you are confident that you have arrived at the correct answers about religious practices and have the knowledge that is Truth for everyone in the universe then you run the risk of being deluded, just as a drunk person doesn't realize her drunkenness. When a person insists she has the Truth about existence for everyone, she likely does not realize her own ignorance. That isn't to say you shouldn't have convictions such as the need to live in brotherhood and peace, and the reality of the afterlife. It just means that with some other issues, such as religious practices, the influence of spirits on people, methods of growing spiritually, and so on, you should, at times, go through periods of reexamination and doubt. If you have no periods of self-doubt and reexamination, you may very possibly be shutting down your openness to new perspectives.

Many children have mediumistic ability because they are more open and naive, but they lose it as they grow older and become more jaded. Poltergeists are often associated with children and adolescents because of this latent medium ability the poltergeists can draw from it to act in the physical realm.

We must all learn to be like children.

--o--

CHAPTER NINETEEN

HYPNOTISM

> *Hypnosis is certainly one of the more unusual things in life and, as yet, it remains completely unexplained. It can be produced by a wide range of stimuli including the firing of a gun, or by stroking or singing.*
>
> *Hypnotized subjects can do all kinds of unusual things including remote viewing and observing things going on behind them. The list is endless.*
>
> *Myself, I am particularly impressed by the man looking right through his daughter and reading the inscription on a watch.*
>
> *Yes, it really is weird!!*

The process of animal hypnosis has been called catatonia, catalepsy, thanatosis, akinesis, and action inhibition; in man it has been known as mesmerism, animal magnetism, somnambulism, reverie, and druidic sleep. In neither case is there any evidence that hypnosis has anything at all to do with normal sleep, but there is widespread disagreement about exactly what hypnosis is.

Leon Chertok, Director of the Paris Institute of Psychiatry, believes that it is a fourth organismic state, which can be added to waking, sleeping, and dreaming (317) It certainly differs in several respects from each of these three states of being, but the difficulty is that although hypnosis is held to be a genuine condition, nobody has yet come up with a satisfactory definition of it. Ivan Pavlov, the celebrated Soviet psychologist, thought that it was a defense mechanism that is similar in many ways to sleep (318). He induced it in dogs by delaying the presentation of food for a long time after the sounding of the signal that the animals had come to associate with food. The dogs' tense expectation often led to catatonic states so severe that they could not move even when food was finally presented. Anatol Milechnin, a Uruguayan physician, uses this and other evidence to support his theory that hypnosis is an emotional reaction that can be produced either by shock techniques, such as the sudden firing of a gun, or by tranquilizing stimuli, such as stroking or soft singing (319).

The British psychiatrist Stephen Black combines both these ideas into the notion that hypnosis could be a reflex conditioned in very early life (320). He suggests that during development of the egg in the uterus an animal is physically restricted and must remain relatively immobile, and that forcible restriction in later life produces a return to this condition of inaction. It is certainly true that most animals, when put into a trance state, or feigning death, do adopt a fetal posture. This theory could also explain why rhythmic stimuli produce hypnosis.

The dominant sound and sensation throughout an embryo's life is the continuous rhythmic beat of its mother's heart, and after birth it is most easily tranquilized either by being held close to its mother's left breast, where it can hear the heart, or by a metronome or a cradle that moves at seventy-two cycles per minute the same rate as the pulse (321). The hypnotic effect of solid-beat music and the trancelike state of some dancers can be explained in the same way.

Alexis Didier

A young Frenchman named Alexis Didier could go into a hypnotic trance, then tell visitors where they had been, what they had been doing, and what their homes looked like. This could have been telepathy; but on one occasion, he was able to tell an official whose clerk had absconded with the funds that the man had gone to Belgium, and to describe his route in detail; he was also able to predict, correctly, that when the man was arrested he would have gambled away all the money. The psychologist Pierre Janet was able to hypnotize one of his patients- a woman called Leonie - at a distance of several miles by merely thinking about her, and induce her to come to his house. The Russian L. L. Vasiliev later demonstrated that distance was unimportant, and hypnotized some of his own patients at a distance of thousands of miles. Dr. Julian Ochorowitz studied a woman who, under hypnosis, could describe what was going on behind her back, and other subjects who could correctly call out the identity of cards that they could not see (322).

Thomson Jay Hudson started from the observation that people under hypnosis can often perform feats that would be impossible for them in a state of wakefulness. He was present in Boston when Professor William B. Carpenter placed a young man, whom he calls C - in a state of trance, then told him that he was about to introduce him to the spirit of Socrates. C looked awestricken, and bowed reverently to an empty chair. At Carpenter's request, he then proceeded to hold a conversation with Socrates and to ask him questions. Carpenter explained that he was unable to hear what Socrates said, and Asked C to repeat it aloud. The result astonished everybody. C proceeded to expound 'a wonderful system of spiritual philosophy'. 'It was so clear, so plausible, and so perfectly consistent with itself and the known laws of Nature that the company sat spellbound through it all, each one almost persuaded that he was listening to a voice from the other world. In fact, some people present became convinced that C really was talking with the ghost of Socrates.

C was introduced to the spirits of many later philosophers. His manner changed with each one, and the ideas were presented in the language appropriate to the philosopher. 'If the person themselves had been present,' says Hudson, 'their distinctive peculiarities could not have been more marked.' And the philosophy expounded continued to be impressive - Hudson calls it 'one of the grandest and most coherent systems of spiritual philosophy ever conceived by the brain of man'.

Once Mesmerism had been thrice condemned by the French Academy of Sciences, it took a brave man to bring the matter up again. But this is exactly what a young lecturer in philosophy and psychology did in 1878 - at the same time moving the study in a new and interesting direction.

Pierre Janet insisted that there was more to being hypnotized than a simple physiological response and determined to find evidence of higher activity. In one fascinating case, he presented a subject with a number of blank white cards and induced the hallucination of a portrait on one of them. He then shuffled the cards, dealt them out on the table and asked his subject to pick out the one with the "portrait". She was always able to do so without hesitation, no matter how well the blank target card was mixed in with large numbers of others, or how often the imaginary picture was shifted by suggestion to other cards. (323)

I have tried to duplicate this experiment of Janet's several times - and it works. The reason it does so is that attention during suggestion becomes so acute that, while imagining a face on the target, the subject becomes aware of the most minute peculiarities in the card itself. Even if the experimenter does not know where the target lies, subjects are able to pick out the appropriate card by tiny markings on it, or by a microscopic defect at its edge, or even by the pattern of the fibre in the paper itself - and will, under hypnosis and careful questioning, identify the cues they use.

The amazing Eugene Marais was aware of such a talent. He called it "hypnotic hyperaesthesia" and suggested in 1922 that the accumulation of intellect and individual memory took place at the expense of our traditional senses. "Hypnosis proves, however, that this degeneration in man is not organic ... when mentality becomes dormant under hypnosis, the inhibition is removed."

Marais collected twenty empty snail shells that seemed to him to have the same shape, size and weight. He numbered these on the inside and arranged them in numerical order on a table. He hypnotized an eighteen-year-old girl, brought her into the room carefully blindfolded, and allowed her to demonstrate the acuity of her sense of touch by closing her hand over each shell in succession without lifting or moving it. In her absence, the shells were then arbitrarily shuffled, but "brought back still blindfolded, she replaced the shells in their original order, without very much hesitation, and without a mistake. He tested the effect of hypnosis on the sense of smell by getting twenty people each to handle a different object before placing it on a tray. The tray was then presented to another subject, this time a twenty-one-year-old girl, also hypnotized. "The girl, blindfolded, took out one object after another and by smelling the object and the hands of the different people, handed each object back to the person who had handled it first, without a mistake."

Hypersensitivity
And finally, in an inspired experiment, Marais showed that the same hypersensitivity extended to what he called "the sense of locality". He took subjects out on to the Springbok

Flats on the edge of Namaqualand, where it is quite obvious that the world cannot be round. Everything stretches out in all directions, across trackless wastes of identical low shrubs, to a totally featureless and perfectly level horizon. In the middle of this vast monotony, Marais found the nest of a sand grouse - three well-camouflaged eggs in a small depression on the ground - and allowed his subjects as long as they liked to study the surroundings. Each was then taken in a straight line 200 yards away from the nest and a further 100 yards beyond that at right angles - putting them, courtesy of Pythagoras, just 224 yards from the nest. Not one was able to find it again. At least, not until hypnotized, then the subjects walked directly back to the target. In later tests, a fourteen-year-old boy was able under hypnosis to return to his starting point from a mile away - and despite every attempt to confuse him, did so unhesitatingly and in a perfectly straight line. "Even when a series of circles were described and numerous zigzags and angled courses, he was never in the least doubt as to the exact direction in which the nest lay. (324)

Committing Murder under Hypnotism
He argues that no one could be made to commit a crime under hypnosis because the prophetic powers of the subjective mind would make it aware that it might lead to disaster. In fact, many crimes have been committed under hypnosis - one of the best known examples being the Copenhagen case of 1951, when a man named Palle Hardrup robbed a bank and murdered the cashier under hypnotic suggestion. Hudson also remarks that committing suicide under hypnosis is as unlikely as committing a crime under hypnosis; in fact, this is precisely what did happen in the Sala case of 1929, when the hypnotist Sigwart Thurneman made a member of his criminal gang commit suicide by hypnotic suggestion (325).

It was, I believe, Colonel de Rochas in the first instance, at least in the Western world and under scientific conditions, who experimented in the employment of hypnotic passes for the purpose of projecting the double of the subjects on whom he was operating.

Before Colonel de Rochas, Reichenbach, in hypnotizing his subjects, had called attention to the fact that the extremities of their bodies emitted luminous rays in the dark, and that this was also the case with magnets and crystals. These he termed odic rays. Following up the experiments of Reichenbach, Colonel de. Rochas, in developing the sensitivity of his subjects, was able to observe these radiations, at second hand, under more favourable conditions than his predecessor. These, he discovered, became more and more pronounced in proportion as his subjects were plunged into a deeper and deeper hypnotic sleep. At first his subjects noticed that these rays formed around their bodies in concentric curves, a sort of aura, extending more or less outside the body of the individual hypnotized. It was also observed that the sensibility of the subject was exteriorized in this aura.

After persevering still further with the hypnotizing process, his subjects noticed luminous clouds issuing from their persons, both to the right and to the left. These clouds were of a reddish tint on the one side, and bluish on the other, and by degrees, as the passes were persisted in, the two clouds united, and their colours coalesced until a phantom figure resembling the subject was formed. This phantom, it was observed, reproduced any move made by the individual who had been hypnotized.

Condensing the Phantom

These experiments were not pressed beyond a certain point by Colonel de Rochas. The matter, however, was taken up at a later date by Hector Durville who operated much on the same lines as Colonel de Rochas, but, after he had obtained very similar results, he was able by means of still further hypnotization, to condense this cloud-like phantom until its contour became gradually more and more clearly developed, in the first instance this development being more marked in the upper part of the form, and also exhibiting a certain degree of luminosity, especially at the head. Finally, the figure acquired the whole attitude of the subject. Its reflection was visible in a looking-glass, and it could be photographed by an ordinary camera. It will, of course, be understood that this is not exteriorization, in the same sense as Oliver Fox's or Sylvan Muldoon's. The phantom form does not walk like a normal being; it glides rather like a ghost, and the legs are not fully formed, but like the exteriorized double, it is linked to the subject by means of an etheric cord. When seated on a chair by the side of the subject the latter is abnormally sensitive to any physical contact which may be applied to the phantom form, and reacts violently to any shock its etheric duplicate may sustain (326).

I would like to relate an occurrence I witnessed in the 1970s. My father had hired a professional hypnotist to entertain a group of friends at his house and had invited me to attend the event. After quickly determining the hypnotic susceptibility of the various individuals present, the hypnotist chose a friend of my father's named Tom as his subject. This was the first time Tom had ever met the hypnotist.

Hypnotized Man sees through his Daughter
Tom proved to be a very good subject, and within seconds the hypnotist had him in a deep trance. He then proceeded with the usual tricks performed by stage hypnotists. He convinced Tom there was a giraffe in the room and had Torn gaping in wonder. He told Tom that a potato was really an apple and had Tom eat it with gusto. But the highlight of the evening was when he told Tom that when he came out of trance, his teenage daughter, Laura, would be completely invisible to him. Then, after having Laura stand directly in front of the chair in which

Tom was sitting, the hypnotist awakened him and asked him if he could see her.

Tom looked around the room and his gaze appeared to pass right through his giggling daughter. "No," he replied. The hypnotist asked Tom if he was certain, and again, despite Laura's rising giggles, he answered no. Then the hypnotist went behind Laura so he was hidden from Tom's view and pulled an object out of his pocket. He kept the object carefully concealed so that no one in the room could see it, and pressed it against the small of Laura's back. He asked Tom to identify the object. Tom leaned forward as if staring directly through Laura's stomach and said that it was a watch. The hypnotist nodded and asked if Tom could read the watch's inscription. Tom squinted as if struggling to make out the writing and recited both the name of the watch's owner (which happened to be a person unknown to any of us in the room) and the message. The hypnotist then revealed that the object was indeed a watch and passed it around the room so that everyone could see that Tom had read its inscription correctly.

When I talked to Tom afterward, he said that his daughter had been absolutely invisible to him. All he had seen was the hypnotist standing and holding a watch cupped in the palm of his hand. Had the hypnotist let him leave without telling him what was going on, he never would have known he wasn't perceiving normal consensus reality.

Obviously Tom's perception of the watch was not based on information he was receiving through his five senses. Where was he getting the information from? One explanation is that he was obtaining it telepathically from someone else's mind, in this case, the hypnotist's. The ability of hypnotized individuals to "tap" into the senses of other people has been reported by other investigators. The British physicist Sir William Barrett found evidence of the phenomenon in a series of experiments with a young girl. After hypnotizing the girl he told her that she would taste everything he tasted. "Standing behind the girl, whose eyes I had securely bandaged, I took up some salt and put it in my mouth; instantly she sputtered and exclaimed, 'What are you putting salt in my mouth for?' Then I tried sugar; she said 'That's better'; asked what it was like, she said 'Sweet.' Then mustard, pepper, ginger, etcetera were tried; each was named and apparently tasted by the girl when I put them in my own mouth (327).

Anne and Bill go into their own hypnotic World

Tart found two graduate students, Anne and Bill, who could go into deep trance and were also skilled hypnotists in their own right. He had Anne hypnotize Bill and after he was hypnotized, he had Bill hypnotize her in return. Tart's reasoning was that the already powerful rapport that exists between hypnotist and subject would be strengthened by using this unusual procedure.

He was right. When they opened their eyes in this mutually hypnotized state everything looked gray. However, the grayness quickly gave way to vivid colours and glowing lights, and in a few moments they found themselves on a beach of unearthly beauty. The sand sparkled like diamonds, the sea was filled with enormous frothing bubbles and glistened like champagne, and the shoreline was dotted with translucent crystalline rocks pulsing with internal light. Although Tart could not see what Anne and Bill were seeing, from the way they were talking he quickly realized they were experiencing the same hallucinated reality.

Of course, this was immediately obvious to Anne and Bill and they set about to explore their new found world, swimming in the ocean and studying the glowing crystalline rocks. Unfortunately for Tart they also stopped talking, or at least they stopped talking from Tart's perspective. When he questioned them about their silence they told him that in their shared dream world they were talking, a phenomenon Tart feels involved some kind of paranormal communication between the two.

In session after session Anne and Bill continued to construct various realities, and all were as real, available to the five senses, and dimensionally realized, as anything they experienced in their normal waking state. In fact, Tart resolved that the worlds Anne and Bill visited were actually more real than the pale, lunar version of reality with which most of us must be content. As he states, "after they had been talking about their experiences to each other for some time, and found they had been discussing details of the experiences they had shared for which there were no verbal stimuli on the tapes, they felt they must have actually been in the non-worldly locales they had experienced" (328).

--O--

CHAPTER TWENTY

AFTERLIFE

If you have read nothing else in this book then I hope that you will read this chapter, as this is what it is all about.

There is a tremendous amount of information and evidence about the Afterlife, very much more than I have space for. However I will try to, at least, deal with some of the more convincing evidence including The Scole Experiments, Cross Correspondence, Materializations, and the Proxy Sittings.

All of the evidence proves that the personality lives on, and that when we die we will all meet our loved ones again. I hope that, like me, it brings you a great deal of peace. It certainly brings me peace knowing that I will see Margaret again.

I know that there are sceptics now and there will continue to be sceptics. Dr. James Hyslop, Professor of logic and ethics at Columbia University puts it this way:

"I regard the existence of discarnate spirits as scientifically proved and I no longer refer to the sceptic as having any right to speak on the subject. Any man who does not accept the existence of discarnate spirits and the proof of it is either ignorant or a moral coward. I give him short shrift, and do not propose any longer to argue with him on the supposition that he knows anything about the subject."

Michael Roll, a lecturer in sub-atomic phenomena in Bristol, England, is not a sceptic. He succinctly comments: "In a nutshell, our physicists have discovered other dimensions of existence with people in them who are exactly the same as we are. Some really good mediums are able to bridge the gap between these different dimensions of existence. They are speaking to people whose surroundings are as solid and as natural to them as ours are to us. They exist in our space, but as their sub-atomic particle building blocks are moving at such staggering speeds, they are out of range of our physical senses. A good example is to be found in radio and television. All the channels are operating in the same space, but at different frequencies (subatomic vibrations). The supernatural and paranormal are natural and normal after all.' (329)

Religions & the Afterlife
And what about religions in the Afterlife?

Well, those in the afterlife all agree there are no churches or religions, although some people still cling to dogma and beliefs from the Earth plane for a while until they grow out of them. God is at the base of all existence, the power behind all consciousness. God is pure love that permeates matter, energy, consciousness and the seen and unseen realms.

There are no 'holy scriptures' no rituals, and no dogma among those who have released themselves from the Earth plane's belief systems. Some people temporarily cling to the old beliefs, staying in groups with others who have the same worldviews. Everyone enters the next plane of life with the same assumptions and perspectives they had on Earth. As a result, there are some Christian groups living together there who are sure they are in a holding pattern waiting for the rapture and the return to a physical existence on the Earth plane. Some, who believed that the spirit sleeps until the resurrection, are "sleeping." They're given guidance and inspiration to begin understanding that they're already in the next stage of their eternal life (330)

When I was a boy I used to attend the Bethel Mission in St. Helens. I went there for years and was very keen. Some Sundays I would attend as many as five meetings. When I was 11 we moved to another part of St. Helens but I continued to attend Bethel Mission, but it meant quite a bit of travelling so I eventually started at St. Marks (C of E) church. I got confirmed and married in that church and attended it for many years.

I was convinced that God didn't Exist

My wife and I travelled to Saudi Arabia in 1985 so that put an end to St. Marks. We were in Saudi Arabia for 17 years and came into contact with many religions and non-believers. Not long before we left for Saudi Arabia I lost my belief in God. In consequence I had many discussions with Muslims about the universe and where it came from. At that point I was a "Darwinist," and I used to argue with the Muslims about how they couldn't possibly know what was going on; where we came from, or where the universe came from. In fact at that stage I used to think that they were a lot of nutters.

We get older and (hopefully) wiser. I had always read scientific journals such as Scientific American and I began to read more about Quantum Mechanics and the weird stuff that scientists said was going on. It grabbed my interest and I read a lot more about it. It talked of an absence of time; an object being in a number of places at the same time, and about multiple universes. Suddenly, I could feel all my previous arguments falling away and I had a feeling that there was a great deal more to this life than we could sense with our normal senses. I began to realize that it was NOT the Muslims who were nutters, it was me.

We eventually came back from Saudi Arabia and within a few years my wife died of cancer. It was after that, that I started attending a Spiritualist Church. By that time I had read quite a bit about the afterlife and I was hopeful that I would get messages from "the other side." I didn't have to wait long. I got messages from my wife, Margaret; my mum, Ann; and other members of the family. Most of them were verifiable messages, and I am now absolutely convinced that this is only a temporary "stop over" for us on earth and that we will all re-join our loved ones in the next life. I see the proof every week.

If you think that its telepathy or mind reading, then forget it. Often the person who receives the message has to go away and confirm what they have been told. On a number of occasions people have been told to go away and look for a certain photograph in an attic album – only to find a picture there of the person sending the message from the Afterlife. On more than one occasion it has been a soldier killed in the trenches in the First World War

Once you are on this planet Earth, it is extremely important to know what is going to happen to you when you die. But how can you find out?

Whilst I respect your beliefs, what you will read in this book has nothing to do with religion. It is based on information gathered by hundreds of courageous open-minded investigators over the last hundred and fifty years who used careful empirical observation and analysis.

Why does the empirical information have more authority than the descriptions of the afterlife given by the Christian, Hindu, Jewish, Islamic, Buddhist and other religions?

First, beliefs about the afterlife in religions that rely on a "holy book were written down by people who lived some thousand or more years ago and based up their own psychic experiences. One big problem is that often the original documents do NOT exist any more and over the centuries they have been changed by unknown copyists.

The Bible has changed many times over the Centuries
We do NOT have the original, authentic Biblical texts. We have copies of Biblical copies that we know have been changed a number of times over the centuries, and therefore we can only analyze what we have today. Historians and Biblical experts agree that what information from the ancient texts we have today is highly unreliable.

Would it not be reasonable to investigate who these people were, where they came from, the extent of their learning and experience, their character, their beliefs, their motivation, who asked them to write, their intentions in writing and on what basis they stated the things they stated? But we can never answer these questions. We, the people of the world, are asked to believe in these religious writings just because our parents and our ancestors believed in them.

Those who do want to believe what was written over two thousand years ago, by people about whom we know nothing, have to balance those beliefs against the documented experiences of millions of people recorded using strict empirical methods in modern psychic science.

For example, those who want to believe that the dead lie in unawareness until the sounding of the trumpet on the day-of-judgment have to balance that belief against the experience of millions who have seen and spoken to their loved ones after their death.

Not too many people in the world today accept that some people will be punished in "hell for all eternity in the afterlife. But some religions still teach that.

So why should you accept the empirical explanation as to what is going to happen to you when you die and the conditions that exist in the afterlife when you inevitably cross over? (331)

The great scientist Dr. Robert Crookall, D.Sc., PhD, undertook a systematic study of hundreds of such communications from the afterlife obtained through many of the above avenues and published the results in his book *The Supreme Adventure* (1961).

His work is considered "scientific" because it painstakingly and objectively examines the evidence, it is internally coherent and it provides hypotheses consistent with a great mass of factual evidence.

Consistent Reports about the Afterlife

Crookall was amazed at the consistency of the evidence coming from all over the world. Communications from every country and continent, from Brazil, from England, from South Africa, from Tibet, from Europe, from India and from Australia are all consistent. He was surprised that they were identical with the beliefs held by the natives of the Hawaiian Islands, cut off from other civilizations for years prior to their "discovery" by Captain Cook in 1788.

He also noted the consistency of the evidence given by people who had out-of-body experiences, near-death experiences and the communications of high level mediums.

Crookall was a member of the Churches' Fellowship for Psychical Study, which came into being in England to allow those who had personal experiences of a psychic and spiritual nature to share them and examine them in the light of traditional church teachings on the afterlife.

The preface to his book *(A Lawyer Presents the Case for the Afterlife) was* written by a former Chief Justice of the British High Court, who said that, "It behoves every ordained Minister in the land to use it."

Another brilliant and highly respected investigator was Arthur Findlay, a practical businessman and successful stockbroker, who approached the task of psychic investigation with a cool and rational mind. For five years he undertook a special investigation with John Sloan, one of the most gifted direct voice mediums of all time. (332)

I have created conditions so as to make fraud and impersonation impossible, and, by persistent enquiry have obtained information about the Etheric (Spirit) World, its inhabitants and how communication takes place which should satisfy the average individual. I have dealt with hard facts all my life. I have acquired knowledge of economics and mathematics in my business life, and, outside of this, my special interest has been in physics. I have therefore approached this subject in a matter-of-fact way, and have obtained information which makes the phenomena, to my unbiased person, both reasonable and natural.

His first book *On the Edge of the Etheric. The Afterlife Scientifically Explained* (1931) made it very clear that the subject of survival after death comes from subatomic physics. *Where Two Worlds Meet* (1951) is the verbatim record of a series of nineteen séances with John Sloan, Glasgow direct voice medium. *The Way Of Life* (1953) is gathered from various works written by Mr Findlay; it tells inquirers all we should know about the journey through death to a much more intense and wonderful life in the spirit world.

George Meek
At the age of 60, George Meek retired from his career as an inventor, designer and manufacturer of devices for air conditioning and treatment of waste water. He held scores of industrial patents that enabled him to live comfortably and devote the next twenty five years of his life to self-funded, full-time research into life after death.

Meek undertook an extensive library and literature research program and travelled the world to locate and establish research projects with the top medical doctors, psychiatrists, physicists, biochemists, psychics, healers, parapsychologists, hypnotherapists, ministers, priests and rabbis. For years he conducted his own investigations and worked closely-with the pioneers of ITC in America and Europe. 'His last book, *After We Die What Then* (1987), outlines the conclusion of his years of full-time research on the nature of the afterlife.

The name "Allan Kardec" was the pen name of H Leon Denizard Rivail, a French educator and philosopher born in Lyon on October 3, 1804. He spoke several languages, and taught courses in comparative physiology, astronomy, chemistry and physics in a prestigious scientific school in Paris. He also organized and taught free courses for the underprivileged.

In 1854, at the age of 50, Rivail heard of the mysterious paranormal phenomena that had taken America and Europe by storm. Despite his scepticism he was convinced by close friends to attend an experimental séance where he was able to witness such occurrences first-hand.

Like most intelligent people he was sceptical at first and searched for a rational explanation. Using the same logical rigor that he had applied to his work in education and science, Rivail set out to understand and test the phenomena. He compiled hundreds of questions on the afterlife and sent them to the best mediums he could find, in different countries.

He was absolutely stunned to find that the answers coming back were totally consistent. The answers were compared, analyzed, and organized for inclusion in *The Spirits' Book*, which was first published in 1857. This was followed by a number of other books also compiled by seeking answers from spirits of high degree speaking through different mediums in different countries.

His books include: *The Gospel* - Explained by the Spiritist Doctrine; Christian Spiritism; *The Medium's Book*; Heaven and Hell; Genesis, and Posthumous Work.

Leslie Flint was a direct voice medium. The hundreds of communications received would have been shared by only those people present, and then lost, had they not been carefully recorded by Sidney George Woods who sat with Leslie Flint from 1946 onwards and Mrs Betty Greene who joined him in 1953.

Messages via Leslie Flint
In 1956, the voice of Ellen Terry, a famous actress of the British stage, who died in 1928, came through and said to them: You are going to have some remarkable communications. And I suggest you keep these contacts going regularly to build up the power, and to make possible this link which has been deliberately arranged for your tapes. The tapes you record give us the opportunity to reach many people in all parts of the world. We shall bring various souls from various spheres to give talks and lectures. We need willing helpers on your side.

This marked the beginning of their self-sacrificing work which continued for seventeen years until Mrs Greene's death in 1975. George Woods (1890-1983) was to keep the work of distributing cassettes going in spite of his age for eight years more until he joined her. Leslie Flint died in 1994.

In the Woods-Greene collection of recordings, which are now easily accessible on the Internet, you can hear person after person, talking in their own voice, about what happened to them after they died.

Another excellent detailed source of information about living in the afterlife is contained in the work of attorney, Edward C.

Randall, who sat with direct voice and materialization medium, Emily French, on more than seven hundred occasions taking detailed "statements" from witnesses The reader is referred to N. Riley Heagerty's compilation of his work *The French Revelation* (Heagerty 1995).

Another argument that was raised in the early days of psychic research was that the mediums were getting the information by telepathy from the unconscious minds of the people who came to sit with them.

Proxy Sittings
The early psychic investigators overcame this objection through what they called "proxy sittings" - where one person who knew nothing about a certain person took that person's place and went to see the medium on behalf of that other person.

The Reverend Charles Drayton Thomas, a Methodist minister who became a psychic researcher, spent many years as a proxy sitter investigating the mediumship of Mrs. Leonard and recording his results for the Society for Psychical Research. He would go to a sitting knowing only the name of the deceased and the name of the person who desired communication.

In one instance in 1936-1937, Thomas went to four sittings on behalf of Emma Lewis, a person he did not know. Through the medium, Mrs. Leonard, he was able to gain seventy pieces of information which Emma later said confirmed beyond all doubt that it was her father, Frederick William Macaulay, who was communicating.

The reader has to keep in mind that the Rev. Thomas, who insisted on using scientific methods to ascertain what was being transmitted, thoroughly investigated the medium Gladys Osborne Leonard, one of the most gifted mediums of the twentieth century. We are informed that he had over 500 sittings with her over a period of twenty years. After Mrs. Leonard's death in 1945, he joined Leslie Flint, the gifted direct voice medium, and did a great deal of valuable work with him.

The only possible objection a sceptic can make in relation to proxy sittings is fraud. There is simply no other possible or probable explanation for the information coming through the medium about someone who has passed on and who had no connection whatsoever with any of the sitters who were with the medium at the time.

But so far, in the last fifty years or so, no one has been able to even suggest fraud in the proxy sittings conducted by the Reverend Drayton Thomas. Again, psychic researchers are impressed by the conspicuous absence of criticism of these particular proxy sittings.

Professor Dodds, the rationalist President of the Society for Psychical Research from 1961-63, supervised a series of proxy sitting tests with the medium Nea Walker and was much impressed.

Dodds concluded that the hypothesis of fraud, rational inference from disclosed facts, telepathy from the actual sitter, and coincidence cannot either singly or in combination account for the results obtained (Dodds1962). (333)

The Scole Experiments
The Scole Experiment was a recent example of physical mediumship and materialization, which are dealt with in more detail in Chapter 6 of his book. It is a very well-documented current experiment, witnessed by a number of people of the highest credibility, many of who are still very much alive.

When sceptics attack the evidence for the afterlife, you will find that they are all strangely silent about The Scole

Experiment. While they theorize about how physical mediums could have cheated, not one of them has offered to conduct even one demonstration to produce even a fraction of the phenomena that these wonderful experiments produced, on a weekly basis, for over six years in several different countries under the strictest scrutiny in premises that were often assigned to the group on short notice.

Scole is a village in Norfolk, England. Using it as a base, several experimenters of the Scole Group, including mediums Robin and Sandra Foy and Alan and Diana Bennett, produced brilliant evidence for the afterlife in experiments conducted in England, the United States, Ireland and in Spain.

Senior scientists and investigators who participated in The Scole Experiment included Professors David Fontana, Arthur Ellison and Montague Keen. Of course, over the six years there were many others who attended as senior scientists and guests in the actual experiments: Dr. Hans Schaer, a lawyer; Dr. Ernst Senkowski; Piers Eggett; Keith McQuin Roberts; biologist Dr. Rupert Sheldrake; Professor Ivor Grattan-Guiness, all with scientific or other relevant background, and a host of other highly credible witnesses who have had years of experience in dealing with the paranormal. (334)

Materialization of Objects
Soon the messages came in the form of voices which could be heard by all in the room. Many of the experimenters experienced physical touch and the levitation of a table took place. Then came the actual materialization of the people and objects from the non-physical side.

More than fifty small objects were materialized, including a silver necklace, a Churchill coin, a small rose, quartz crystal ball, a 1940 British penny, a 1928 one-franc piece, a silver charm of the "Grim Reaper," an original copy of The Daily Mail dated l April, 1944; an original copy of The Daily Express dated 28 May 1945; and many others.

Interesting experiments were undertaken with photography. Images were imprinted on unopened rolls of film inside a locked box. These images included actual photos of people and places, sometimes from the past, and various obscure verses and drawings that took some effort to identify. There were also pictures of other dimensions and the beings that inhabit them. Eventually video cameras were able to record disincarnate images.

One of the most spectacular phenomena of The Scole Experiment was the materialized psychic lights that whirled around the room performing various maneuvers. Occasionally, these lights would throw out beams, as well as pass through solid objects. When they touched people, there was a definite sensation, and when they entered a person's body, a healing.

The speed, the different configurations and other phenomena performed behind the lights were just overwhelming, especially when all witnesses attested it was impossible that the lights could have been in any way fraudulently physically manipulated. All of these phenomena were accompanied by sudden and dramatic drops in temperature.

This is how Piers Eggett, one of the eyewitnesses, described the light: "This was a small ball of white light which moved around the room in all directions, sometimes at great speed, leaving a trail like a firework by persistence of vision. At times the light hovered in mid-air, and then touched some of the sitters, giving them a small electric shock.

According to other eye witnesses the normally single light point would:

- dart around at great speed and perform elaborately patterned dances including perfect, sustained circles executed at high velocity and with a precision which appeared inconsistent with physical manipulation
- settle on outstretched hands and jump from one to the other
- enter a crystal and remain as a small point of light moving around within the crystal
- strike the top of the table with a sharp rap on the glass of the dome of a dish with an appropriate "ping" and do this repeatedly while remaining visible as a sharp pinpoint of light
- respond to requests, such as alighting on and irradiating parts of the witnesses bodies
- move in time to tape-recorded music
- produce "lightning flashes" in an area of a large room some three to three and a half meters distant from the group sitting round a table (in Spain).
- undertake several aerial "bombing raids" on the table top, hitting it very audibly and visibly, and appearing to emerge from an area immediately below the table (Los Angeles)
- change shape, from a pinpoint of light to a generalized irradiation
- move at very high speed, describing at times perfect geometric shapes within a foot or two of visitors' faces, but without making any sound or creating any perceptible air movement. (335)

For those of us fortunate enough to have the personal experience, these materialization experiments are overwhelmingly convincing evidence for the existence of the afterlife.

"The ultimate in personal experiences came when my wife Irene, who passed four years ago, manifested to me on no less than four occasions with individual mannerisms and characteristics so familiar to me. With her final visit she brought a single red rose and kissed me. Well, what can one say in the light of such happenings, except that it was not only very moving but the most wonderful experience of my life." (Allan Crossley Psychic Investigator)

Professor W.J. Crawford, who was a lecturer in mechanical engineering at Queen's University, Belfast, conducted long and meticulous studies of ectoplasm. He wrote three classic books. (336)

He found that during one materialization the weight of his medium dropped from 120 pounds to 66 pounds. Professor Crawford found that all of the physical manifestations of his mediums - lifting of tables, moving of objects etc. - were achieved by the construction of ectoplasmic rods, struts and cantilevers. In his *Psychic Structures* he provides photographs of ectoplasm being used to lift tables. In his expert opinion as a professor of mechanical engineering:

All of the mechanical results without exception agreed with the mechanics of a beam fixed to the medium's body at one end and with the latter projecting into the séance room" (337)

George Meek (1987) found that during a materialization experiment there is a temporary weight loss from both the medium and the sitters as a substance is withdrawn from their bodies. In his own experiments he found a weight loss of 27 pounds - about 10 kilos - shared among the medium and fifteen physicians, psychologists and others who made up the research team. (338)

Evidence for materialization is substantive not only in England and the United States but also in other countries such as Brazil, where materializations took place in daylight when Carmine Mirabelli (1889-1950) produced fantastic physical phenomena witnessed by scientists from many parts of the world and which up until today have not been seen again in the presence of hundreds of hard-core sceptics.

In 1927 there appeared in Brazil a book entitled *O Medium Mirabelli*, containing a 74-page account of phenomena which occurred in broad daylight, at times in the presence of up to as many as sixty witnesses representing the leading scientific and social circles of Brazil. Among those who gave their names as witnesses were the President of Brazil, the Secretary of State, two professors of medicine, 72 doctors, 12 engineers, 36 lawyers, 89 men of public office, 25 military men, 52 bankers, 128 merchants and 22 dentists as well as members of religious orders (339).

The testimony of so many prominent credible witnesses cannot easily be overlooked, and in Brazil a committee of twenty leading men, headed by the President, was set up to interview witnesses and to decide what should be done to scientifically investigate Mirabelli's powers.

In the past 100 years, occasional small groups of serious-minded people have carried on research that resulted in materializations no less dramatic than those recorded in the Bible. Sir William Crookes in England, Schrenck-Notzing in Germany, Pavlowski and Kluski in Poland, Carlos Mirabelli in Brazil, and Harry Edwards in his work in England and South Africa have succeeded in producing materializations. These materializations have been no less dramatic and real than those of Moses and Elijah, and that of Jesus appearing to and speaking with the apostles on two occasions after His burial. Some readers may find these modern examples more credible than the Biblical references.

He Materialized without Clothes
The problem of the clothes of ghosts has vexed many a critical mind. Here is a veritable poser for them, a poser, however, that may be capped by a record which the late W. T. Stead gave in his magazine, *Borderland*. Here, a

man supposed by his friends to be dead suddenly became conscious outside his physical form, but in doing so realized that he was naked. There were ladies standing round his supposed deathbed, and his embarrassment may be imagined. Here again, however, the shock of finding himself in such an awkward situation seems to have had the desired effect for, almost immediately after, he discovered to his surprise that he was properly dressed. Needless to say, dressed or undressed, he remained invisible to those present. There must, one would think, be something very remarkable about the power of the imagination on another plane to effect these instantaneous transformations. (340)

There is No Death
There is No Death. I am standing on the seashore. A ship at my side spreads her white sails to the morning breeze and starts for the blue ocean. She is an object of beauty and strength, and I stand and watch her until at length she is a speck of white cloud just where the sea and sky come to mingle with each other.

Then someone at my side says, "There! She's gone!" Gone where? Gone from my sight, that is all. She is just as large in mass and hull and spar as she was when she left my side, and she is just as able to bear her load of living weight to her destined harbour.

Her diminished size is in me, not in her. And just at the moment when someone at my side says, "There! She's gone!" there are other eyes watching her coming, and other voices ready to take up the glad shout, "Here she comes!" And that is dying. (341)

Shamanic Traditions
Holger Kalweit, a German ethnopsychologist with degrees in both psychology and cultural anthropology, goes the one better. An expert on shamanism who is also active in near-death research, Kalweit points out that virtually all of

the world's shamanic traditions contain descriptions of this vast and extradimensional realm, replete with references to the life review, higher spiritual beings who teach and guide, food conjured up out of thought, and indescribably beautiful meadows, forests, and mountains. Indeed, not only is the ability to travel into the afterlife realm the most universal requirement for being a shaman, but NDEs are often the very catalyst that thrusts an individual into the role. For instance, the Ogiala Sioux, the Seneca, the Siberian Yakut, the South American Guajiro, the Zulu, the Kenyan Kikuyu, the Korean Mu dang the Indonesian Mentawai Islanders, and the Caribou Eskimo-all have traditions of individuals who became shamans after a life-threatening illness propelled them headlong into the afterlife realm. (342)

Whitton has found that, although a person's material conditions can vary greatly from one life to the next, their moral conduct, interests, aptitudes and attitudes remain the same. Individuals who were criminals in their previous existence tend to be drawn to criminal behaviour again; people who were generous and kind continue to be generous and kind, and so on. From this Stevenson concludes that it is not the outward trappings of life that matter, but the inner ones, the joys, the sorrows, and "inner growths" of the personality, that appear to be most important. (343)

Reincarnation
Whitton is not the only reincarnation researcher who has uncovered evidence that our unconscious has more of a hand in our lives than we may realize. Another is Dr. Ian Stevenson, a professor of psychiatry at the University of Virginia Medical School. Instead of using hypnosis, Stevenson interviews young children who have spontaneously remembered apparent previous existences. He has spent more than thirty years in this

pursuit and has collected and analyzed thousands of cases from all over the globe.

According to Stevenson, spontaneous past-life recall is relatively common among children, so common that the number of cases that seem worth considering far exceeds his staff's ability to investigate them. Generally children are between the ages of two and four when they start talking about their "other life," and frequently they remember dozens of particulars, including their name, the names of family members and friends, where they lived, what their house looked like, what they did for a living, how they died, and even obscure information such as where they hid money before they died and, in cases involving murder, sometimes even who killed them. (344)

> Indeed, frequently their memories are so detailed Stevenson is able to track down the identity of their previous personality and verify virtually everything they have said. He has even taken children to the area in which their past incarnation lived, and watched as they navigated effortlessly through strange neighborhoods and correctly identified their former house, belongings, and past-life relative's and friends.

Like Whitton, Stevenson has gathered an enormous amount of data suggestive of reincarnation, and to date has published six volumes on his findings. And like Whitton, he also has found evidence that the unconscious plays a far greater role in our makeup and destiny than we have hitherto expected.

> No longer can the scramble to meet the monthly payments on a never-ending list of material wants -or the effort to climb a little higher in the economic or social rat-race-be quite so irresistible.

No longer can we fail to recognize that no matter how dull, dreary and unrewarding this moment of life may be, the path which begins with the next moment can be the stepping stone into a glorious and ever-unfolding future of great promise.

No longer can a political system fall to recognize that its citizens are far more than one-lifetime, soulless cogs in a materially-oriented world, who face personal extinction at death.

And if the term "Immortality" has any negative connotations for you, perhaps we should take a lesson from the men who edited the Bible. "Immortality" is not mentioned in the Bible. 'Life Eternal" is mentioned 72 times (345).

We have already mentioned independent and dependent apparitions. In your own experiments some important factors must be taken into consideration. There are definite problems concerned with any possible communications with apparitional personalities, and some of these should be more thoroughly discussed.

It is highly difficult to prove the validity of apparitional communication, communication which is allegedly established with personalities who have survived physical death. For one thing, even if the data is legitimate, we often take it for granted that such personalities operate in the same manner as we, and this, I believe, is a mistake. Their psychological structure may have altered in some respects; the ego, for example, may not be as necessary to a non-physical being. The ego is extremely specialized, geared toward material orientation.

It is most probable that such personalities would display instead characteristics of consciousness with which we have become familiar in dream, trance and other dissociated states. Communication would be more associative, intuitive and symbolic than that which appertains to the waking state. We can hardly suppose that the psychological structure of a personality who has survived physical death is the same as our own. We cannot, therefore, expect that communication will follow the lines which are familiar to us. To expect this is asking too much, and may lead us in the wrong direction (346).

The Christian Bible as well as most religious writings are replete with stories of people who "heard" voices, "saw" visions and foretold the future. In ages past, these rare people were called prophets, sages, seers and mystics.

In the early days of the American colonies, people with such abilities were sometimes called "witches" and were, in some cases, tortured and even burned at the stake. Even in this century in England, such people were ostracized and even imprisoned until the repeal of the Witchcraft Act in 1951.

Only within the last 140 years, has serious research into the abilities of such people been conducted. Even up to the present moment such researchers are looked at askance by their peers. Hence, there are only a few intrepid souls in England, the United States, the Soviet Union, and Brazil who are today seriously engaged in conducting research in the area of communications from spirits.

During the past 16 years, my fellow researchers and I (George W. Meek) have searched the world over to locate and work quietly with deep trance mediums who are not in "the business of mediumship." These people never advertise their abilities. In fact, some of our most useful and highest-level contacts with the world of spirit came into our laboratory through a 60-year-old man who had gone into trance once each month for twenty years in the presence of only his two closest friends (347).

More objective proof that the mediums are speaking to living people in the afterlife comes from the research called "cross correspondence" that has been carried out to ensure that the information mediums receive isn't simple psychic knowledge. In cross correspondence, a series of messages are given by someone in the afterlife to different mediums in different parts of the world. Individually, the messages are not meaningful. Together, however, they have a clear message. That means a single medium couldn't be receiving psychic information. Instead, the deceased has carefully planned to give the messages to a number of mediums. That requires a living person in the afterlife to plan and execute the communication.

The Myers Cross -Correspondence
The Myers Cross-Correspondence is the best known example of such a study. Frederick W.H. Myers was a Cambridge Classics scholar and writer in the nineteenth century and he was one of the founders of the Society for Psychical Research. He originated the concept of cross correspondence.

After Myers died in 1901, over a dozen mediums in different countries began receiving incomplete scripts through automatic writing that were all signed by Frederick Myers. The scripts were all about obscure classical subjects (that would be known to Myers, a Classics scholar at Cambridge). When all the scripts were assembled, like a jig-saw puzzle, they formed a complete message. Frederick W. H. Myers, living in the afterlife and communicating through the mediums, had planned and executed the writings so that they proved no single medium was receiving psychic knowledge. Instead, it proved that it was communication from a deceased person.

Later, two other leaders of the Society for Psychical Research died: Henry Sidgwick and Edmund Gurney. Soon after each of their deaths, fragments of messages came to mediums around the world from them, and the Myers "study" was replicated successfully. Over the next thirty years, more than three thousand such scripts were transmitted to mediums around the world, some as long as 40 typed pages. They now fill 24 volumes of 12,000 pages. As investigators involved in the research died, they joined the study on the other side by communicating incomplete messages through a number of mediums around the world that formed complete wholes when brought together. (349) Hundreds of other accounts of such cross correspondence are recorded in the Proceedings of the Society for Psychical Research.'" (348).

Another proof that the contact in medium readings and séances is with the actual, living person on the next plane of life comes from "proxy sittings," (as previously mentioned). In a proxy sitting, someone comes to the medium reading or séance for a reading for someone else, not for himself or herself. The proxy sitter knows only the name of the deceased and the name of the person wanting to have contact with the deceased. That decreases the likelihood that the medium is just, doing a psychic reading of the person, without really receiving communication from the loved one speaking from the next plane of life.

The Reverend Charles Drayton Thomas, a Methodist minister, repeatedly acted as a proxy sitter investigating the mediumship of Gladys Osborne Leonard for the Society for Psychical Research. For example, from 1936 to 1937, Thomas went to four sittings with Leonard as a representative for a woman about whom he knew only her name, Emma Lewis, and that she wanted to contact her father, Frederick William Macaulay. With those two pieces of information, Leonard provided seventy items of information, which Thomas recorded and conveyed to Emma Lewis. She confirmed, beyond a doubt, that they came from her father because of the unique content only he would have known (350).

"The most convincing proof of the reality of
life after death ever set down on paper."
(351).

Colin Wilson"

Ask any critic of the paranormal to account for the evidence
of the cross-correspondences and you can be assured of
bewilderment or, at best, ignorant dismissal."

Montagtie Keen

A recurring argument in psychic research is that the
information produced by mediums as evidence for the
afterlife could have come from the medium's own
unconscious or from reading the mind of the sitter.
However, psychic science has been most successful in
showing that, with genuine mediums, neither telepathy nor
their unconscious has anything to do with information
transmitted from the afterlife.

The Myers Cross-Correspondences have now become
classic evidence for survival and are most influential and
persuasive in helping many people come to terms with life
after death.

The method he thought up was cross-correspondence - a
series of messages to different mediums in different part
of the world that on their own would mean nothing, but
which, when put together, would make sense. He and his
fellow leaders of the Society for Psychical Research felt
that if such a thing could be accomplished it would have
very high level of proof of continued existence.

After he died in 1901, more than a dozen different mediums
in different countries began receiving a series of incomplete
scripts through automatic writing signed by Frederick Myers.
Later there were scripts signed by his fellow leaders of the

Society for Psychical Research, Professor Henry Sidgwick and Edmund Gurney, as they too died.

The mediums used by Myers and the others from the afterlife were not professors of the classics. They were not highly educated and all messages transmitted were outside their learned knowledge and experience. On one occasion, one of the mediums, Mrs. Coombe-Tennant, was conducting a discussion using "automatic writing" between the spirit entity of Professor Sidgwick and his living colleague G. W. Balfour on the "mind-body relationship," "epiphenomenalism and interactionism." She complained bitterly that she had no idea what they were talking about and lost her temper that she was asked to transmit such difficult things.

Myers did say it was extremely difficult to transmit his messages from the spirit world across to the mediums. He described as it being like... standing behind a sheet of frosted glass which blurs sight and deadens sound, dictating feebly to a reluctant and somewhat obtuse secretary (352)

The information transmitted in the Myers experiments was so accurate that it stunned the members of the Society for Psychical Research. At one stage those who were investigating the Myers Cross-Correspondences hired private detectives to put Mrs. Piper, one of the mediums involved, under surveillance. Her mail was opened, private detectives followed her, and questions were asked about her friends and about those she spoke to. All the investigations proved her innocent of fraud, conspiracy and trickery.

The evidence is absolute. All the original documents are on file and there are at least eight complete sets of copies in existence for any investigator to study. For those who have initiative to investigate, sufficient information is available. And whilst for the investigator of the Myers Cross-

Correspondences the information available is challenging, the rewards are evidentiary proof of the afterlife.

One person who took the time to study the Cross Correspondences in depth was the former secular-humanist Colin Brookes-Smith. After researching them he stated in the Journal of the Society for Psychical Research that survival should now be regarded as a sufficiently well-established fact to be beyond denial by any reasonable person. Furthermore, he argued that this conclusion should not be kept in the obscurity of research records but should be presented to the public as a momentous scientific conclusion of prime importance to mankind. (353)

Another very convincing piece of evidence for the afterlife was provided by one of the mediums who had received some of the Myers communications. After her own death in 1956 at the age of 81, Mrs. Coombe-Tennant, using her pen-name Mrs. Willett, transmitted a long and detailed book of personal reminiscences containing incredibly intimate details about her own life through the medium Geraldine Cummins, who had never met her or her children. Published as *Swan On a Black Sea*, the Willett scripts, as they are sometimes also known, are considered by many, including Colin Wilson, to be: "The most convincing proof of the reality, of life after death ever set down on paper" (354)

Colin Wilson, himself a former sceptic, and now a writer with an international reputation, did investigate.
He writes:
Taken as a whole, the Cross Correspondences and the Willett scripts are among the most convincing evidence that at present exists for life after death. For anyone who is prepared to devote weeks to studying them, they prove beyond all reasonable doubt that Myers, Gurney and Sidgwick went on communicating after death. (355)

The Myers Cross Correspondences have successfully showed that what was transmitted from the medium was not from the medium's own unconscious.

Only the Body Dies

Only the body dies. The mind but ever continues unchanged and unaffected.

Thus the results of Crystal Ball gazing cannot be too highly lauded. For this practice can lead the Magician to the loftiest pinnacles of the Tree of Life where the air is pure and the viewpoint clear and unsullied. There is, of course, the preliminary danger of either getting lost on the uncharted byways of that plane, or become ensnared within the seductive grasp of bright forms and the fleeting astral visions of the depths. However, all this is elementary. If the aspiration be kept untarnished and pure, and if the sceptical principles of the Qabalah are applied, there should be little danger of this happening. Then the Magician may calmly wing his way beyond his personality, beyond the glittering phantoms of the Astral, past the splendid faithless visions with their allure and witchery, to the inner heart of the Heavenly Men, where the Lord of all is enthroned (356).

Undeniable Evidence presented by a Senior Lawyer

There is undeniable scientific evidence today for the afterlife. I (Victor Zammit) am a former practicing attorney-at-law formally qualified in a number of university disciplines. I am also an open-minded sceptic.

The argument that follows is not just an abstract, theoretical, academic legal argument. As an open-minded investigator, I set out to investigate the existing evidence for survival after death and, with others, to test claims that communication with intelligences from the afterlife is possible.

After many years of serious investigation, I have come to the irreversible conclusion that there is a great body of evidence which, taken as a whole, absolutely and without a doubt proves the case for the afterlife. I will not be arguing that the objective evidence has high value as proof. Nor am I suggesting that this evidence be accepted beyond reasonable doubt. I am stating that the evidence taken as a whole constitutes overwhelming and irrefutable proof for the existence of the afterlife.

There have been millions of pages written about psychic phenomena and scientific research into the afterlife. Using my professional background as an attorney, and my university training in psychology, history and scientific method, I have very carefully selected aspects of psychic research and afterlife knowledge that would constitute objective evidence. This evidence would be technically admissible in the Supreme Court of the United States, the House of Lords in England, the High Court of Australia and in every civilized legal jurisdiction around the world.

When the objective evidence - modern materializations, near-death experiences, out-of-body experiences, after-death contacts, voices on tape, psychic laboratory experiments, the best mediums, the cross correspondences, The Scole Experiment, proxy sittings, poltergeists and all of the other evidence contained in this work - is seen collectively, the case for survival after death is absolutely stunning and irrefutable. (357)

Yes, of course, there is a funeral at the end of the road - be you a mighty ruler, an office or factory worker, banker, scientist, international financier, priest, rabbi, janitor, homemaker, billionaire industrial tycoon, or pope.

Every one of the billions of souls occupying a physical body travels a similar road. But now you understand the seeming magic by which your soul and mind, memory banks, and personality will still be very much alive. You can now understand that you cannot cop out by the drug or suicide route. There is just no way that you can terminate the wonderful, total being that is you. This is the magic of living forever: you cannot die! And though you will be living forever, the quality of life, here and hereafter, depend on you.

All of which leads me inexorably - and not without a certain concern, because I remain a Western-trained scientist with all the pragmatism that entails - to the conclusion that living things are part of some larger process. And that they can, under certain circumstances, exploit that relationship in ways that give them access to supernormal powers - making them better fitted for survival. And proof of this ability is, I suggest, evident in some peculiar aspects of animal behaviour. (358)

Animals can show determination in this life as well as the next:
    In August 1914, Private James Brown of the 1st North Staffordshire Regiment was sent to join the Great War in France. On 27th September, his wife wrote to him with the bad news that Prince, his favourite Irish terrier, was missing. He wrote back: "I am sorry that you have not found Prince. You are not likely to. He is over here with me. " The dog, it seems, travelled over 200 miles through the south of England, succeeded somehow in crossing the Channel and then negotiated another 60 miles of war-torn French country-side to the one set of trenches on the front line near Armentieres, where its master could be found. (359)

The Scole Experiments (see previous)
For six years, a group in Norfolk, England, conducted experiments of contact with the afterlife. The following professionals participated in the experiments: Dr. David Fontana, Professor Arthur Ellison, Montague Keen, Dr. Hans Schaer, Esq., Dr. Ernst Senkowski, Piers Eggett, Keith McQuin Roberts, Dr. Rupert Sheldrake, and Professor Ivor Grattan-Guiness. A group of NASA scientists participated, as well as professionals from the Institute of Noetic Sciences.

The experiments resulted in communication with a variety of deceased people, revelations of information that nobody but the deceased could know about, appearance of objects that came from nowhere, voices of the deceased heard by all experimenters in attendance, and materialization of people who were deceased. Rolls of film were placed in locked boxes by experimenters and images appeared on them. Video cameras recorded the appearance of deceased people.

A scientific report titled "The Scole Report" was produced by the Society for Psychical Research based on the experiments. The conclusion was, "None of our critics has been able to point to a single example of fraud or deception. (360)

A stage magician, James Webster, was brought in to see if any magic tricks could produce the phenomena. Webster had more than fifty years experience in psychic research, applying his knowledge of magic tricks to such phenomena. On three occasions he attended sittings with the Scole group and published this conclusion in an English newspaper in June 2001: "I discovered no signs of trickery, and in my opinion such conjuring tricks were not possible, for the type of phenomena witnessed, under the conditions applied." (361)

Yram writes: "When I project my body in my bedroom, it is my custom to kiss my wife before proceeding with my experiments. One day, when I was projected in the astral and standing beside her, she said, "Stay near me!" Instead of that, I rejoined, "you come with me."

This was the beginning of these mutual adventures if we may accept Yram's account at all literally, love on another plane is as real, if more spiritual in its raptures, as any earthly affection. "Her love" (he says) "penetrated into my being under the guise of a general warmth, while a feeling of absolute confidence filled my spirit. On the other hand, my aura penetrated hers, and I had the sensation of melting into her. So intense were the vibrations that I experienced a kind of giddiness. In the atmosphere in which we had projected ourselves I could see our more material doubles united in the form of a cloud, and as the cloud became nearer I had the impression of taking off a series of clothes and becoming more and more intimately united with my wife. Words are powerless to describe the sensations of this state of super consciousness. In no other experience have I had so wide-awake a consciousness, no love so powerful, nor a calm and serenity so profound."

Some would describe these emotions as the cosmic consciousness of twin souls. At least we may find in the description the inadequacy of which the writer is only too ready to admit, a hint that the love element, wherever love is a reality, is not destroyed, but only intensified by the loss of the physical form (362).

Voice Communication & Spiricom
In the last few years there have been great advances in electronic communication with those in the Afterlife:
1971
Paul Jones, G.W. Meek, and Hans Heckmann, first research to create a two-way voice communication system far more sophisticated than in the EVP approach.
1978
William J. O'Neil, using a modified side-band radio, has brief but evidential contact with an American medical doctor said to have died five years earlier.
1982
G. W. Meek makes a trip around the world to distribute taped recordings of sixteen excerpts of communication between William J. O'Neil and an American scientist who died fourteen years earlier. He also distributes a one-hundred-page technical report giving wiring diagrams, photos, technical data, and guidelines for research by

others. Upon return, he holds a press conference in Washington, D.C., and distributes (free) the tape cassettes and technical manuals to the representatives of the press, radio, and TV

1982-88
Hans-Otto Koenig, Germany, develops sophisticated electronic equipment using extremely low-beat-frequency oscillators, ultraviolet and infrared lights, and so on.

1985-88
Jules and Maggy Harsch-Fischbach, Luxembourg, with spirit help, develop and operate two electronic systems superior to any of the EVP equipment up to this time. The communications become significantly more dependable and repeatable than the systems developed earlier.

1980s
Researchers in several countries have pictures of the dead appear sporadically on their TVs. There is no control over the appearance of the images.

1985
Klaus Schreiber, Germany, with technical assistance from Martin Wenzel, begins to get images of dead persons on TV picture tubes, using optoelectronic feedback systems. There is positive identification in many cases by accompanying audio communications, including audio-video contact with Schreiber's two deceased wives. This work is the subject of a documentary TV film and a book by Rainer Holbe of Radio Luxembourg.

1987
Jules and Maggy Harsch-Fischbach, with assistance from an earthside colleague and from the spirit world, get TV picture sequences of good quality.

Finding myself to exist in the world, I believe I shall in some shape or other always exist; and, with all the inconveniences human life is liable to, I shall not object to a new edition of mine, hoping, however, that the errata of the last may be corrected.

Benjamin Franklin

Spiritualism
Regardless of race, color, caste, or creed, each of us, totally alone, walks through the door called Death. Then certain basic questions cry out for answers. Nothing could be more important than to know them beforehand.

The material that follows is possible only because of the inquisitive minds of dedicated researchers during the past century. First I honour the most dedicated of the serious (and honest) deep-trance mediums, primarily in England, Scotland, Brazil, the United States, Canada, Ireland, Italy, and South Africa. Second, I acknowledge the work of thousands of persons traditionally known as "sitters," whose presence seems to provide subtle energies that facilitate the best contacts with communicators from other levels of life.

These valuable contributions would have been lost, however, had it not been for dedicated psychic researchers and scientists who had the moral courage to investigate and report the work of these mediums and their sitters or "circles." These researchers, even down to the year 1991, have had to suffer ridicule from their peers and loss of their professional status. Men like Sir William Crookes in England, Schrenk-Notzing in Germany, Nobel prize-winner Charles Richet in France, Ernest Bozzano in Italy, Dr. Holtacher in South Africa, T. Glen Hamilton, M.D., in Canada, William Tiller, Ph.D., in the United States, and Dr. Hernani Andrade in Brazil all paid a price for their pioneering work.

Although the accumulated communications and data were fragmentary and often extremely contradictory, in fine it became possible to piece together a reasonably consistent and experimentally valid picture of life after death.

Finally, in the 1980s, this type of research intensified. Communications under laboratory conditions from recently "deceased" communicators with medical and scientific backgrounds have added still more validity to the emerging picture. These have greatly enhanced our understanding of the process of death and rebirth. It has pushed our knowledge far beyond that which grew out of the first hundred years of spiritualism.

We live on!

--o--

These findings should not be kept obscure. They are a momentous scientific achievement of prime importance to mankind

--o--

CHAPTER TWENTYONE

WITCHES

I believe that this book would not be complete without saying something on the important subject of Witches.

There has been some amazing testimony about Witches. Some quite incredible and, sometimes, quite devastating things have been attributed to them.

It was only in 1951 that the Witchcraft Act was repealed after many, so called Witches had been burned at the stake.

The Evil Eye

I never really believed that there was such a thing as 'the evil eye'. It sounded preposterous.

But then, I had a friend named Pat. He was a good friend and would do absolutely anything for someone he liked. However, there was another side to Pat. If someone really annoyed him or hurt him, then watch out!

There had been a number of people (fortunately I wasn't one of them) who fell into the latter category. Their demise was vengeful and normally quite quick.

I remember him explaining to me that he didn't have to stick pins into dolls or anything like that. He simply had to think about them and turn on his hate. Some of them really suffered.

No, I never really believed
in 'the evil eye' but I do now.

Nasty Jane Brooks

On Sunday, 15th of November, 1657 (so runs the narration), about three of the clock in the afternoon, Richard Jones, then a sprightly youth about twelve years old, son of Henry Jones of Shepton Mallet in the County of Somerset, being in his Father's house alone and perceiving one looking in at the windows went to the door where one Jane Brooks of the same town (but then by name unknown to this boy) came to him. She desired him to give her a piece of close bread, and gave him an apple. After which she also stroked him down on the right side, shook him by the hand and so bade him good night. The youth returned into the house where he had been left well when his Father and one Gibson went from him, but at their return which was within an hour or thereabout, they found him ill and complaining of his right side, in which the pain continued the most part of that night. And on Monday following in the evening the boy roasted the apple he had from Jane Brooks and having eaten about half of it was extremely ill and sometimes speechless, but being recovered he told his father that a woman of the town on Sunday before had given him that apple and that she stroked him on the side. He said he knew not her name but should know her person if he saw her. Upon this Jones was advised to invite the women of Shepton to come to his house upon the occasion of his son's illness and the child told him that in case the woman should come when he was in a fit, if he were not able to speak, he would give him an intimation by a nod, and desired that his Father would then lead him through the room, for he said he would put his hand upon her, if she were there. After this, and continuing very ill, many women came daily to see him. And Jane Brooks the Sunday after came in with two of her sisters, and several other women of the neighborhood were there.

"Upon her coming in, the boy was taken so ill that for some time he could not see nor speak, but having recovered his sight he gave his Father the item and he led him about the room. The boy drew towards Jane Brooks, who was behind her two sisters among the other women, and put his hand upon her, which his Father perceiving immediately scratcheth her face and drew blood from her. The youth then presently cried out that he was well and so continued seven or eight days. But then meeting with Alice Coward, sister of Jane Brooks, who passing by said to him: 'How do you do, my Honey?' he presently fell ill again, and after that the said Coward and Brooks often appeared to him. The boy would describe the clothes and habit they were in at the time exactly, as the Constable and others have found upon repairing to them, though Brooks' house was at a good distance from Jones's. This they often tried and always found the boy right in his descriptions."

Here follows the most significant incident in the narration. "One Sunday about noon the boy was at home with his Father and his Father's friend Gibson when he suddenly cried out that he saw Jane Brooks on the Wall, pointing to the spot where he saw her. Where-upon Gibson promptly struck the place with a knife which he had with him. Upon this the boy exclaimed that Gibson had cut Jane Brooks' hand and that it was bloody."

We will let the erudite Joseph Glanville, chaplain-in-ordinary to His Majesty and fellow of the Royal Society; continue the account of this curious episode in his own words.

"The Father and Gibson immediately went to the Constable, a discreet person, and acquainting him with what had passed, desired him to go with them to Jane Brooks' house, which he did. They found her sitting on a stool with one hand over the other. The Constable asked her how she did. She answered 'Not well.' He asked again why she sat with one hand over the other. She replied she was wont to do so. He enquired if anything were amiss with her hand. Her answer was, it was well enough. The Constable desired he might see the hand that was under, which she being unwilling to shew him, he drew it out and found it bloody according to what the boy had said.

Being asked how it came so, she said 'twas scratched with a great pin. ' "

In conclusion, we learn that Jane Brooks was arrested and subsequently condemned and executed at Chard assizes on March 26th, 1658.

The Somerset Witches
If we accept the 'belief in an astral (or etheric) form to which the consciousness can, under certain circumstances and by the adoption of certain methods, be transferred at will, we go far to explain many of the freely volunteered confessions of the accused at the witch trials of the past which apart from some such hypothesis leave us totally at a loss for any plausible explanation. That their experiences were a reality to many of those on trial for witchcraft the evidence leaves no manner of doubt. That the accused in such cases made no distinction between their sensations in their physical and in their astral or etheric bodies is in the highest degree probable. Devoid of all knowledge of theosophical conceptions and of psychical theory it was but natural that they should confuse their alternating in the body and out of the body existences and that one should appear to them just as real and as actual as the other. Even the dreamer, when a dream is exceptionally vivid, cannot always determine whether what he recalls has taken place in the physical world or is merely part and parcel of his dream life. It can hardly be doubted today that the methods adopted by the witches of the past had for their object the extrusion of the astral body from its physical envelope, and it was a

knowledge of certain recipes of a presumably occult character that enabled them to compound the unguents that set in motion the phantasmagorical phenomena of the Witches Sabbath. That this explanation does not cover the whole field I readily admit. There were, unquestionably, numerous cases in which an ordinary man of flesh and blood in his physical form took advantage of the superstitions of the day to pose as "The Dark Master". Some of the records given in the very learned work of Margaret Alice Murray (362), leave us in little doubt of this, but there are a number of others to which such an explanation is quite inapplicable. Among these must be mentioned especially those which involve what this author terms "the marvelous and magical means of locomotion" by which the devotees of his Satanic Majesty betook themselves to the Witches' Sabbath and other such gatherings of the Devil's Disciples. "The belief in the power of witches to ride in the air" (she writes), "is very ancient and universal in Europe. They flew either unsupported, being carted by the Devil, or were supported on a stick; sometimes, however an animal which they rode passed through the air. The flying was usually preceded by an anointing of the whole or part of the body with a magical ointment."

Sometimes, especially if the meeting place was near at hand, the witches attended it on foot, according to the records supplied, but in others, as in the case of Isobel Goudie, they rode or at least imagined themselves to do so. Isobel Goudie confessed: "I haid a little horse and wold say, 'Horse and Hattock in the Divellis' name!'" And then, she declared, they would fly away where they would like straws fly upon the highway. "All the Coeven" (she is reported as saying) "did flie lyk cattis and I still read on an horse, quhich ve vold mak of a straw or a beeinstalk."

Two of the New England witches confessed to riding on a pole and others appear to have (as they imagined) adopted the same method of locomotion. The Somerset witches stated that they were in the habit of flying through the air by means of a magical oil with which they anointed themselves.

Sometimes the witch's themselves took animal shape and one would ride to the Sabbath upon the back of another. We read, in these confessions, of enchanted bridles which transformed their wearers into horses. There is in fact no limit to the illusions which accompanied these nocturnal experiences. Margaret Johnson, one of these witches, confessed (1633) that if they desired to be at anyplace on a sudden "their devil or spirit would presently convey them thither upon a rod, dog or anything else". The patent absurdity of such experiences, must not, it seems to me, blind one to the fact that to the witches themselves they possessed a strong element of reality. We may in short fitly employ the old expression "glamour" with regard to them.

Paul Grilland (1537) gives an instance of an Italian witch who flew in the air with the help of a magic ointment in the year 1526. Various formulae for the composition of this ointment are given in old French magical tomes. Two may be cited as examples.

They are translated from the French originals:
(1) Water parsnip, sweet flag, cinquefoil, bat's blood, deadly nightshade and oil.
(2) Baby's fat, juice of water parsnip, aconite, cinquefoil, deadly nightshade and soot.

Some of these ingredients are poisonous when taken internally. Whether they would have the effect of exteriorizing the etheric body, when used as an unguent is more than I can say, but certainly this appears to have been the object with which they were employed.

Autosuggestion

Taken to its limit, autosuggestion can even kill. Every year thousands of people die simply because they believe that it is inevitable. Witchcraft may have powers that are truly supernatural, 'but it does not need them while people are capable of wishing themselves to death. It is not even necessary to consciously believe in forces of evil; the unconscious can manage very well on its own. There are vivid and graphic descriptions of otherwise rational people in New York and London wasting away when they have been told that someone is abusing a doll constructed in their image, and of these same people making rapid and complete recoveries when they knew, or even thought, that the doll had been destroyed.

Milan Ryzl a Czechoslovakian physician now working in the United States, tells of a series of telepathic experiments in which the sender tried to transmit bursts of emotion. When the sender concentrated on the anxiety of suffocation and conjured up racking attacks of asthma, the receiver several miles away suffered an intense choking fit. When the sender concentrated on gloomy emotions and was given a depressant drug, the receiver showed the appropriate EEC response and began to experience strong head pains and a feeling of nausea that lasted for hours. This sheds an entirely new light on the old notion of black magic. There is no doubt that someone who believes that he has been bewitched can think himself into illness and even death, but this new work makes it look as though you don't necessarily have to think your own destructive thoughts. Someone else can think them up and point them at you.

William Seabrook lived for years among the Malinke people in old French West Africa and tells of a Belgian hunter who abused and murdered his local bearers until as a matter of private justice, they arranged for a sorcerer to lay on a death-sending for him. In a clearing in the jungle the witch doctors set up the corpse of a man requisitioned from a nearby, village, dressed it in one of the Belgians shirts, combed some of his hair in among its Own, fastened some of his nail parings to its fingers, and rebaptized the body with the hunter's name. Around this object of sympathetic magic, they chanted and drummed, focusing their malignant hatred on the white man miles away. A number of his employees, pretending sympathy for him, made certain that the Belgian knew that all this was going on and would continue until he died. He soon fell ill and did die, apparently from auto-suggestion. The accepted explanation for events of this kind is that an unconscious belief in the power of the spell, even if one has not in fact been cast, can kill. But the discovery of what seems to be illness transmitted by telepathy suggests that the ceremony itself may be important. The frenzy of hate around the corpse in the jungle would certainly have a hypnotic effect on the participants and would produce exactly the conditions now known to be necessary for creating a telepathic state, the token doll in this case perhaps serving only as a focus for emotions that were in themselves doing damage at a distance.

The evidence still extant with regard to the trials of witches points unmistakably to the fact that, however such phenomena have been derided in modern times, to the witches themselves they had all the reality of actual occurrences, though it is obvious that they could not have been present and undergone these experiences in their physical forms.

Of the records of witch phenomena the one best known and from the high repute of the author most reliable, is that contained in Dr. Glanvil's *Saducismus Triumphatus*. (363) A modem work of great importance in this connection is *The Witch Cult in Western Europe* (364). In fiction two romances dealing with this subject stand out conspicuously owing to the vividness of their descriptive power, and their sympathetic appreciation of the occult in nature. These are J. W. Brodie Innes's novel, *The Devil's Mistress*, dealing with

Isabel Goudie, the so-called Witch of Aulderne, and the other a story entitled "*Secret Worship*" in Algemon Blackwood's, *Dr. John Silence* (365).

> The value of Mr. Brodie Innes's contribution to the subject lies in the fact that owing to his official position he had access to the records of witch trials preserved in the archives of the judiciary Court in Edinburgh and his story, highly coloured as it is, is actually founded on fact and introduces us to actual historical personages and among them to the celebrated witch who was eventually sentenced to death and paid the penalty for her traffic with the "Dark Master". The fascination of the book lies indeed in its adherence in its main features to the original accounts as elicited at the trial in Edinburgh and the curious may still inspect the spot where Isabel Goudie, the fair but frail wife of the farmer of Lochloy, admitted to having first encountered her Demon lover, and may visit the ruins of the old church in which she confessed to having been baptized by his Satanic Majesty.

Such phenomena have indeed long been set down to the disordered imagination of a diseased brain, but the convincing character of the evidence in regard to them has nowhere been avowed with such startling candour as in the pages of the late W. E. H. Lecky's *History of the Rise and Progress of Rationalism in Europe*, a volume the dispassionate and judicial character of which has been widely acclaimed and never called in question.

> "It is," writes Mr. Lecky, "difficult to examine the subject with impartiality without coming to the conclusion that the historical evidence establishing the reality of witchcraft is so vast and so varied that nothing but our overwhelming sense of its antecedent improbability and our modern experience of the manner in which it has faded away under the influence of civilization can justify us in despising it. The defenders of the belief who were often men of great and distinguished talent maintained that

there was no fact in all history more fully attested, and that to reject it would be to strike at the root of all historical evidence of the miraculous. The subject was examined in tens of thousands of cases in almost every country in Europe by tribunals which included the acutest lawyers and ecclesiastics of the age, on the scene and at the time when the alleged acts had taken place, and with the assistance of innumerable sworn witnesses. If we considered witchcraft probable, a hundredth part of the evidence we possess, would have placed it beyond the region of doubt. If it were a natural but very improbable fact, our reluctance to believe it would have been completely stifled by the multiplicity of the proofs."

Throughout the ages, witches and 'magicians' have produced manifestations very similar to those of the spiritualist mediums; in past centuries, mediums were known as 'scryers', meaning 'descryers of spirits'. Dr. John Dee, the famous Elizabethan magician, wrote a lengthy work (369), describing the spirits who communicated through his scryer, Edward Kelley. Witches throughout the ages have claimed to perform their magical acts through the intervention of spirits of the dead (hence the word 'necromancy'). Whatever our views on the existence of the spirits, the one thing that seems clear is that the manifestations seldom take place without the presence of a medium or scryer. The common assumption being that the medium somehow provides the necessary energy. Poltergeists are usually associated with children or adolescents, who play the part of unconscious mediums; as we have seen, there were two such in the Fox household.

It seems to me that there is incredible evidence of the power of witches and of some of the evil which they brought onto people. My friend, Pat, with his evil eye demonstrated that power very well.

--o--

CHAPTER TWENTYTWO

WHY ARE WE HERE?

> *Now that's a big question, a question man has asked for as long as he has existed.*
> *However, many great scientists, philosophers, and mystics, have come up with the same answer. 'We are here to develop our spiritual souls, and to learn tolerance, understanding and unconditional love.*

In fact, the life review bares a marked resemblance to the afterlife judgment scenes described in the sacred texts of many of the world's great religions, from the Egyptian to the Judeo-Christian, but with one crucial difference. Like Whitton's subjects, NDEers universally report that they are never judged by the beings of light, but feel only love and acceptance in their presence. The only judgment that ever takes place is self-judgment and arises solely out of the NDEers own feelings of guilt and repentance. Occasionally the beings do assert themselves, but instead of behaving in an authoritarian manner, they act as guides and counselors whose only purpose is to teach.

This total lack of cosmic judgment and / or any divine system of punishment and reward has been and continues to be one of the most controversial aspects of the NDE among religious groups, but it is one of the most oft reported features of the experience. What is the explanation? Moody believes it is as simple as it is

AFTERLIFE – THE PROOF

polemic. We live in a universe that is far more benevolent than we realize.

Some religions and individuals suggest that our purpose in life includes considerations other than those described by people now in the afterlife. We have clear descriptions of eternal life and the afterlife now in recordings of people on the next plane of life speaking and in the descriptions given to mediums. We know what is true now and what has come from the imaginations of people through the centuries. The most prominent assertions taught by religions and individuals that are not supported by those in the afterlife follow.

Those speaking from the afterlife do not describe our purpose in life as becoming perfected so we merge into a super-consciousness or ground of all being. They describe themselves as being exactly the same after death as they were before; progressing through eternity in spiritual development as the individuals they were on Earth, but on a vast number of unique spheres that the individual enters according to his or her state of mind. They do describe group souls and developing into higher planes of being, but they always maintain their individuality. During some of the periods of their eternal lives, they explain, they may have experiences as other individuals to grow and mature spiritually, but the core person remains. Loved ones stay with them and they have access to both those who have gone into the afterlife before and those still alive on the Earth plane, even though they can't freely interrupt the lives of people still engaged in learning lessons on the Earth plane.

Those in the next planes of life do not describe the purpose of life as progressing individually in spirituality without progressing with a community. None suggest self denial, or becoming a hermit as desirable means of growing spiritually. They speak of simultaneous development in individual spiritual maturity and in brotherhood and peace in humankind. We are to love and be loved in a spiritual community.

We are eternal beings having an Earthly episode in our eternal life. The eternal self exists apart from energy and matter. It's outside of the body and outside of the Earth, meaning consciousness (the mind) is elemental. It exists independent of matter and energy.

Jesus

That explains how we can know things before they happen. It explains how I'm able to sit in my office and see things on a stranger's table hundreds of miles away. And why Yeshua ben Yosef (Jesus) and other luminaries were so certain that death is only a transition into another part of our eternal existence. We have an immense amount of knowledge that we are eternal spirits and there is no rebuttal of it!

Knowing that to be true is important to your spiritual growth. If you believe you are limited in time and space to this short lifetime and you are the bag of flesh you see in a mirror, then you will be less interested in loving others, being a servant to others, listening to the Higher Power, feeling your inner self has worth, and conserving nature. You'll try to get all you can get because life is short and you have only one time around. Knowing that you are an eternal being having an Earth episode of your eternal existence is critical to spiritual growth. And if everyone has that knowledge, then society as a whole will grow spiritually as well.

--o--

CHAPTER TWENTYTHREE

MONEY AND MATERIAL POSSESSIONS

The happiest person who "has the most" is someone who lives in accordance with the rhythms of the natural world, free from the conventions and values of civilized society, and is "content with the least."

Diogenes of Sinope
(404 to 323 BC)

And to his disciples Jesus said, "It is easier for a camel to go through the eye of a needle than for a rich man to enter into the kingdom of God.

Yeshua ben Yosef
(Jesus)
(Mark: Ch10 Verse25)

Human Trafficking

Quite by accident I started watching a programme on GOD Channel. That's a channel which (for some reason) I have always avoided. However this particular programme was very good. The presenter (on stage) was Christine Caine (GLORIOUS). She couldn't half deliver a message, and very directly to those listening. She went on with real feeling about human trafficking and about how girls are kidnapped and forced into prostitution. Apparently about 20 million are missing worldwide. It is said that one girl can earn the trafficker as much as £300,000 / year. It is a horrendous life for the girls who have to have sex with as many as 40 men a day. Christine Caine told the story of 60 girls being shipped in a container. Thirty were later found to be dead. The remaining 30 were shifted to a boat (heading for Greece I think). However the Coast Guard showed up so the traffickers threw the girls overboard. A lot of them couldn't swim and only 5 got to shore!!!). Apparently this was part of Human Trafficking Weekend).

> *Do I continue to walk by on the other side and say that it is nothing to do with me?*

Materialism

I recently had cause to visit a Care Home. I have been to some very good Care Homes but this particular one was terrible. It had code locks at the entrance and at the top and bottom of the internal stairs. The atmosphere in the place was terrible. There were people wailing, and one man kept shouting out at the top of his voice "Why am I here? Why am I here?"

I discovered that some children get one or both parents put in there so that they can get their hands on their money!!! What does it say about those who willingly lock their parents up in a place like that just so that they can get their hands on their money? (They used to do the same thing in the old days but in those days they called them 'Lunatic Asylums').

> Where does Love come into this?
> I cringe when I think about it.

It was a calm, starlit night, and the two men discussed the great issue that tormented the Victorians: the problem of scientific materialism. Both men had been brought up in devoutly religious households; both had come to reject the Church of England and, as a consequence been forced to resign fellowships at Trinity.

Yet neither could accept the idea that man is stranded in a meaningless, empty universe that has been created by pure chance. And it was Myers who asked, with a kind of desperation, whether, since philosophy has failed to solve the riddle of the universe, there was just a chance that the answer might lie in the realm of ghosts and spirits. If, after all, it could be proved that there was life after death, the philosophy of materialism would vanish like a bad dream.

--o--

CHAPTER TWENTYFOUR

GOD

If you have managed to wade through all of the previous pages then you may be amazed, as I am, at just what goes on in this universe; the mysteries of the atom; the weird world of quantum; the peculiarities of time; the miracles of the disappearing kenari trees; the weird ways in which our minds can affect machines; the mysteries of the human double; seeing things at a distance; seeing future events, and more.

The advances of science in the modern age have come at the cost of certain traditional reasons for belief in God. When we had no idea how the universe came into existence, it was easier to ascribe it all to an act of God, or many separate acts of God. Similarly, until Kepler, Copernicus, and Galileo upset the applecart in the sixteenth century, the placement of Earth at the center of the majestic starry heavens seemed to represent a powerful argument for the existence of God. If He put us on center stage, He must have built it all for us. When heliocentric science forced a revision of this perception, many believers were shaken up.

But a third pillar of belief continued to carry considerable weight: the complexity of earthly life, implying to any reasonable observer the handiwork of an intelligent designer. As we see, science has now turned this upside down. But here, as with the other two arguments, I would like to suggest that science should not be denied by the believer, it should be embraced. The elegance behind life's complexity is indeed reason for awe, and for belief in God, but not in the simple, straight-forward way that many found so compelling before Darwin came along.

The "ARGUMENT FROM DESIGN" dates back at least to Cicero. It was put forward with particular effectiveness by William Paley in 1802 in a highly influential book, *Natural Theology, or Evidences of the Existence and Attributes of the Deity Collected from the Appearance of Nature*. Paley, a moral philosopher and Anglican priest, posed the famous watchmaker analogy:

In crossing a heath, suppose I pitched my foot against a Stone, and were asked how the stone came to be there; I might possibly answer that, for anything I knew to the contrary, it had lain there forever. Nor would it perhaps be very easy to show the absurdity of this answer. But suppose I had found a watch upon the ground, and it should be inquired how the watch happened to be in that place; I should hardly think of the answer, which I had before given, that for anything I knew, the watch might have always been there ... the watch must have had a maker. That there must have existed, at some time, and at some place or other, an artificer or artificers, who formed it for the purpose which we find it. Who comprehended its construction, and designed its use....Every indication of contrivance, every manifestation of design, which existed in the watch, exists in the works of nature; with the difference, on the side of nature, of being greater or more, and that in a degree which exceeds all computation.

The evidence of design in nature has been compelling to humanity throughout much of our existence. Darwin himself, before his voyage on the HMS Beagle, was an admirer of Paley's writings, and professed to be convinced by this view.

Quantum Weirdness

The "quantum weirdness" of nature has profound implications. Most significantly it tells us that the world simply is not as it seems. A superficial reading of nature finds differentiation; disparate entities: stars and stones and bottled water and even life and death. At a deeper level that same nature reveals unity. I'm on our balcony. The afternoon Jerusalem sun is filtering through the yellow-green finger leaves on a row of eucalyptus trees planted a century ago to mark the property line. ("So the field of Ephron, and the cave which was therein and all the trees that were in the field, that were in all the border round about were made over to Abraham," Genesis 23.. 17, 18).

De Broglie tells me the leaves and the light are one. Not poetically, though that also, but physically they are one. The fact that he has been proven correct fills me with joy. The universe quietly reveals its unity. God is polite, knocking only gently. We have to listen carefully if we are to hear the report.

What all of these conjectures have in common is that some-thing, or more accurately stated some non-thing, an eternal whatever, predates our universe. This whatever-it-is has no bodily parts, is totally nonmaterial, is eternal, and though being absolutely nothing physically has the infinite potential to produce vast universes. Sounds familiar. Kind of like the biblical description of God. In fact it is the biblical description of God with one significant difference. A "potential field" doesn't give a hoot about the universes it spins off. The Bible, however, claims that the Creator is intimately interested and involved in his creations. Is there any hint of a metaphysical interest in our universe?

Consider the "coincidences" of the first several minutes, and later as planets formed and cooled, coincidences that led to life and consciousness. From a ball of energy that turned into rocks and water, we get the consciousness of a thought. And all by random, unthinking reactions. Even to an atheist, this line of reasoning must seem a bit forced.

This is not a statement of the anthropic principle: "Gee, our universe is so well tuned for life that there must be a Tuner." No, what we see here is far more significant than fine-tuning. We see the consistent emergence of wisdom, of ordered complex information that is nowhere hinted at either in the governing laws of nature or in the particles of matter that form the brain that lies below the mind's thought.

There is a premise commonly applied in physics: Occam's razor, the idea that, all things being equal, the simplest, most elegant explanation tends to be true. A recent book about string theory even used the title The Elegant Universe. Why should the universe be elegant? Why should Occam's razor be true? Why are the laws of nature elegant, and from where did they acquire the wisdom to produce intelligent life? Where indeed? Could it be the metaphysical shining through?

In the twenty-first century, in an increasingly technological society, a battle is raging for the hearts and minds of humanity. Many materialists, noting triumphantly the advances of science in filling the, gaps of our understanding of nature, announce that belief in God is an outmoded superstition, and that we would be better off admitting that and moving on. Many believers in God, convinced that the truth they derive from spiritual introspection is of more enduring value than truths from other sources, see the advances in science and technology as dangerous and untrustworthy. Positions are hardening. Voices are be-coming more shrill.

Is Science a Threat to God?

Will we turn our backs on science because it is perceived as a threat to God, abandoning all of the promise of advancing our understanding of nature and applying that to the alleviation of suffering and the betterment of humankind? Alternatively, will we turn our backs on faith, concluding that science has rendered the spiritual life no longer necessary, and that traditional religious symbols can now be replaced by engravings of the, double helix on our altars?

Both of these choices are profoundly dangerous. Both deny truth. Both will diminish the nobility of humankind. Both will be devastating to our future. And both are unnecessary. The God of the Bible is also the God of the genome. He can be worshiped in the cathedral or in the laboratory. His creation is majestic, awesome, intricate, and beautiful and it cannot be at war with itself. Only we imperfect humans can start such battles. And only we can end them.

There are many subtle variants of theistic evolution, but a typical version rests upon the following premises:

1.
The universe came into being out of nothingness, approximately 14 billion years ago.
2.
Despite massive improbabilities, the properties of the universe appear to have been precisely tuned for life.
3.
While the precise mechanism of the origin of life on earth remains unknown, once life arose, the process of evolution and natural selection permitted the development of biological diversity and complexity over very long periods of time.

4.
Once evolution got under way, no special supernatural intervention was required.
5.
Humans are part of this process, sharing a common ancestor with the great apes.
6.
But humans are also unique in ways that defy evolutionary explanation and point to our spiritual nature. This includes the existence of the Moral Law (the knowledge of right and wrong) and the search for God that characterizes all human cultures throughout history.

If one accepts these six premises, then an entirely plausible, intellectually satisfying, and logically consistent synthesis emerges: God, who is not limited in space or time, created the universe and established natural laws that govern it. Seeking to populate this otherwise sterile universe with living creatures. God chose the elegant mechanism of evolution to create microbes, plants, and animals of all sorts. Most remarkably, God intentionally chose the same mechanism to give rise to special creatures who would have intelligence, a knowledge of right and wrong, free will, and a desire to seek fellowship with Him. He also knew these creatures would ultimately choose to disobey the Moral Law.

This view is entirely compatible with everything that science teaches us about the natural world. it is also entirely compatible with the great monotheistic religions of the world. The theistic evolution perspective cannot, of course, prove that God is real, as no logical argument can fully achieve that. Belief in God will always require a leap of faith. But this synthesis has provided for legions of scientist-believers a satisfying, consistent, enriching perspective that allows both the scientific and spiritual worldviews to coexist happily within us. This perspective makes it possible for the scientist-believer to be intellectually fulfilled and spiritually alive, both worshiping

God and using the tools of science to uncover some of the awesome mysteries, of His creation.

Do Scientists Believe in God?
And what about spiritual belief amongst scientists? This is actually more prevalent than many realize. In 1916, researchers asked biologists, physicists, and mathematicians whether they believed in a God who actively communicates with humankind and to whom one may pray in expectation of receiving an answer. About 40 percent answered in the affirmative. In 1997, the same survey was repeated verbatim and to the surprise of the researchers, the percentage remained very nearly the same.

So perhaps the "battle" between science and religion is not as polarized as it seems? Unfortunately, the evidence of potential harmony is often overshadowed by the high-decibel pronouncements of those who occupy the poles of the debate. Bombs are definitely being thrown from both sides. For example, essentially discrediting the spiritual beliefs of 40 percent of his colleagues as sentimental nonsense, the prominent evolutionist Richard Dawkins has emerged as the leading spokesperson for the point of view that a belief in evolution demands atheism. Among his many eye-popping statements. "Faith is the great cop-out, the great excuse to evade the need to think and evaluate evidence. Faith is belief in spite of, even perhaps be-cause of, the lack of evidence. Faith, being belief that isn't based on evidence, is the principal vice of any religion."

On the other side, certain religious fundamentalists attack science as dangerous and untrustworthy, and point to a literal interpretation of sacred texts as the only reliable means of discerning scientific truth. Among this community, comments from the late Henry Morris, a leader of the creationist movement, stand out: "Evolution's lie permeates and dominates modern thought in every field. That being the case, it follows inevitably that evolutionary thought is basically responsible for the lethally ominous political developments, and the chaotic moral and social disintegrations that have been accelerating everywhere. When science and the Bible differ, science has obviously misinterpreted its data."

When I am, as it were, completely myself, entirely alone, and of good cheer - say, travelling in a carriage, or walking after a good meal, or during the night when I cannot sleep; it is on such occasions that ideas flow best and most abundantly. Whence and how they come, I know not; nor can I force them. Nor do I hear in my imagination the parts successively but I hear them, as it were, all at once. The committing to paper is done quickly enough, for everything is already finished; and it rarely differs on paper from what it was in my imagination."

Inspiration
This enviable flow of inspiration, fully formed, was Mozart's great glory - the result, it seems, of an unusual ability to sustain the intuitive moment beyond the brief flash that leaves most of us blinking and fumbling for answers that were clear in the moment of illumination, but seldom last long enough for us to put them into words or get them down on paper.

Bach had some of Mozart's flair. "I play," he said, "the notes in order, as they are written. It is God who makes the music." Milton wrote that the Muse "dictated" to him the whole "unpremeditated song" that we now know as *Paradise Lost*. Robert Louis Stevenson dreamed the plot of *Doctor Jekyll and Mister Hyde*. Samuel Taylor Coleridge awoke with what he called "a distinct recollection" of the whole of "*Kubla Khan*", which he wrote down without conscious effort, pausing only when interrupted by the infamous Visitor from Porlock. By the time that Coleridge returned to his room, the end of the poem was lost forever. It had "passed away like the images on the surface of a stream into which a stone has been cast." The flow was broken and the work remains tantalizingly incomplete.

We humans like to label things, to wrap our minds around a concept, to define and package it; in essence to limit it so that the concept finds harmony within our human definition of logic. But how does someone label or even think about that which is not part of our physical world? Confining the metaphysical to a physical description totally misses the "meta" aspect.

And Jacob asked him, and said "Tell me your name." And he said "Wherefore is it that you ask after my name?"(Genesis 32:30)

And [the people] will say to me "What is His name?" What shall I say to them? And God said to Moses, 'I will be that which I will be." And He said thus shall you say to the children of Israel "I will be" send me to you.... This is My name Leolam. (Exod. 3:13-15)

Leolam, a Hebrew word with three root meanings: forever, and also hidden, and also in the world. This is my name forever hidden in the world. So how to recognize the presence of the metaphysical?

In that day [the Eternal] shall be one Lord, and his name one. (Zech. 14:9)

The Eternal is One. (Deut. 6:4)   (366)

So there is science and there is God, and, although it hasn't always been that way, I (John Burrows) know now, in my heart of hearts that there is a God.

--o--

CLOSING REFLECTION

Love the Lord God with all your Heart
Love your neighbour as yourself

--o--

Help make this World a better place

--o--

--END--

APPENDIX 1

PYRAMIDS

There has been a lot of research into the peculiar effects observable inside of pyramids. Pyramids have been found to:

1 Restore the lustre to tarnished jewellery and coins.
2 Purify water.
3 Mummify meat, eggs and other food stuffs.
4 Maintain the freshness of milk and prevent souring without refrigeration.
5 Dehydrate flowers without losing their form or colour.
6 Increase the growth of plants.
7 Help attain increased relaxation.
8 Improve the taste of coffee, wine and certain fruit juices.
9 Promote the healing of cuts, bruises and burns, as well as reduce pain from toothaches and headaches.
10 Improve health.
11 Re-energise people.
12 Trigger sex urges.
13 Effect the penetration of cosmic rays.
14 Removes wrinkles

In 1968 a team of scientists from the United States and from the Ein Shams University in Cairo began a million-dollar project to X-ray the pyramid of Chephren, successor to Cheops. They hoped to find new vaults hidden in the six million tons of stone by placing detectors in a chamber at its base and measuring the amount of cosmic ray penetration, the theory being that more rays would come through hollow areas. The recorders ran twenty-four hours a day for more than a year until, in early 1969, the latest (at the time), IBM 1130 computer was delivered to the university for analysis of the tapes. Six months later the scientists had to admit defeat: the pyramid made no sense at all. Tapes recorded with the same equipment from the same point on successive days showed totally different cosmic-ray patterns. The leader of the project, Amr Gohed, in an interview afterward said, "This is scientifically impossible. Call it what you will – occultism, the curse of the pharaohs, sorcery, or magic, there is some force that defies the laws of science at work in the pyramid.

But that is not the end of it. It has been found that other geometric shapes have mystifying properties as well, the sphere, the cube and the hexahedron, all have their own special properties.

> I find this all very mystifying,
> but I'm grateful we have
> such a mysterious universe.

--o--

APPENDIX 2

RESONANCE

When I was a young man I worked as an apprentice in the Electric Shop of Pilkington Brothers Plate works in St. Helens.

It was a very substantial building with large double, steel, columns which carried an overhead crane down the central length of the building. I worked in a lower roofed side section, a bit like the side aisle in a church.

One day I was working at my bench when, above the noise of everything else, I could clearly hear a high pitched buzzing. I had always had an inquisitive nature so I tried to figure out where the noise was coming from. I eventually discovered that it was coming from a fuse box about 10 feet up on the crane columns.

I looked all around the columns but couldn't figure out what was causing the noise. Maybe there was some kind of electrical fault in the fuse box.

Then just as quickly as it started, it stopped. No more buzzing.

I got back to work again but then, later, there it was again. This time I decided to explore immediately before it disappeared again. Maybe it was a fault in the fuse box. There was no signs of what was causing it. I started to explore further down the building but then the noise stopped again.

I continued to explore the noise each time it reappeared and it took me three days to realize that it was caused by a small grinding machine at the bottom end of the building. There was no buzzing from anything else around the grinding machine or the fuse box, but that was what it was. Every time the grinder started the fuse box buzzed. It was just like turning a light switch on and off. I was amazed.

For me, it was a great demonstration of resonance, or 'sympathetic vibration' as it is sometimes called.

We used to have an upright piano and, sometimes if I listened quietly, I could hear a note coming from it. I did a bit of experimenting with it and, even with my imperfect voice, I found that if I sang a steady note, the piano would sing the same note back to me.

Resonance is a wonderful thing, but, as I have discovered since, it is not always wonderful. Given the right frequency and the right conditions, it can cause solid buildings to collapse.

Many scientists believe that resonance is responsible in Psychokinesis where similar vibration patterns in different objects cause them to move, jump, or topple over from the effect of a person's mind

--o--

END NOTES

(1)   The Psychic Detectives (Colin Wilson) pages 20 & 21
(2)   The Adventures of Self Discovery (Grof) page 266
(3)   The Adventures of Self Discovery (Grof) page 149
(4)   Your Eternal Self, page 60 (Craig Hogan)
(5)   The Adventures of Self Discovery (Grof) page 261
(6)   The Hidden Face of God (Schroeder) page 3
(7)   The Language of God (Collins) pages 63 to 66
(8)   The Hidden face of God (Schroeder) page 45
(9)   The Language of God (Collins) pages 66 & 67
(10) A Penzias quoted by M. Browne, "Clues to the Universe's
      Origin Expected, "New York Times (March 12, 1978)
(11) Supernature (Watson) pages 123 & 124
(12) The Hidden face of God (Schroeder) page 4
(13) The Holographic Universe (Talbot) page 33
(14) After We Die, What Then?, page 78 (Meek)
(15) The Holographic Universe (Michael Talbot) pages 41 & 42
(16) The Hidden face of God (Schroeder) pages 26 & 27
(17) The Hidden face of God (Schroeder) page 25
(18) The Hidden face of God (Schroeder) page 25
(19) Beyond Supernature, page 235 (Lyall Watson)
(20) The Holographic Universe (Michael Talbot) page 47
(21) Tales of Power (Carlos Castaneda) page 300
(22) The Holographic Universe (Talbot) page 254
(23) The Mystery of the Human Double pages 41 to 42 (Shirley &
      Shepard).
(24) Supernature (Watson) pages 294 & 296
(25) The Holographic Universe (Talbot) Page 207
(26) Heading toward Omega (Ring) pages 217 & 218
(27) Your Sixth Sense (Steiger, B) New York Award Books,
      (1966)
(28) The Mystery of the Human Double pages 36 to 38 (Shirley &
      Shepard).
(29) ESP Power, page 239 (Jane Roberts)
(30) Beyond Supernature (Watson) page 267
(31) Beyond the Brain (Grof) page 31
(32) Tales of Power, page 100. (Catanada)
(33) The Doors of Perception – (Huxley) (1954)
(34) Beyond Supernature pages 265 and 266
(35) Natural History Of The Mind page 7 (Taylor)
(36) The Holographic Paradigm (Karl Pribram) page 24
(37) ESP Power, page 142 (Jane Roberts)
(38) Beyond the Brain, page 31 (Grof)
(39) The Holographic Universe, page 31 (Talbot, Michael)
(40) The Neurophysiological Basis of Mind. Oxford: (Eccles, J.

C.) The Clarendon Press 1953 (Referred to on page 150 of Lyall Watson's 'Supernature'.).

(41) The Natural History Of the Mind (Taylor) page 295

(42) (The Body) (Smith) (1985).

(43) The Hidden face of God (Schroeder) page 5

(44) The Natural History Of the Mind (Taylor) page 234

(45) Your eternal Self (Hogan) pages 9 and 10

(46) Enjoy Your Own Funeral (Meek) pages 14 & 15

(47) Value and Need as Organic factors in Perception (Journal of Abnormal & Social Psychology, pages 42 & 33 (Bruner & Goodman)

(48) The Natural History of the Mind, pages 314 & 315 (Gordon Rattray Taylor)

(49) The Natural History of the Mind, pages 275 & 276 (Gordon Rattray Taylor)

(50) The Art of Memory (Yates) 1906

(51) The Detailed Texture of Eidetic Images) (Stromeyer & Psotka) 1970

(52) The Mystery of the Human Double page 106 (Shirley & Shepard)

(53) Autobiography of a Yogi, (Paramahansa Yogananda) (page 134)

(54) Hunt, 1985 (page 5).

(55) Roy, 1996 (page 176).

(56) Supernature, page 119 (Lyall Watson)

(57) Belief in God in an Age of Science, pages 18 to 19) (Polkinghorne) (1998)

(58) Supernature pages 106 & 107 (Lyall Watson)

(59) The Psychic Detective page 36 (Wilson)

(60) The Sea Around Us, (Carson) (1951)

(61) Initial results of the IMP-1 magnetic Field Experiment, (Goddard Space Flight Centre) (1964)

(62) Dating the Past, (Zeuner) (1950).

(63) Planetary Position Effect on Short Wave Signal Quality, (Nelson) (Electrical Engineering 72: 421, 1952)

(64) Tree Potential and Sunspots (Burr) (Cycles 243: October 1964)

(65) Methodes pour etudier la repartition des astres dans le mouvemnent diurnr, (Paris) (1957) (120)

(66) A Theory on the Structure of Water, (Pople) (Proceedings of the Royal Society, 1950).

(67) The Morning of the Magicians, (Pauwels & Bergier) (1964)

(68) Ober eine neue bioglisch wirksame Kompente der Sonnenstrahlung page 486) (TAKATA) (1951)

(69)   Cymatics, (Jenny) (1966)
(70)   Psychic Discoveries behind the Iron Curtain,
       Ostrander) (I97I)
(71)   Modern Miracles, p[ages 26 & 27 (Haraldsson) (1987)
(72)   (Modern Miracles. An Investigative Report into Psychic
       Phenomena Associated with Sathya Sai Baba pages 35 to
       36) (Haraldsson) (1987)
(73)   Shamanism, ESP, and the Paranormal, page 135, (Scott
       Rogo) (1987)
(74)   The Ancient Wisdom in Shamanic Cultures, page 10,
       (Harner & Doore) (1987).
(75)   The Way of the Shaman, page 17 (Michael Harner)
       (1980).
(76)   Beyond Human Knowledge, (Von Urban) (1958).
(77)   The Way of the Sharman, (Harner) (1980)
(78)   Gifts of Unknown Things, pages & 204, (Lyall Watson)
       (1976)
(79)   The Paranormal (Inglis) (1985)
(80)   Dowsing, (Graves) (1976)
(81)   Sex, Customs and Parapsychology, (Laubscher) (1938)
(82)   PSI Abilities of Primitive Groups) (Proceedings of the
       Para psychological Association) (Van De Castle) (1970).
(83)   Intuitive Archaeology, (Emerson) (1973).
(84)   Archaeological Map Dowsing, (Ross) (1975)
(85)   The Holographic Universe, page 158 (Talbot)
(86)   Habitual Short-Term Memories & Luck (Taylor) (1967)
(87)   Why Some Succeed and Others Fail (Van Lennep) (1962)
(88)   Winning at Casino Gambling (Rouge Et Noir) (1966)
(89)   The Adventures of Self-Discovery, pages 156 & 157
       (Grof, Stanislov)
(90)   An Interview with Whitley Strieber page, 41 (Daab &
       Langevin) (1990)
(91)   A Casebook of Alien Contact, page 269, (Jacques Vallee)
       (1988)
(92)   The Interrupted Journey, page 9, (John G. Fuller)
       (1966).
(93)   The Kulagina Cine Film, (Journal of Para physics) (1969).
(94)   Beyond Supernature, pages 200 and 201 (WATSON,
       LYALL)
(95)   A PK test with Electronic Equipment – Journal of
       Parapsychology 1970) (Schmidt)
(96)   Parapsychology and the Nature of Life, (Randall) (1975)
(97)   Psychic Discoveries behind the Red Curtain (Ostrander
       and Schroeder) (1971)
(98)   Psychic Discoveries behind the Red Curtain (Ostrander
       and Schroeder) (1971).

(99)   When Apples Fall (Kolodny) 1968.
(100)   Psychic Discoveries behind the Red Curtain (Ostrander
        and Schroeder) (1971).
(101)   A New Theory of the Relationship of Mind & Matter, page 122
        (David J. Bohm) (1987)
(102)   Physical Investigation of Psycho-kinetic Phenomena
        in Rosenheim, (Karger & Zicha) (1968)
(103)   Your Eternal Self (Craig Hogan) pages 186 & 187
(104)   Radin, page 167, (1997)
(105)   Tiller, (1999).
(106)   Directory of spontaneous phenomena 3: 183, (1969)
(107)   Where are We Going? (Reference 115) (Weizenbaum)
(108)   Feedback techniques for deep relaxation, (Parapsychology 6:
        371, 1969.)
(109)   The Koestler Chair of Parapsychology, (Journal of the Society
        for Psychical Research 53: 196) (1985)
(110)   Emoto, (2005)
(111)   Mass Dreams of the Future, page 218 (New
        York: McGraw-Hill,1989) (Snow, Chet B. and
        Wabash, Helen)
(112)   Attention units in the auditory cortex, Science: 129, 1279,
        (1959) (Hubel BD. H.)
(113)   The Neurophysiology of remembering) (Scientific
        American 228: 73, 1989) (Pribram K. H.)
(114)   Beyond Supernature, page 96 (Lyall Watson)
(115)   The Holographic Universe, page 127 (Talbot)
(116)   Miracles of Healing in Anglo-Celtic Northumbria as
        recorded by the Venerable Bede and his contemporaries,
        (British Medical Journal 287 – December 1983)
(117)   (Braud) (1990)
(118)   The Adventures of Self Discovery (Grof) (Page 158)
(119)   Probing the Enigma of Multiple Personality – (New York Times,
        June 25, 1988) page C1
(120)   Private Communication with Michael Talbot, January 11, 1990
(121)   The Holographic Universe, pages 90 & 91 (Talbot)
(122)   The Medusa and the Snail, page 63 (Lewis Thomas)
        (1980)
(123)   The Holographic Universe, pages 93 & 107 (Talbot)
(124)   Physiological variables in Human Cancer, (Journal of
        Prospective Techniques 31), pages 331 to 340)
        (Bruno Klopfer) (1967)
(125)   Getting Well Again (Simonton, Simonton & Creighton)
        pages 6 to 12 (1980)
(126)   (ASPR Newsletter page 20 (Achterberg)
(127)   The Natural History of the Mind, page 5 (Gordon Rattray Talor)

386

AFTERLIFE – THE PROOF

(128) The Influence of an Unorthodox Method of Treatment of
       Wound Healing of Mice (Grad) (1961).
(129) SUPERNATURE pages 162 & 163 (Lyall Watson)
(130) The Laying on of Hands: Implications for Psychotherapy,
       Gentling & the Placebo Effect (page 256) (Journal of the
       American Society for Psychical Research) (1967)
(131) The Mystery of the Human Double, Pages 15 To 17)
       (Shirley & Shepard)
(132) After We Die What Then? Pages 22 & 23 (Meek)
(133) The Holographic Universe, pages 167 & 168 (Talbot)
(135) Communication with Michael Talbot, (February 7, 1990)
(136) Adventures in the Supernormal (Garrett) (1959).
(137) The Human Atmosphere (Kilner) (1911)
(138) Hands of Light, page 26 (Barbara Ann Brennan) (1987)
(139) The Holographic Universe, page 179 (Talbot)
(140) Multiplicity and the Mind-body Problem, page 19 (Thomas
       J. Hurley III) (1985).
(141) The Body Electric (Becker & Selden) (1985)
(142) Your Life in their Hands (Hutchinson) (1967).
(143) Supernature, pages 196 & 197 (Lyall Watson)
(144) Pre-School, page 38 (Omni 11, no. 11) (August 1989)
       (Pamela Weintraub)
(145) Hostility Boosts Risk of Heart Trouble, page 60
       (Science News135 no. 4 (January 28, 1989 (Kathy A.
       Facklelmann)
(146) Longevity (November 1988) (as quoted in Your Mind's
       Healing Powers) (Science News, page 5) (1989)
(147) Emotion-Immunity Link in HIV Infection (Science News
       134 no. 8) (August 20, 1988) (page 116)
(148) Your Attitude Can Make You Well, (Reader's Digest, April
       1987, page 75)
(149) Daniel Goldman in the New York Times, (April
       20, 1989) (as quoted in - Your Mind's Healing
       Powers) (Reader's Digest , September 1989, page 6)
(150) Robinson, (Reader's Digest, page 75)
(151) Signe Hammer, (The Mind as Healer) (Science
       Digest 92, no. 4, April 1984, page 100)
(152) Signals of What?, (Leonidov) (Soviet Union 145: 1962)
(153) Psychic discoveries behind the Iron Curtain, (Ostrander
       and Schroeder) (1973)
(154) After We Die, What Then? pages 55 & 56 (George W.
       Meek)
(155) The Alternative Health Guide, Michael Joseph:
       London, 1983) (Inglis B. & West R.)
(156) Report on Radionics, Spearman, London, 1973
       (Russell E. W.)

(157) The Mind Fields, Omni: August 1984, (McAuliffe, K.)

(158) The Mystery of the Human Double pages 46 to 48, and 52 (Shirley and Shepard)

(159) The Mystery of the Human Double, page 52 (Shirley and Shepard)

(160) The Mystery of the Human Double page, 56 & 57 (Shirley and Shepard)

(161) The Mystery of the Human Double, pages 58 & 59 (Shirley and Shepard)

(162) The Mystery of the Human Double pages 62 & 63 (Shirley and Shepard)

(163) The Mystery of the Human Double pages, 64 to 69 (Shirley and Shepard)

(164) The Mystery of the Human Double pages, 71 to 74 (Shirley and Shepard)

(165) The Mystery of the Human Double pages, 79 to 81 (Shirley and Shepard)

(166) The Mystery of the Human Double, page 188 (Shirley and Shepard)

(167) Probing the Enigma of Multiple Personality – (New York Times, June 25, 1988) page C1

(168) Private Communication with Michael Talbot, January 11, 1990

(169) The Mystery of the Human Double pages 21 to 26 (Shirley & Shepard.

(170) The Mystery of the Human Double. University Books: New York, 1965, (Shirley, R.)

(171) A Cross-Cultural Survey of Beliefs in Out-Of-The-Body Experiences, Journal of the Society for Psychical Research 49: 697, 1978, (Sheils, D.)

(172) The Holographic Universe (Talbot) Page 69

(173) The Adventures of Self Discovery (Grof) page 90

(174) The Mystery of the Human Double pages 111 & 112 (Shirley and Shepard)

(175) The Mystery of the Human Double page 154 to 156 (Shirley and Shepard)

(176) The Psychic Detectives page 54 (Colin Wilson)

(177) A study of Psychological Variables Associated with Out-of-Body Experiences, Ref 251 (Hartwell J. – in – Morris)

(178) The Use of Detectors for Out-of-Body Experiences, (Ref. 313) (Morris R. L.- in – Roll).

(179) An Experimental approach to the Survival Problem (Theta 33; 1971) (Morris R. L.)

(180) The Romeo Error (Watson L.) (1974)

(181)   A Journey out of the Body (Doubleday: New York, 1971) (Monroe R. A.)
(182)   Census of Hallucinations (Society for Psychical Research) (1894)
(183)   A Selection of Cases from a Recent Survey from Spontaneous ESP Phenomena (Journal of American Society for Psychical Research) (56: 3) (1962) (Dale L.A.)
(184)   Phantasms of the Living (TRUBER: London) (1886) (Gurney E.)
(185)   ESP Projection (Journal of American Society for Psychical Research) (48: 121) (1954) (HART H.)
(186)   Results of an Out-Of-Body Survey (ref: 284) (POYNTON J. C.)
(187)   Results of an Out-of-Body Survey (Ref. 284) (Poynton J. C.)
(188)   A Cross-Cultural Survey of Beliefs in Out-Of-Body Experiences (Journal of the society for Psychical Research) (49: 697) (1978) (SHEILS D.)
(189)   Beyond the Body (Heinemann, London, 1982) (Blackmore S. J.)
(190)   PSI (Dutton: New York, 1977) (TART C. T.)
(191)   Perceptual Experiments on Out-Of-body experiences (Osis K. - in – Morris: ref. 251)
(192)   After We Die What Then? pages 42 and 43 (Meek, George W.)
(193)   Astral Travel (New Age Journal, November / December, 1988) (Page 45) (Bassior, Jean-Noel
(194)   New ASPR Research on Out-Of-Body Experiences (Newsletter to the American Society for Psychical Research 14 (1972) (Karl Osis) See also - Out Of-Body research at the American Society for Psychical Research – in Mind Beyond the Body) (New York Penguin, 1978. pages 152 to 169)
(195)   Psychic Breakthroughs Today (Wellingborough, Great Britain; Aquarian Press, 1987) pages 163 to 164) (Scott Rogo, D.)
(196)   Out of Body Experiences (New York: Ballantyne Books, 1987, page 81) (Mitchell, Janet Lee)
(197)   In the Minds of Millions (Allen: London, 1977) (Manning M.)
(198)   Psi. Dutton, New York (1977) (Tart C. T)
(199)   Mind Reach (Delacorte: New York, 1977) (Targ R. & Puthoff H.)
(200)   The Mind Race (Villard: New York, 1984) (Targ, R. & Harary K.)

(201) Mind at Large (Praeger: New York, 1979) (Tart C. T.)
(202) The Mind Race (Villard: New York, 1984) (Targ, R. & Harary, K.)
(203) Research in Parapsychology (1979) (Scarecrow: New Jersey, 1980) (Targ, R. et al)
(204) Images from H. E. Puthoff (CIA Remote Viewing at Stanford Research Institute)
(205) Radin (1997) (page 104)
(206) (Utts, 1995)
(207) A Lawyer Presents the case for the Afterlife, pages 133 to 136 (Zammit, Victor)
(208) McMoneagle (2000:176-177).
(209) Major General Edmund R Thompson, U.S. Army Assistant Chief of Staff for Intelligence (1977-81; Deputy Director for Management and Operations, DIA, 1982-84) (Cover of Schnabel 1997)
(210) The Human Double, pages 150 & 151 (Shirley, Ralph & Shepard, Leslie)
(211) The Psychic Detectives, pages 57 & 58 (Wilson, Colin)
(212) The Near-Death Experience, (Chicago: Charles C. Thomas, 1984) as quoted by Stanislov Grof in 'The adventures of Self Discovery (Albany, N. Y.: SUNY Press, 1988, pages 71 to 72
(213) See also chapter 3
(214) Targ and Puthoff 1978, Targ and Harary 1984
(215) Ideas and Opinions (Einstein, A) Crown: New York, 1973)
(216) Extrasensory Perception (Boston: Bruce Humphries) (1934) (RHINE J. B.)
(217) The Focusing of ESP Upon Particular Targets (Journal of Psychology 27: 4. 1963) (Ryzl M. & Pratt J. G.) Psychology 27: 4. 1963) (Ryzl M. & Pratt J. G.)
(218) Prediction of ESP Performance on Selected Focusing Effect Targets (Journal of American Society for Parapsychological Research 63, 1969)
(219) Psychic (London: Barker, 1962) (HURKOS P.)
(220) Clairvoyance (The Psychic Detectives, page 83) (Wilson, Colin)
(221) ESP Power, page 69 (Roberts, Jane)
(222) ESP Power, pages 255 & 257 (Roberts, Jane)
(223) Extrasensory Communications and Dreams (in *Handbook of Dreams*, ed Benjamin B. Wolman) (New York: Van Nostrand Reinhold, 1979) (pages 178 to 179)
(224) Private Communication with Michael Talbot, October 31, 1988.]
(225) Wholeness and Dreaming (in *Quantum Implications*. Ed. Basil

390

J. Hiley and F, David Peat) (New York: Routledge & Kegan
Paul, 1987) (page 393)
(226)   Some Cases of Prediction, (London: Bell, 1937) (Lyttelton,
        Edith)
(227)   Frequency of Types of Experience in Spontaneous
        Precognition) (*Journal of Parapsychology* 18, no. 2,
        1954) (see also Precognition and intervention)
        (*Journal of Parapsychology* 19 (1955), and *Hidden
        Channels of the Mind* (New York: Sloane Associates,
        1961)
(228)   Precognition and Retrocognition in *Psychic Explorations,*
        ed. Edgar G. Mitchell and John White) (New York: G. P.
        Putnam's Sons, 1974) (page 163).
(229)   ESP Tests with American Indian Children, (*Journal of
        Parapsychology* 7, no. 94 (1943); Dorothy H. Pope) (ESP
        Tests with Primitive People) (*Parapsychology Bulletin* 30,
        no. I (1953); Ronald Rose and Lyndon Rose, Psi
        Experiments with Australian aborigines) (*Journal of
        Parapsychology* 15, no. 122 (1951); Robert L. Van de
        Castle, ed. Edgar D. Mitchell and John White (New York:
        G. P. Putnam's sons, 1974); and Robert L, Van de
        Castle, Psi Abilities in Primitive Groups) (*Proceedings of
        the Parapsychological Association i7, no. 97 (1970).*
(230)   Precognition of Disasters, (*Journal of the American
        Society for Psychical Research* 64. no. 2 (1970)
(231)   Space and Time variables in ESP, (*Journal of the
        American Society for Psychical Research* 58) (1964)
        (Osis, Karlis & Fahler J.)
(232)   Parapsychology and Contemporary Science, trans.
        Aleksandr Petrovich (New York: Consultants Bureau,
        1982) (pages 93 to 104) (Dubrov Alexander P. and
        Pushkin Veniamin N,)
(233)   *The Future is Now: (The Significance of Perception)* (New
        York: University Books, 1961) (Osborn, Arthur)
(234)   Extrasensory Perception, (SPR: Boston, 1934)
        (Rhine J. B.)
(235)   The Elusive Science, (John Hopkins University:
        Baltimore, 1981) (Mauskopf, S. H. & McVaugh).
(236)   The Australian Aborigines. (Angus & Robertson: Sydney,
        1942) (Elkin A. P.)
(237)   Aboriginal Men of High Degree. (St. Martins: New York,
        1977) (Elkin A. P.)
(238)   Hogan's Personal Communications, (1984) (Travis
        W.)
(239)   (Penman, 2007)
(240)   (Radin, 1997, page 101)

(241) Your Eternal self, page 42, (Hogan, R. Craig)
(242) A Lawyer Presents the Case for the Afterlife pages, 52 & 53 (Zammit, Victor)
(243) Ring & Cooper (1999)
(244) Dossey (1989, page 18)
(245) A Lawyer Presents the Case for the Afterlife, pages 55 to 57 (Zammit, Victor)
(246) Heading Towards Omega, pages 143 to 164 (Ring)
(247) Heading Towards Omega, pages 114 to 120 (Ring)
(248) Increase in Psychic and Psi-related Phenomena following Near Death experiences (*Theta,* as quoted in Ring, Heading Towards Omega, page 180)
(249) Nature as Creativity (*Re Vision 5,* no. 2) (Fall 1982, page 40)
(250) Near death Experiences (The Holographic Universe, page 240 (Talbot, Michael)
(251) (Moore) (2006)
(252) (Wagner) (2007)
(253) (Morse with Perry) (1990)
(254) (Komp) (1992)
(255) (Kubler-Ross) (1983)
(256) (OSIS) (2007)
(257) A Lawyer Presents the Case for the Afterlife, pages 138 & 139 (Victor Zammit)
(258) A Lawyer Presents the Case for the Afterlife, pages 199 to 204 (Victor Zammit)
(259) The Mystery of the Human Double, page 187 (Shirley and Shepard)
(260) A Brain rewires Itself in a Test Tube (New Scientist, 6 January, 1972) (Seeds N.)
(261) Exploring English Character (London: Cresset, 1955) (Gorer, G.)
(262) The Psychic Detectives, page 93 (Wilson, Colin)
(263) After We Die What Then? Page 44 (Meek, George W.)
(264) The Fairy Faith in Celtic Countries (Oxford: Oxford University Press, 1911) (page 111) (Evanz-Wentz, W. Y.)
(265) Ghosts (Editors of Life-Time Books) (Alexandria, Va.: Time-Life Books, 1984) (page 75)
(266) Your Eternal Self, pages 245 & 246 (Hogan, R. Craig)
(267) The Psychic Detectives, pages 38 to 40 (Wilson, Colin)

(268)   In the Minds of Millions (1977)
(269)   A Lawyer Presents the Case for the Afterlife pages, 169
        to 171 (Victor Zammit, Victor)
(270)   Lawyer Presents the Case for the Afterlife, pages 164
        to 167 (Zammit, Victor)
(271)   A Lawyer Presents the Case for the Afterlife pages,
        169 to 171
(272)   Interested readers will find more information in the
        writings of Charles Tart (Tart 1975a, 1977), Stanley
        Krippner (Krippner 1977, 1980), Jules Eisenbud
        (Eisenbud 1967), Russell Targ and Harold Puthoff
        (Targ and Puthoff 1978, Targ and Harary 1984), and
        Hans Bender (Bender 1984ab, 1985)
(273)   (Hazlewood, J). in Steiger
(274)   Can We Explain the Poltergeist? (New York: Garrett
        Publications, 1964) (Owen, A. R. G.)
(275)   Beyond Supernature, pages 189 & 190 (Watson,
        Lyall)
(276)   Magic & Religion (London, 1901) (Lang, A.)
(277)   Between Two Worlds (Parker: New York, 1964)
        (Fodor, N.)
(278)   Your Eternal Self, pages 171 & 172 (Hogan, R. Craig)
(279)   McKenna & O'Bryen, (1997)
(280)   Radin and others, (2000)
(281)   Playfair, (2003)
(282)   ESP Power, pages 88 & 89 (Roberts, Jane)
(283)   Quasi-sensory Communications, *(Journal of Personality
        and Social Psychology,* 14: 281, 1970) (McBAIN, W. N.)
(284)   The Living Stream, (London: Collins, 1965) (Hardy A.)
(285)   Rhythms of Success in PK Test Data, *(Journal of
        Parapsychology* 11: 26, 1947) (Pratt J. G)
(286)   Psychic Discoveries Behind the Iron Curtain,
        Englewood Cliffs. N.J.: Prentice Hall, 1971)
        (Ostrander, S. & Schroeder I.)
(287)   The Psychic Detectives, page 45 (Wilson, Colin)
(288)   Beyond Supernature, pages 142 & 143 (Watson,
        Lyall)
(289)   The Airmen who would Not Die, Putnam: New York,
        1979) (Fuller J. G.)
(290)   Parapsychology and the Nature of Life *(Souvenir:
        London, 1975)* (Randall, J. L.)
(291)   The Mentality of Apes, Kegan Paul: London, 1927.
        (Kohler W.)
(292)   Telepathy at Times of Crisis – Supernature, pages 260 &
        261 (Watson, Lyall)
(293)   Psi Developments in the USSR, *(Bulletin of the*

Foundation for Research on the Nature of Man 6:
1967) (FRNM)

(294) Supernature, page 267 (Watson, Lyall)

(295) Experiments in Mental Suggestion, (Hampshire: Galley
Hill Press, 1963) (Vasiliev L. L.)

(296) The Psychic Detectives (Wilson, Colin) back cover

(297) The Secret Vaults of Time, (New York: Grosset &
Dunlap, 1978) : Stanislaw Poniatowski,
"Parapsychological Probing of Prehistoric Cultures,"
in *Psychic Archaeology,* ed. J. Goodman (New York:
G. P. Putnam & Sons, 1977); and Audrey
Borzmowski "Experiments with Ossowiecki,"
International Journal of Parapsychology 7, no. 3
(1965). Pages 259 to 284

(298) The Psychic Detectives, pages 44 to 46 & 47 (Wilson,
Colin)

(299) The Psychic Detectives, page 93 (Wilson, Colin)

(300) The Psychic Detectives page 49 (Wilson, Colin)

(301) The Psychic Detectives pages 50 to 53 (Wilson,
Colin)

(302) A Step in the Dark (London: Routledge & Kegan
Paul, 1967)

(303) Psychic Discoveries behind the Iron Curtain, (Englewood Cliffs,
N. J.: Prentice Hall, 1971) (Ostrander, S. & Schroeder, L.)

(304) Parapsychological Probing of Prehistoric Cultures, (in
Goodman, Ref. 128) (Pontiatowski, S.)

(305) Psychic Archaeology, (Putnam: New York, 1977)
(Goodman, J.)

(306) The Enchanted Boundary, (Little, Brown: Boston, 1930)
(Prince, W. F.)

(307) Clairvoyant Reality, (Turnstone: London, 1974)
(Leshan, L.)

(308) The Psychology of Consciousness (Robert Ornstein)
(1972)

(309) After We Die What Then?, page 123 (Meek, George
W.)

(310) (*Light*, pages 103 to 107) (Moody and Perry)

(311) Supernature, page 242 (Watson, Lyall)

(312) Beyond Supernature, pages 204 & 205 (Watson,
Lyall)

(313) (Hertzog & Herrin) (1985)

(314) (Gabbard & Twemlow) (1985)

(315) (Morse) (1994)

(316) The Evolution of Research into Hypnotism, (In
Psychophysiological Mechanisms of Hypnosis. New York:

394

AFTERLIFE – THE PROOF

Springer-Verlag, 1969) (Chertok, L.)

(317)   *Uber die sogenannte Tierhypnose,* Berlin: Akad. Verlag, 1953) (Pavlov, I. P.)

(318)   *Hypnosis,* (Bristol: John Wright, 1967) (Milechnin, A.)

(319)   *Mind & Body,* (London: William Kimber, 1969) (Black, S.)

(320)   *The Naked Ape,* (London: Jonathan Cape, 1987) (Morris, D.)

(321)   The Psychic Detectives, pages 62 & 63 (Wilson, Colin)

(322)   The Mental State of Hystericals (Putnam: New York, 1901) (Janet P.)

(323)   The Soul of the Ape (Blond: London, 1969) (Marais E.)

(324)   Antisocial or Criminal Acts and Hypnosis (Reiter, Paul J.)

(325)   The Mystery of the Human Double, pages 148 & 149 (Shirley, Ralph & Shepard, Leslie)

(326)   Hypnotism and the Supernormal, (London: Aquarian Press, 1967, as quoted in Supernature by Lyall Watson) (Bantam Books, 1973, page 236)

(327)   Hypnotism and the Supernormal, (London: Aquarian Press, 1967, as quoted in Supernature by Lyall Watson) (Bantam Books, 1973, page 236)

(328)   After We Die What Then?, page 76 (Meek, George W.)

(329)   Your Eternal Self (Hogan. R. Craig) page 251

(330)   A Lawyer Presents the Case for the Afterlife, pages 218 to 220 (Victor Zammit)

(331)   A Lawyer Presents the Case for the Afterlife, pages 222 to 227 (Victor Zammit)

(332)   A Lawyer Presents the Case for the Afterlife, pages 131 & 132 (Victor Zammit)

(333)   A Lawyer Presents the Case for the Afterlife, pages 71 & 72 (Victor Zammit)

(334)   A Lawyer Presents the Case for the Afterlife, pages73 to 75 (Victor Zammit)

(335)   The Reality of Psychic Phenomena (1916), Experiments in Psychic Science (1916) and The Psychic Structures in the Goligher Circle (1921)

(336)   Butler 1947:78

(337)   Meek 1987:69

(338)   Zeitschrift fuer Parapsychologie, (1927:450-462)

(339)   The Mystery of the Human Double page, 145 (Shirley and Shepard)

(340)   Enjoy Your Own Funeral, page 108 (Meek, George W.)

(341)   Dream Time and Inner Space (Boston: Shambhala Publications. 1994, pages 12 and 13) (Kaweit, Holger)

(342)   The Holographic Universe, page 218 (Talbot, Michael)

(343)   Twenty cases Suggestive of Reincarnation (Ian Stevenson) (University Press of Virginia, 1974).

AFTERLIFE – THE PROOF

(344)   After We Die What Then?, page 96 (Meek, George W.)

(345)   ESP Power, pages 244 & 245 (Roberts, Jane)

(346)   After We Die What Then?, pages 80 & 81 (Meek, George W.)

(347)   Your Eternal Self, pages 129 & 130 (Hogan, R. Craig)

(348)   A Lawyer Presents the case for the Afterlife, page 131 (Zammit, Victor) (2006)

(349)   (Dodds) (1962)

(350)   (Wilson, 1987:176).

(351)   (Murphet, 1990:64).

(352)   (Wilson, 1987:183).

(353)   (Wilson, 1987:179).

(354)   The Tree of Life, page 164 (Regardie, Israel)

(355)   A Lawyer Presents the Case for the Afterlife, pages 7 & 8 (Zammit, Victor)

(356)   Beyond Supernature, page 79 (Watson, Lyall)

(357)   (Animals Are Equal) (Wildwood: London, 1980) (Hall, R.)

(358)   (Keen & Ellison), (1999)

(359)   The Devil's Mistress, (Brodie, J, W.)

(360)   History of the Rise and Progress of Rationalism in Europe, (Lecky, W. E. H.)

(361)   The Long War against God, (New York: Master Books, 2000) (Morris, H. R.)

(362)   Saducismus Triumphatus. (Glanvil, Dr.)

(363)   The Witch Cult in Western Europe

(364)   Secret Worship in Dr. John Silence (Blackwood, Algemon).

(365)   The Eternal is One. (Deut. 6:4)

BIBLIOGRAPHY

Aitken A. C.	51,
Alin	293,
Andrade, Dr. Hernani	381,
Arigo,	151, 152,
Armstrong, Anne	233,
Atwater, Phyllis	258,
Bacon, Francis	20,
Bayliss,	264,
Becker, Robert	158, 170,
Bender (Professor)	290,
Bennett, Alan and Diana	357,
Bierman, Professor Dick J.	248,
Black, Stephen	334,
Blackmore, Susan	212,
Blyth, Benjamin	54,
Bohm, David	27, 31, 33, 49,
Bozzano, Ernest	381,
Brennan, Barbara Ann	140, 141, 144, ,
Brion, Marcel	293., 293
Brookes-Smith, Colin	343,
Brooks, Jane	353-355,
Carpenter, Professor William B.	309,
Carrington, Hereward	193,
Carter, Jimmy, Former President	206, 208,
Chertok, Leon	307.
Cobb	238,
Colburn, Zera	49,
Crawford, professor W. J.	332,
Cridge, Anne	287, 288,
Croiset, Gerard	36, 215, 217, 219, 297.
Crookall, Dr. Robert D.Sc., PhD	203, 211, 260, 350,
Crookes, Sir William	333, 350,
Crossley, Allan	332,
Currie,	244,
De Broglie	31, 37,
Dee, Dr. John	361,
Denton, Elizabeth	288, 291,
Didier, Alexis	309,
Dodds, Professor Eric R.	328,
Dossey, Dr. Larry	230,
Dostoevsky	185,
Dove, Elaine & Evelyn	273,
Dubos, Professor Rene	148,
Dunn, Dr. Earl	245,
Dunne	35, 105, 106, 221,

398

AFTERLIFE – THE PROOF

400

--o--

INDEX

Printed in Great Britain
by Amazon

31631320R00231